Narrating Muslim Sicily

The Early and Medieval Islamic World

Published in collaboration with the Society for the Medieval Mediterranean

As recent scholarship resoundingly attests, the medieval Mediterranean and Middle East bore witness to a prolonged period of flourishing intellectual and cultural diversity. Seeking to contribute to this ever-more nuanced and contextual picture, The Early and Medieval Islamic World book series promotes innovative research on the period 500–1500 AD with the Islamic world, as it ebbed and flowed from Marrakesh to Palermo and Cairo to Kabul, as the central pivot. Thematic focus within this remit is broad, from the cultural and social to the political and economic, with preference given to studies of societies and cultures from a socio-historical perspective. It will foster a community of unique voices on the medieval Islamic world, shining light into its lesser-studied corners.

Series editor
Professor Roy Mottahedeh, Harvard University

Advisors
Professor Amira Bennison, University of Cambridge
Professor Farhad Daftary, Institute of Ismaili Studies
Professor Simon Doubleday, Hofstra University
Professor Frank Griffel, Yale University
Professor Remke Kruk, Leiden University
Professor Beatrice Manz, Tufts University
Dr Bernard O'Kane, American University in Cairo
Professor Andrew Peacock, University of St Andrews
Dr Yossef Rapoport, Queen Mary University of London

New and forthcoming titles

Cross Veneration in the Medieval Islamic World: Christian Identity and Practice under Muslim Rule, Charles Tieszen (Fuller Theological Seminary/Simpson University)

Power and Knowledge in Medieval Islam: Shi'i and Sunni Encounters in Baghdad, Tariq al-Jamil (Swathmore College)

The Eastern Frontier: Limits of Empire in Late Antique and Early Medieval Central Asia, Robert Haug (University of Cincinnati)

Writing History in the Medieval Islamic World: The Value of Chronicles as Archives, Fozia Bora (University of Leeds)

Female Sexuality in the Early Medieval Islamic World: Gender and Sex in Arabic Literature, Pernilla Myrne (University of Gothenburg)

Narrating Muslim Sicily

War and Peace in the Medieval Mediterranean World

William Granara

I.B. TAURIS
LONDON • NEW YORK • OXFORD • NEW DELHI • SYDNEY

I.B. TAURIS
Bloomsbury Publishing Plc
50 Bedford Square, London, WC1B 3DP, UK
1385 Broadway, New York, NY 10018, USA

BLOOMSBURY, I.B. TAURIS and the I.B. Tauris logo are
trademarks of Bloomsbury Publishing Plc

First published in Great Britain 2019
Paperback edition first published 2021

Copyright © William Granara 2019

William Granara has asserted his right under the Copyright,
Designs and Patents Act, 1988, to be identified as Author of this work.

For legal purposes the Acknowledgements on p. viii constitute
an extension of this copyright page.

Cover design: Adriana Brioso
Cover image: Arabonormand style portrait of Roger II of Sicily (1095–1154),
Cappella Palatina del Palazzo Reale (Palatine Chapel of the Royal
Palace) Palermo, Italy. (© The Yorck Project, 2002)

All rights reserved. No part of this publication may be reproduced or
transmitted in any form or by any means, electronic or mechanical,
including photocopying, recording, or any information storage or retrieval
system, without prior permission in writing from the publishers.

Bloomsbury Publishing Plc does not have any control over, or responsibility for,
any third-party websites referred to or in this book. All internet addresses given
in this book were correct at the time of going to press. The author and publisher
regret any inconvenience caused if addresses have changed or sites have
ceased to exist, but can accept no responsibility for any such changes.

A catalogue record for this book is available from the British Library.

A catalog record for this book is available from the Library of Congress.

ISBN: HB: 978-1-7883-1306-3
PB: 978-0-7556-3854-3
ePDF: 978-1-7867-3613-0
eBook: 978-1-7867-2607-0

Series: Early and Medieval Islamic World

Typeset by Integra Software Services Pvt. Ltd.

To find out more about our authors and books visit
www.bloomsbury.com and sign up for our newsletters.

Contents

List of Illustrations	vi
Notes on Transliteration and Translation	vii
Acknowledgements	viii
Preface	x
1 Sicilian Islamic History as *Grand Récit*	1
2 Treason as Historical Anecdote and Literary Trope in Narrating Muslim Sicily	35
3 Land, Law and Jihad: Al-Dawudi's Anti-Fatimid Polemics	69
4 Of Minarets and Shipwrecks: Ibn Hamdis and the *Poetics of Jihad*	99
5 In Praise of Norman Kings: Arabic Panegyrics beyond Its Boundaries	143
Postscript	181
Notes	187
Bibliography	200
Index	205

Illustrations

List of Plates

1 Jug of Mazzara del Vallo, Museo, Regionale Galleria, Palermo
2 The Church of Saint John of the Hermits (San Giovanni degli Eremiti): A sixth-century church converted into a mosque during Muslim rule and restored as a church by Roger II *c.*1136, Palermo
3 Mosaic of Christ Pantocrator in the royal Palatine Chapel (Cappella Palatina) commissioned by Roger II *c.*1132, Palermo
4 Statue of William II at the front of the Cathedral of Monreale (begun by William II *c.*1174), Monreale (Sicily).

List of Maps

1	Sicily: The Provinces	xvi
2	Sicily: The Cities	xvi
3	Sicily: The Cities in Arabic	xvii
4	Southern Italy: The Cities	xviii
5	Sicily, North Africa and Europe.	xix

All maps and images have been provided by the author.

Notes on Transliteration and Translation

For the transliteration of Arabic names, terms and bibliographical citations, I follow the Library of Congress system with some modifications; I omit both macrons for long vowels and diacritics for 'emphatic' consonants. I use the apostrophe for the *hamza* and the inverted apostrophe for the *'ayn*.

All translations from Arabic, French and Italian are my own unless otherwise indicated.

Acknowledgements

This book has been in the making for a long time. It was conceived in my graduate school days at the University of Pennsylvania, where I began to take an interest in medieval Sicily, especially Islamic Sicily. My professor and mentor, George Makdisi (RIP), immediately pointed me in the direction of Michele Amari, and his *Biblioteca Arabo-Siciula* and *Storia dei Musulmani di Sicila* became my scholarly scriptures. Professor Makdisi's guidance throughout my early years of research and writing was invaluable.

I thank my colleague and friend, Professor Roy Mottahedeh, for his mentoring, wise counsel and encouragement to bring this book to fruition. To Thomas Stottor, Rory Gormley, and the staff at I. B. Tauris, I extend my gratitude. I thank my copy editor Kate Rouhana for her exceptional skills and guidance, and to Eric Edstam for his skill and patience in helping me through the final editing. I also thank the Office of the Divisional Dean of Arts and Humanities at Harvard for its generous support for this project.

A special round of thanks as well goes to Robert Wisnovsky and Wilfred Rollman who took the time to read my completed manuscript and offer important suggestions.

Since joining the faculty in the Department of Near Eastern Languages and Civilizations at Harvard in 1993, I have had the privilege of working with a bright constellation of scholarly luminaries. The late Wolfhart P. Heinrichs (RIP) was the first to nudge me to publish a lecture I delivered at Harvard's Humanities Center on Ibn Hamdis. He spent many hours with me working through some of the more obscure verses of Ibn Hamdis. His vast knowledge and erudition and his passion for Arabic poetry continue until now to be most infectious. I also thank my colleagues Khaled Al-Masri and Shady Nasser, who sat patiently with me reading and rereading literally hundreds of lines of Ibn Hamdis and arguing convincingly over variant interpretations. I also owe a debt of gratitude to my dear friends, former Shawwaf visiting professors at Harvard, Gaber Asfour and Ridwan Al-Sayyid, who shared my interest in Sicily and imparted their knowledge of Arabic literature and Islamic law onto me. I have been honoured to work and supervise a number of graduate students, and I cite Nicola Carpentieri and Ali Asghar Alibhai, whose work on medieval Sicily has enriched me tremendously.

I express my gratitude and respect as well to two eminent scholars of medieval Sicily, Jeremy Johns and Alex Metcalf, whose magnificent work has been indispensable to my own research.

My hearty thanks and affection as well go to my 'gang' of friends and scholars who, over the many years, have patiently listened to me go on and on about Sicily, Palermo, Ibn Hamdis and the Normans – more often than not 'as exuberant topers grasping the silver cup of grape-induced intoxication', as Ibn Hamdis would put it. I toast Laila Parsons, Rob Wisnovsky, Ilham Khuri-Makdisi, Eve Troutt Powell, Sahar Bazzaz, Ayman El-Desouky and Sinan Antoon.

Finally, I thank my parents, Eugene J. and Irene Pellegrini Granara for encouraging me and supporting the many years of my education, and to whom I dedicate this book.

Preface

This book is a collection of essays about Sicily, from the early ninth until the late twelfth century of our Middle Ages, during the period ranging from Arab political sovereignty to Islam's final years of lingering cultural and socio-economic influence. More precisely, it is a book about writing about Sicily. It considers how Arabs and Muslims viewed the island from historical hindsight or memory, including eyewitnesses from the high years of Sicily's Islamic period, to later Muslim historians who worked through the archives to resurrect or to reimagine its history. Most of what we know today of medieval Sicily comes to us from the pens of these later scholars who, ploughing through the increasingly disappearing historical records and collating snippets of information and marginalia from 'history books', attempted to weave a cohesive narrative about a discrete history of a time and place that, like most nations, experienced a rise and fall. Even back then, writing about Sicily was about writing the past or the soon-to-be past. Writing 'Sicily' entailed memory, conjecture and heeding history's lessons about why nations and people rose and fell. My goal in this book is to focus on Muslim Sicily as historical subject and literary trope.

My book will, presumably, take its place among a relatively small library of modern scholarship on medieval Arab Muslim Sicily. It does not deal primarily with Romans, Byzantines or Normans, although the informed reader will be able to detect and locate their peripheral presence. It takes a close look at Arabic writing in its various genres, from historiography, geography, biography, jurisprudence and poetry, and considers how these generic domains explained and preserved the memory of a 'state' that burst onto history's radar screen in a flash and left it in a comparable hurry.

This book follows in succession a corpus of scholarship to which I refer especially the newcomers to this field: Michele Amari (1806–1889), Sicilian historian and Italian patriot, the 'father' of modern scholarship on Muslim Sicily, authored, among others, two monumental works that are indispensable to our subject: *Biblioteca Arabo-Sicula* (1859) is a massive compendium of all Arabic sources extant during the nineteenth century that deal in any way, shape or manner with medieval Arab and Muslim Sicily; and *Storia dei Musulmani di Sicilia* (completed in 1879, edited and reissued posthumously in 1933 by Amari's disciple Carlo Alfonso Nallino) is an extensive five-volume history of Sicily in the Muslim era. It is to Amari's disciples and to the Italian school of Orientalism – notably Celestino Schiaparelli (d.1919), Francesco Gabrieli (d.1996), Umberto Rizzitano (d.1991), Adalgisa De Simone and Antonino Pellitteri – that we are indebted for continuing and building on Amari's foundational work and expanding the small field of Sicilian Islamic studies throughout the twentieth century. Historians of the medieval Mediterranean – Henri Bresc, Jeremy Johns and Alex Metcalfe, to name a few of the most outstanding – have added richly to our knowledge of Sicily in the Middle Ages. Mohamed Talbi and Farhat Dachraoui, both modern Tunisian historians who wrote on the Aghlabid and Fatimid periods of North African history, both produced groundbreaking works indispensable to our subject. Finally, throughout the Arab world, new generations of Arabic readers continue to be informed about the Sicilian chapter of their history and literary heritage by way of the works of Ihsan 'Abbas. All of the above have made significant contributions to Siculo-Arabic scholarship in their own specialized ways.

In 973, the traveller-geographer Ibn Hawqal spent a brief period in Sicily and logged his shocking and shocked impressions of Arab Sicilians and their society into his journal, which eventually morphed into his magnum opus, *Surat al-Ard*. His Sicilian chapter, although not the first sample of writing Sicily within the Arabic Sicilian *biblioteca*, nonetheless provides us with a kind of first primary source of note, marking a new beginning in writing about Arab Sicily. He was an eyewitness above all, and the information he provides remains unmatched. After Ibn Hawqal, travellers, chroniclers, biographers and poets added their voices to describing, documenting, analysing, critiquing and remembering that relatively brief period in history when the largest island in the Mediterranean was securely ensconced within *Dar al-Islam* (the Muslim world).

Chapter 1 of this volume deals with historiography as a discursive mode of writing. It looks at the master chroniclers, the recorders of world or universal history of their day, who, in their meticulous accounts of people and events, year by year, government by government, create in unison a master narrative or *grand récit* of Muslim Sicily. The histories of Ibn al-Athir (d.1233), al-Nuwayri (d.1333) and Ibn Khaldun (d.1406), as Amari long ago pointed out, provide the major bulk of the political or dynastic history of the Arabs in Sicily. In my own reconstruction of a chronologically cohesive narrative, I highlight some of the hallmark features of Muslim Sicilian history: the dominant role of jihad in the conquest of the island and the formation of a *ghazi* (warrior) society; the rise of civilian and intellectual institutions that parallel the evolution of Palermo from a garrison town to a grand metropolis; the formation of a Sicilian-Arab specificity and its affinities with the North African (Ifriqiya) motherland; and the persistent complicated and codependent political, social and economic relationship with it.

Chapter 2 follows a single trope: that of betrayal or treason – one that punctuates the historical and literary sources and disturbs any imagining of a united or monolithic Muslim Sicily. As a frontier society (*thaghr*), Sicily has often lived between and on the edges of imperial empires, with conquering peoples presiding over conquered majorities. Since large swathes of the new population included men of war (conscripted and mercenary), slaves and captives, political exiles and refugees, travelling merchants, pirates and fortune seekers, heretics and tricksters, and generally men and women living on the margins of an unstable and fluid society, loyalties were not always fixed and reliable but rather quite often fickle and negotiable. In war and in conquest, institutions that bound people to networks of loyalty were being destroyed and replaced by new ones. Betrayal as *petit récit* challenges both medieval and modern preconceptions of a world neatly divided between Islam and Christianity, where actors and actions under the rubric of jihad and crusade happened in accordance with logical patterns and conformed to familiar expectations of behaviour, belief and bonding.

Chapter 3 offers a rereading of a series of *fatwas* (solicited legal opinions) to questions pertaining to the status of Sicilian land and other properties seized, confiscated or distributed as booty by the Muslim governors at the time of the Islamic invasions. In a jihadist society such as Muslim Sicily, land was of paramount military, economic and social importance. Because Islamic law requires the equitable distribution of property (including land) among the participants in a battle, allotting conquered land or granting conditional rights to unmovable properties was not only essential in motivating Muslim soldiers to fight effectively in battle but also a highly effective incentive for retiring soldiers to settle down and cultivate the land in the new 'Muslim' province. Abu Ja'far al-Dawudi (d.1011), (Sunni) Maliki jurist and anti-(Shi'ite) Fatimid polemicist, provides us with a series of questions and responses that shed precious light on the contemporaneous contentious politics of land distribution that bear resemblance to modern political practices and concepts, such as 'eminent domain', political favouritism and nepotism, and loopholes and tax evasion. Al-Dawudi's chapter, 'Spain, Sicily and North Africa', also provides us with glimpses and insights into the complex of military, political and economic dependencies between the (rural) province and the (urban) major centre of power.

Chapter 4 is a study of 'Abd al-Jabbar ibn Hamdis (c.1055–1133), itinerant court poet, perennial exile and Muslim Sicily's most famous native son. He left the island at the tender age of twenty-four, during the first stirrings of the Norman Conquest, to enhance his career as a professional poet. But he was fated never to return to the island, although he lived to be eighty years old. However, Ibn Hamdis never stopped thinking about, longing for and writing about his beloved homeland. Although precious little is known about his personal life, the powerful autobiographical voice that resonates throughout his extensive *diwan* (his edited anthology contains roughly 370 poems) tells us much about his life and the times in which he lived.

Ibn Hamdis is best known for a small number of poems that address the anguish of exile and longing for his homeland, referred to by literary historians as his *siqilliyat* or Sicilian poems, and it is these pieces to which later scholars and critics devoted their attention. In Chapter 4, I trace the *topos* or theme of jihad as a way of understanding how Ibn Hamdis used his literary craft to write about and memorialize his falling homeland. I argue that, contrary to critical consensus, his evocation of jihad was less a matter of religious conviction and belief than it was a strategy to rally the Muslim population to the Sicilian cause and to assign to his beloved homeland a secure place in the Arabic literary canon.

Chapter 5 surveys the twelfth-century political and cultural landscape of Christian-Muslim relations in Sicily in the post-Norman conquest, by way of (re)reading Arabic panegyrics towards the Norman kings Roger II (r.1105–54) and William II (r.1166–89). My intention is to read in equal measure the philology of the texts (i.e. introductions to encyclopaedic works (al-Idrisi), travel accounts (Ibn Jubayr) and poems (al-Atrabanshi, Abu al-Daw' Siraj, Ibn Qalaqis, et al.), against the political, social and religious contexts reconstructed from historical accounts. In considering contemporary notions of *la convivencia* and myths of inter-faith utopia, I read these texts against a Sicilian Arabic poetics vilifying the Norman Conquest (Ibn Hamdis) as well as accounts of oppression and abuse that pepper Ibn Jubayr's travelogue.

I argue for a 'zone of contradiction' that lies at the subtexts of all of my proof-texts. Key to understanding the complexities of contradiction is the persistent presence of *fitna*, especially as pronounced by Ibn Jubayr, which spans the lexical range from 'civil-strife' to 'seduction'. I aim to show how we might expand the contexts of reading Arabic panegyrics to the Norman kings between the fading glory of Norman royal patronage and the emergence of a belligerent post-Norman hostility towards the Muslim community percolating throughout the island.

***

A recurring theme that lies subtly throughout the subtexts of the works under discussion here is the tension or challenge of writing Muslim Sicily between war and peace. These texts reflect and bear witness to a world that does not fit neatly into the folds of the *Dar al-Islam* (the Muslim world) versus *Dar al-Harb* (the non-Muslim world) dichotomy that has dominated so much of Arabo-Sicilian literature. All of the authors of the above-cited and soon-to-be treated works are writing, at least on the surface, within the established boundaries of classical Arabic canons, accepting and adhering to the legitimacy of orthodox Sunni Islam, the primacy of classical Arabic literary and cultural tradition, and the allegiance to Islam's religious and political ascendancy. But beneath the lines lurks the strong sense that both divisive relationships with fellow Muslims and peaceful coexistence with the Christian 'other' disturb a facile but comfortable world view of a united *jihadist* society in constant struggle with the non-Muslim world.

A quick look to Ibn Hawqal, whom many suspect to have been a Fatimid Shi'ite sympathizer, gives us perhaps the most dramatic example of writing Sicily with this sense of disturbance at not finding this *jihadist* frontier according to normative Muslim expectations. His visit to the outer peripheries of Palermo around 973 exposed him to Muslim Sicilians married to Christian women who raised their daughters as Christians. He refers to the majority of Sicilians as 'tricksters' (*musha'midhiin*),[1] negligent in their religious obligations and cavalier in the ways they lived their lives as Muslims. The description, even if we assume its exaggeration, nonetheless reflects the substantial degree of peaceful coexistence that evolved in one of *Dar al-Islam*'s holy war provinces. Writing Sicily in all its complexities and contradictions seems to me to have been a challenge to Ibn Hawqal and other historians of the Middle Ages far greater than encountering and reaffirming a united and homogeneous Sicilian Islam.

Finally, I evoke a passage from the ninth-century Sahnun Ibn Sa'id (d.855), in which he defined four different kinds of jihad: jihad of the **heart**, of the **tongue**, of the **hand** and of the **sword**.[2] Sahnun was the legal scholar and jurist who presided over the instillation and maintenance of orthodox Islam according to the teachings of Malik ibn Anas (d.795) throughout North Africa, Sicily and Spain. His thesis of the various kinds of jihad allows for a broader conceptual approach in understanding how a predominantly military campaign and a band of soldiers could transform a garrison town and a handful of military outposts into a highly sophisticated and fully developed 'state' where military interests gave way to aspects of civil society. His notion of a jihad of the tongue – the use of speech as a weapon to combat, appeal and persuade people and events to one's cause – perhaps best captures the desire or impulse to write historical accounts, journals and anecdotes, geographical descriptions, legal treatises, biographies, and polite prose and poetry while struggling to find an equilibrium between war and peace, the religious and the secular, and Islam and Christianity.

William E. Granara
Harvard University
30 January 2018

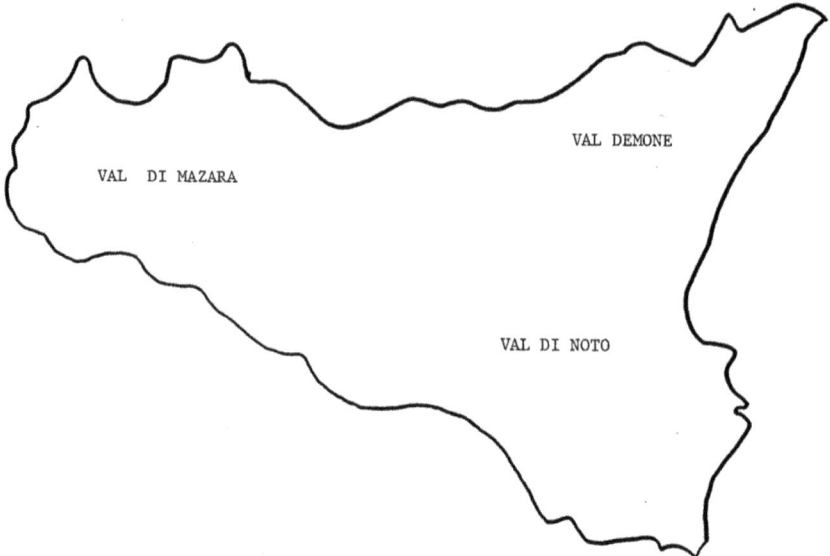

Map 1 Sicily: The Provinces.

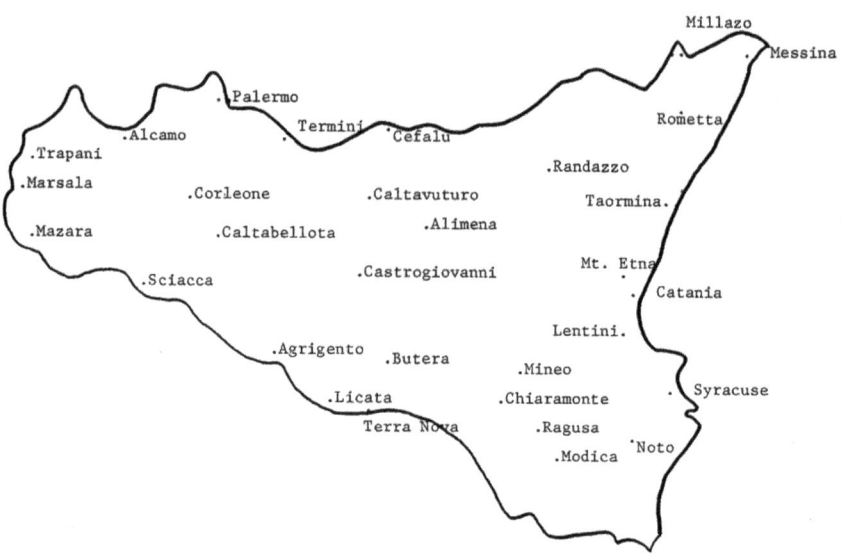

Map 2 Sicily: The Cities.

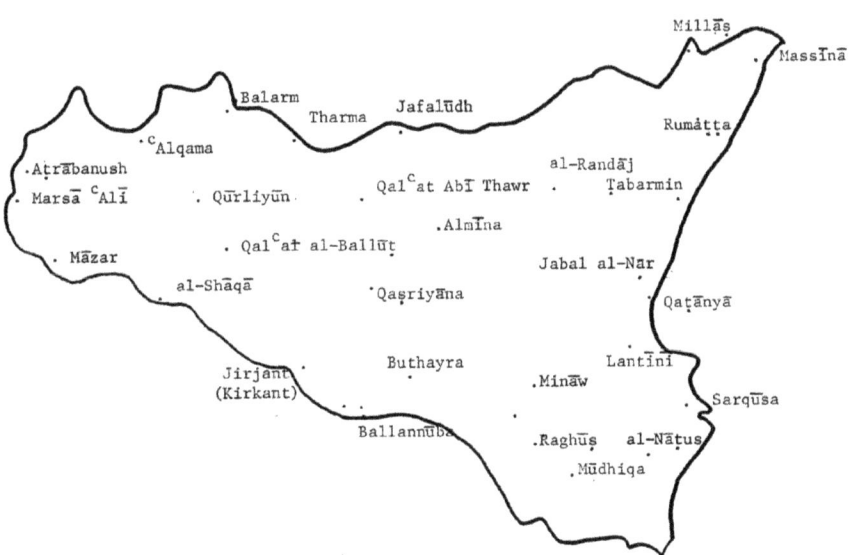

Map 3 Sicily: The Cities in Arabic.

Map 4 Southern Italy: The Cities.

Map 5 Sicily, North Africa and Europe.

1

Sicilian Islamic History as *Grand Récit*

Looking back: Framing Muslim Sicily's history in a rise and fall dialectic

The eminently renowned Ibn Khaldun (1332–1406), historian, sociologist and philosopher, bequeathed to human civilization a corpus of writing and ideas on the nature and evolution of human societies. Paramount in his thought was the idea of civilizational decline or, in other words, the study of the rise and fall of nations.

Ibn Khaldun lived in the most interesting of times. His world, spanning the late medieval Islamic West and the Islamic East, was moving at a frenetic pace, and many and much of who and what surrounded him succumbed to wars, rebellions, famine (he lived through the Black Plague), and the political machinations and ambitions of men who make history. His elite classical education and his pursuit of scholarship, on the other hand, allowed him to observe, study, analyse and explicate the problems and complexities of his own times against the lessons of human history.

'Abd al-Rahman bin Muhammad Ibn Khaldun was born in the city of Tunis in 1332, the scion of an Arab family who had settled in the city of Seville during the early years of the Islamic conquest of Spain (al-Andalus). His family (the generation of his great-grandfather) resettled in North Africa at the onslaught of the Spanish Christian Reconquista, and both great-grandfather and grandfather, religious and legal scholars, became actively involved in the political intrigues of their times. His own father, Muhammad, followed the family's scholarly traditions but eschewed political life, while the young 'Abd al-Rahman was destined to follow in his grandfathers' footsteps.

In thinking about, reflecting on and postulating theories about rises and falls of nations great and small, Ibn Khaldun had much to work with in his own time and place(s). His parents died from the Black Plague when he was just an adolescent, and he witnessed the Marinid invasion of his Hafsid Tunis in the same period of his life. He spent time in prison for being on the wrong side of power, and in 1362 he was warmly received in Granada by its emir, Muhammad ibn Ahmar, and his controversial vizier, Lisan al-Din ibn al-Khatib (1313–1374), with whom Ibn Khaldun enjoyed a long but cautious friendship. Ibn al-Khatib's many political ups and downs and his ultimate murder while in prison exemplify the mercurial nature of public life at that time. Ibn Khaldun's diplomatic mission to negotiate with the Christian enemy Pedro the Cruel in 1364 would be replicated later in his life with a similar mission in 1400 to the camp of the Mongol Tamerlane. The many government and teaching posts he occupied from Fez to Damascus made him privy to all that was happening throughout the inner sanctums and corridors of power and provided him with insights, information and perspectives – all the raw material he needed to analyse the processes of history.

As a fully educated scholar in the classical Arab Muslim tradition, Ibn Khaldun had even much more to rely on in his formation as a world historian: literally thousands of pages and centuries of Arabic historiographical writing that bear witness to a long and dynamic process of historical consciousness. From the earliest Bedouin oral narratives of recounting a glorious past (*akhbar al-'arab*) to the many references to names, places and events evoked in pre-Islamic poetry, the Arabs succeeded in expanding their historical consciousness by way of understanding and explaining a new Muslim world view as reflected in the genres of *sira* (biographies of the Prophet), *maghazi* (accounts of his campaigns) and *hadith* (records of his saying and deeds). Local and universal chronicles and histories, biographical dictionaries and works of expansive encyclopaedic breadth were penned throughout the Arab Muslim world, addressing questions from the nature of power and the Sunni-Shi'ite divide to the shift from an Arab, Levantine Ummayad caliphate to a multi-ethnic Mesopotamian Abbasid caliphate. Monumental events and changes, such as the conquest of lands far beyond the borders of the Arabian peninsula, the intellectual interface with classical Greek and Persian learning, the Crusades, the demolition of Baghdad by the Mongol hordes and the emergence of mystical Islamic practices (Sufism) that came to threaten the hold of the old-guard religious elite over large swathes of the populace, were all inscribed in the pages of the many genres of Arabic historiography, contributing in varying ways and degrees to an ever-changing and expansive historical consciousness that forced Arabs to think and rethink their past and present.

In sum, Ibn Khadun's theories and scholarship were not produced ex nihilo. The combination of his very public and professional life and his erudition in the school of Arab Islamic letters gave him insights and knowledge of historical processes that culminate in his socio-philosophical *Muqaddima* as well as his opus on positive history, *Kitab al-'Ibar*. The history of Islamic Sicily, spanning roughly 827–1060, indeed must have presented to him a discreet and highly illustrative model on which to reflect on rise(s) and fall(s).

Ibn Khaldun's by now well-known and oft-cited thesis of the five cycles in the life span of a nation (*atwar al-dawla*) may very well have been shaped, at least in part, by his reading of Islamic Sicily, one that rose and fell many years before. His thesis of cycles includes (i) a period of conquest in which a primitive way of life prevails, based on natural solidarity and religious sentiment; (ii) the years of consolidation of power in the form of a powerful army and a strong government; (iii) a period of financial success, luxury and ease, fortified by a well-developed (urban) infrastructure and civil institutions; (iv) a period of contentment in which luxury is expected, accustomed and constantly pursued; and (v) a final period of waste, deterioration and decline.[1]

The Islamic conquest of Sicily was launched in the full pageantry of jihad that united various and often-contentious groups under the banner of the Aghlabid prince of the semi-autonomous province of Ifriqiya. The campaign was led by a highly respected Muslim jurist and scholar, Asad ibn al-Furat, and it included a remarkable number from the 'religious' establishment. The period of conquest, lasting some seventy years, was followed by a modicum of Aghlabid political consolidation, especially with the development of Palermo as a regional metropolis. By the end of the first century, the Kalbid dynasty, having achieved great success on the military front against Byzantium, came to preside over a royal court that could boast a high culture and a strong and robust economy. Finally, political and social divisions, the result of greed and ambition, led to fragmentation and military defeat at the hands of the Norman militia.

Ibn Khaldun, along with two great master chroniclers who preceded him, Ibn al-Athir (d.1239) and al-Nuwayri (d.1332), is credited, as Michele Amari has observed, with providing the framework for our reconstruction of Muslim Sicily's political or dynastic history. Each one, as I mentioned above, was not only equipped with a plethora of historical documents but also enjoyed the advantage of hindsight, they all faced nonetheless the challenges of making sense of a messy history from a corpus of fragmented reports and narratives.

The Aghlabid court at Qayrawan in search of an external enemy

The Mediterranean island of Sicily was inhabited by Arabs and Muslims from the early ninth century until the early decades of the thirteenth century. From a broad historical perspective, the Arab invasion and settlement of Sicily in the early ninth century may be read within the long continuum of the Islamic wars of conquest that began shortly after the death of the Prophet Muhammad in 632. As the Arab armies moved beyond the borders of the Arabian Peninsula, they spread in every direction. In their movement westward, beyond the lands of Egypt and into the Maghrib, they eventually covered the whole of the African continent north of the Sahara, and from the farthest point west of the Maghreb, they crossed the Mediterranean and entered, conquered and settled the Iberian Peninsula from the year 711.

Medieval Arab (as well as Latin and Greek) chronicles report sporadic Muslim naval incursions into Sicily as early as the mid-seventh century. As the largest of the Mediterranean islands and the most strategically located, Sicily had long been the target of foreign invaders. Phoenicians, Greeks, Carthaginians, Romans and Byzantines all staked their claims to the vulnerable island, invading, occupying and ultimately inscribing 'Sicilian' chapters onto their histories. And so it was natural for the Arab Muslims, in their quest for religious, political, military and commercial sovereignty over the Mediterranean, to cast their sights and carve their name on Sicily as well.

By the beginning of the third Islamic century (ninth century), however, the Islamic Empire had ceased to be a single, monolithic empire with one universally accepted authority. The Islamic 'nation' (*umma*) was politically and religiously divided, and the caliphate in Baghdad was no longer recognized as the sole legitimate authority of all Muslims. The Muslim empire of al-Andalus in the Iberian Peninsula proclaimed its own caliphate in Cordoba, while Sunnis, Shi'ites and Kharijites acted upon their conflicting visions of legitimate authority and rightful rulership throughout North Africa and the Arabian Peninsula. Additionally, the Muslims of the third Muslim century, now long ensconced in their role as conquerors of nations and cultures, harboured few notions of universal Islam, as their political ideas and treatises began to deal with the more complicated questions of peaceful coexistence and the rights of non-Muslims. In sharp contrast to the Muslim invasion of the Iberian Peninsula a century earlier, the Muslim invasion of Sicily was launched against a background of a divided Muslim world, on the one hand, and a series of negotiated peace treaties with the Byzantine warlords of Sicily, on the other.

More precisely, the history of Muslim Sicily begins somewhere along the corridors and inside the grand chambers of the Aghlabid royal palace in the city of Qayrawan (Tunisia) in the early years of the ninth century. The Aghlabids were a dynasty of Arab princes who ruled the province of Ifriqiya, a region extending from Constantine (Algeria) in the west to Tripoli (Libya) in the east, from 800 until 909. Their founder, Ibrahim I ibn al-Aghlab, was granted autonomy by the Abbasid caliph Harun al-Rashid in 800 in exchange of a yearly tribute tax and pledges of allegiance to the Abbasid Court. By the time of Abu Muhammad Ziyadat-allah (r.817–38), the province was facing a host of domestic problems. Ziyadat-allah had to put down a long and violent insurrection led by a disgruntled military officer, Mansur ibn Nasr al-Tunbudhi, in 824, who, through an alliance with various tribal chieftains, succeeded in seizing control over much of the province for several years. Although the rebellious al-Tunbudhi eventually surrendered and was put to death, residual resentment among the army factions towards the Aghlabid palace continued to fester.

Throughout the rural areas within and beyond Aghlabid rule, the political movement of Kharijism held wide popular appeal, especially among the nomadic Berbers. Kharijism was a sect that began in opposition to both Sunni and Shi'ite notions of political and religious authority. Meanwhile, many of the Kutama Berbers adhered to Shi'ism in direct opposition to the Sunni orthodox Aghlabids. Also, tensions between the Arab elite and the Berber masses in the urban centres flared up from time to time, and if this were not enough of a disturbance, the religious scholars (*fuqaha*') emerged as popular supporters for the disenfranchised urban poor. Their public and vociferous criticisms of the ruling family and its special interest groups drew attention not only to the economic and social inequities plaguing the realm but also to the licentious and decadent ways that permeated the highest echelons of government.

In the early months of 827, word reached Ziyadat-allah that the Byzantines of Sicily were holding Muslim soldiers as captives. A renegade Byzantine general from Sicily, Euphemius, had contacted the Aghlabid court with this news as well as with other vital military information he offered in exchange for Aghlabid assistance in overthrowing his enemies in Sicily. The military intelligence was extremely valuable to Ziyadat-allah, considering his domestic problems with a restless army, an aggrieved population and a hostile *ulema*. Sicily, long the target of Muslim raiding expeditions, could easily be reconfigured as enemy territory. At the same time, its strategic location offered exciting prospects for renewed commercial and military ventures. On the domestic front, a war to liberate Muslim captives from enemy lands could redirect the attentions of the masses away from internal problems, and it could provide employment to an idle and troublesome army. However, the question of invading the island was not a simple matter since Ziyadat-allah was bound to a peace treaty with Byzantine Sicily that had been concluded by his successor. In a quandary, the Aghlabid ruler summoned his inner circle for advice.

Two voices emerged during the spirited debates, those of Ziyadat-allah's two chief judges. Abu Muhriz (d.829), a powerful voice among the Qayrawani religious scholarly community, counselled caution and pleaded for a wait-and-see strategy despite the evidence of a possible Byzantine violation of the treaty. His argument was overwhelmingly supported by his peers. Asad ibn al-Furat, a maverick Hanifi-turned-Maliki scholar of great note as well as an Aghlabid loyalist who was instrumental in Ziyadat-allah's successful campaign against al-Tunbudhi, took the opposite position. His advice was couched in religious terms as he quoted the Qur'anic verse: 'So do not become weak-kneed and sue for peace, for you will have the upper hand; as God is with you, and will not overlook your deeds.'[2] By standing on solid scriptural ground, whereby appeasing the religious conservatives, Asad pleaded the case that Ziyadat-allah launch an attack.[3]

The very existence of these debates underscores two important issues at stake at this time. The first issue is the 'legal' dimension of a major decision such as waging a war. Despite being something of an absolute potentate, Ziyadat-allah was bound to higher authorities, distant and abstract as they may have been. The caliph in Baghdad was still held as supreme political authority among the urban Qayrawani orthodox masses in spite of the autonomy granted to the Aghlabid ruling family. Any major undertaking on behalf of *Dar al-Islam* needed at least the nominal blessings of the Baghdad caliphate, or it had to be done in such a way as to not undermine the interests of the larger *umma*. There was also the authority of Islamic law (*al-shariʿa*) itself, in both its scriptural precision and in its evolving, elastic and negotiable interpretations. Chapters on jihad in the early manuals of jurisprudence and the emerging genre of *siyar* literature,[4] as will be seen again in Chapter 3, were moving in directions beyond the early treatises, and the nature and role of legitimate rulership was faring more prominently in the manuals for waging war and peace.

The second issue was the virtual power of the religious and legal scholars, not only as guardians of sacred law and legality but as public critics, political dissidents and protectors of the disenfranchised masses. The mere fact that Ziyadat-allah had two chief judges, a non-standard practice in Islam at the time, not to mention his consultations with them on any potential raid on Sicily, points to the sensitivity of the circumstances as well as the reality of power, politics and religion that held significant sway over this issue. Abu Muhriz was a deeply devout and conservative jurist and a disciple of Malik ibn Anas (d.795), the founder of the Sunni school of Islamic law that came to dominate the Islamic Maghreb (North Africa, Spain and Sicily) for centuries. His appointment to the chief judgeship, grudgingly made by Ziyadat-allah's father, Ibrahim, positioned him among the leadership of the emerging Maliki jurists who engaged in anti-Aghlabid campaigns in an attempt to impose their authority and control over the masses.

Ziyadat-allah broke with tradition and hired a second chief judge for Qayrawan. His choice of Asad ibn al-Furat was a stroke of political genius. Asad was a loyal subject and public servant, a skilled negotiator (he was responsible for convincing the rebellious al-Tunbudhi to surrender to the Aghlabid authorities), and a jurist with outstanding academic credentials. He travelled to Mecca to make his pilgrimage and spent a brief period studying with Malik ibn Anas. He then journeyed to Baghdad where he studied under Muhammad ibn al-Hasan al-Shaybani (d.805), a disciple of Abu Hanifa, and then to Cairo to study with 'Abd al-Rahman ibn al-Qasim, disciple of Malik. He returned to Qayrawan with his own completed compendium on Islamic law, *al-Asadiyya*, which gained immediate and widespread popularity throughout Maghribi scholarly circles. In the process, he had become a rival of Abu Muhriz, as both men came to represent opposing factions among the Qayrawani *ulema*. In their debate on the issue of Sicily, Ziyadat-allah played one faction off the other while paying lip service to all of his potential critics.

On a June morning in the year 827, a fleet was assembled on the orders of Ziyadat-allah at the port city of Susa (eastern coast of modern Tunisia) to set sail towards Sicily. Throngs of people surrounded a cavalry of 700 and an infantry of 10,000, recruited and assembled to board a flotilla of 100 ships. The warriors were Arabs of various tribes, as well as Berbers, Persians, professional soldiers and even members from the scholar/clerical community, many of whom evidently experienced a change of heart in joining the jihad. Asad ibn al-Furat was appointed commander of the fleet, with the royal decree that he maintain his official title as chief judge of Qayrawan. Amid the excitement of the crowds, the neighing of horses, the rolling of drums and the waving of banners, Asad spoke:

> There is no god but God alone; he has no partners. O people, neither a father nor grandfather created a state for me nor chose me to rule. No one before me has even seen such a sight, and I have only read about what you now see. Exert your minds and labor your bodies in the search and pursuit of knowledge; increase it and be patient with its intensity, for you will gain with it this world and the next.[5]

Within three days, the forces of Ziyadat-allah reached Mazara on the southwestern tip of Sicily. A large army, headed by P/Balata, the Byzantine governor of Sicily, was stationed at port in anticipation of their arrival. The actual history of Muslim Sicily commences here.

The Arab invasion of Sicily was clearly propelled by local politics but cast in a wider regional context of Muslim-Byzantine rivalries. In this way, the invasion was unlike the Muslim invasions of the Iberian peninsula a century earlier and may be viewed as separate from the general Islamic wars of conquest (*hurub al-futuh*). In sum, it was conceived and executed by Ziyadat-allah in response to internal conditions. In the words of Georges Marcais, the invasion 'was doubtless inspired by the desire to divert the energies of the Arabs to an external theatre of operations'.[6] It had far-reaching economic and political advantages, giving new opportunities for employment to a restless army as well as to new conscripts. Mohamed Talbi observes: 'The invasion of Sicily brought in booty and enriched the public treasury as well as private coffers; it stimulated the slave trade, and for a variety of reasons stimulated the flow of money.'[7] Politically, the decision to invade buttressed the fragile government of Ziyadat-allah while gaining the approval and blessings of the religious leaders and the general masses. The image of 'defender of the faith' was undoubtedly enhanced and exploited. This was done, and most likely could only have been done, through the scriptural prescriptions, the religio-legal bases, and the political and military pageantry of jihad.

Aghlabid Sicily (827–909)

The first years of the Islamic jihad in Sicily were difficult for the Muslim armies. Despite Euphemius's treason and the divisions within the Byzantine politico-military infrastructure that induced it, the Muslim conquest of the island was not facilitated by a dilapidated government, a bitterly divided church, nor any oppressed segments of the population only too willing to receive and assist the invasion in the ways that it had with the Muslim invasion of the Iberian Peninsula in 711. Resistance to the Arab army, on both the popular and official levels, was fierce. If anything, the invasion seemingly patched up any lingering divisions, and Constantinople was quick and generous in its response with reinforcements. Unfamiliar with the terrain and the climate, the Muslims suffered as many defeats as victories in the early days. An epidemic that struck them within their first year took many lives, including that of their leader, Asad ibn al-Furat.

Upon his death, the military commanders acted quickly and elected one of their own, Muhammad Abu al-Jawari, to lead the jihad. Cut off from their military headquarters and command posts in Qayrawan, the troops on the ground needed to act quickly and independently. This early act of 'auto-election' on the part of the invading troops would calcify into a political bone of contention between the Muslims of Sicily and their North African patrons throughout the entire history of Muslim Sicily, as will be seen repeatedly throughout this chapter. Meanwhile, when it appeared that the Byzantines were able to regroup and regain the upper hand, the Muslims decided to leave the island. But when they discovered that the seaports had been blockaded by a massive flotilla of Byzantine vessels, they burned their own ships and sought shelter inland. During their siege of the city of Mineo, reinforcements came from Qayrawan, and the fortuitous arrival of a passing armada of Spanish Muslim profiteers eagerly offering their assistance helped the Muslim forces get back on their feet. The tides had turned in the Muslim favour, and they succeeded in taking Mineo and the city of Agrigento soon thereafter. In their fourth year, 831, the Muslim armies entered the politically and strategically important city of Palermo and expelled the Byzantine ruling family to whom they granted safe passage. From this time, Palermo became their capital city.

With the Sicilian jihad back on track, the Aghlabid palace in Ifriqiya reasserted its direct control through the process of appointing the commanders, rather than leaving these decisions to the soldiers on the ground. In 832, Ziyadat-allah dispatched his cousin, Muhammad ibn 'Abdallah ibn al-Aghlab, better known as Abu Fihr, as commander. Upon his death three years later Ziyadat-allah appointed Muhammad's brother, Ibrahim, who commanded the Muslims of Sicily until 850. These two decades saw stunning progress with much of the western province of the island, Val di Mazara, securely settling under Muslim rule, while other major urban areas – and Byzantine strongholds – in the centre of the island, such as Castrogiovanni (modern Enna) and Syracuse, were well on their way to becoming part of Muslim territory. By appointing members of his own family, Ziyadat-allah maintained both political control of the newly established Muslim communities and economic control over the vast wealth that the spoils of war wielded in the way of war booty: gold and silver sacked from churches and royal palaces, slaves of various kinds, protection payment (*jizya*) from Christians and Jews who capitulated to Islamic rule, and various land and treaty taxes imposed on both non-Muslim and Muslim subjects.

This Aghlabid policy of scrupulous attention and lavish support for the Sicilian jihad would survive intact long after Ziyadat-allah's death in 838.

With the death in 850 of Ziyadat-allah's appointed governor, Muhammad ibn al-Aghlab, whom the historians describe as never having left his palace in Palermo but opting instead to direct the jihad through military commanders, the Muslim forces on the ground in Sicily elected by acclamation one of their own generals, al-'Abbas ibn al-Fadl, as their commander. They then sent word to Qayrawan notifying the court of their choice. Not content to wait for a response, al-'Abbas set out on a new offensive with the objective of conquering Castrogiovanni, the seat of the Byzantine military command since it was driven out of Syracuse some several years prior. The eleven-year reign of al-'Abbas, for whom an official letter of investiture eventually arrived from Ifriqiya, was marked by a succession of brilliant military victories, aided and abetted by the skills and loyalty of his son 'Abdallah and his uncle Rabbah (Riyah, according to Ibn Khaldun), that culminated in the long, violent but successful conquest of Castrogiovanni. Once again, these two trends bear significance: The Sicilian troops were only too ready and willing to elect one of their own in a leadership vacuum, with or without the consent of Ifriqiya; and any ascension to power and legitimation of that power were first and foremost predicated on an active and decisive role in the jihad campaign.

The unexpected death of al-'Abbas in 861 immediately following the Muslim victory at Castrogiovanni prompted the Muslim forces to repeat what had been proven to be a successful tactic: They elected from within their own ranks. This time it was 'Abdallah, al-'Abbas's son, and they acclaimed him as their leader before writing to Ifriqiya of their choice. Like his father, 'Abdallah chose not to command from behind the scenes but to lead his army personally into new forays onto untrodden enemy territory. But this time, the response from the Aghlabid court was different. In what could very well be interpreted as serious apprehensions about the increasing independent-mindedness among the Muslim troops in Sicily, the palace in Qayrawan immediately dispatched emissaries to inform the troops of its rejection of 'Abdallah and to announce the appointment of Khafaja ibn Sufyan, who arrived in Palermo five months after 'Abbas's death.

To backtrack a step or two, the contrast between Muhammad ibn al-Aghlab, who directed the jihad from the palace at Palermo, and al-'Abbas ibn al-Fadl, professional soldier at the front, may be far more fraught with meaning than a mere difference in leadership styles. In fact, it underscores two new trends in the history of Muslim Sicily: firstly, the establishment of Palermo as a capital city created a new urban centre that gradually developed along the lines of other urban centres of the medieval Muslim world, and one that cultivated social, cultural and economic institutions markedly more civilian than military in nature; secondly, there emerged differences of opinion concerning local 'elections' of leaders and political appointments from Ifriqiya that would create a political fault line between the gradually settling and settled Muslims within Sicily and their patrons and benefactors from Qayrawan, as political, personal and financial interests of both parties would eventually come to diverge.

Khafaja ibn Sufyan's arrival in 861 as governor of Sicily was immediately followed by a two-pronged attack in the east of the island. Along with his son Muhammad, he concentrated his jihad efforts towards the Christian strongholds of Noto in the southeast and Taormina in the northeast. In 869, on his way back to Palermo after an extensive raiding expedition on and around Syracuse, Khafaja was assassinated by a Muslim soldier who was able to escape to Syracuse. His body was returned to Palermo where he was buried, and his son Muhammad was elected by the Palermitans and confirmed with investiture by Qayrawan. In 871, Muhammad was also assassinated, this time by his own eunuch guards who, again, were able to escape.

The political and military history of Muslim Sicily for the remainder of the ninth century runs along similar lines. The jihad campaign was heavily concentrated in the island's eastern cities, and Syracuse was finally captured in 878. The governing of the island and the direction of the jihad campaigns were occupied by a large number of insignificant leaders, either appointed by the palace in Ifriqiya or by the Muslim Sicilian officers with eventual Qayrawani approval. What does come to surface in the chronicles is an increase of civil disturbances among the Muslim Sicilians, often, but not exclusively, drawn along Arab/Berber lines. The assassinations of Khafaja and his son Muhammad, although never stated as such, may have had some connection to these growing rifts among the Muslims.

In 875, Abu Ishaq Ibrahim II ascended the Aghlabid throne by popular acclamation in Qayrawan. His twenty-seven-year reign witnessed a complex of stunning military and cultural achievements on the one hand, and violence and widespread dissent on the other. His public pronouncements for social justice and economic well-being for the poor and his generosity and support for the Sicilian jihad were overshadowed by rising domestic opposition on a number of fronts, compounded by uprisings from the Berbers of Zab (Southeast Algeria) and military threats from the Tulunids of Egypt. The disagreement among the historians in assessing his rule attests to his highly complex and schizophrenic temperament that fluctuated unpredictably between a just and benevolent rule and a murderous paranoia. Ibn al-Athir is the lone voice in favourably judging the rule of Ibrahim II:

> He was just and resolute in his affairs. He secured the land and killed the licentious and corrupt. He used to hold court at the Grand Mosque at Qayrawan on Mondays and Thursdays, hearing cases and mediating. Caravans and merchants traveled safely on the roads. He built fortresses and guarding posts along the coast. He was determined to perform the pilgrimage. He redressed oppressive acts and displayed piety and asceticism. He made his way to Sicily to perform both pilgrimage and holy war.

Ibn Khaldun, writing more than a century later, seizes the opportunity to contradict Ibn al-Athir upon whom he otherwise relies heavily for his information:

> That year a messenger from the caliph al-Mu'tadid came and discharged Ibrahim because of the North Africans' complaints against him. He (Ibrahim) recalled his son Abu al-'Abbas from Sicily and then he himself went there to show repentance and banishment. This is according to Ibn al-Raqiq, who also mentioned that he was a tyrant, oppressive and bloodthirsty, who was afflicted with melancholy at the end of his life, which accounted for his excessive killing ... Ibn al-Athir [on the contrary] praised him for his intellect, his justice and his kindness.[8]

In Sicily, Ibrahim II faced a serious challenge to his rule in an open revolt in 900, and he responded by appointing his own son, Abu al-'Abbas ibn Ibrahim ibn Ahmad ibn al-Aghlab, as governor. Abu al-'Abbas arrived at the western port city of Trapani in August 900 with a flotilla of 160 ships and immediately set up a blockade around the port. At the time of his arrival, the (Arab) Palermitans were fighting with the (Berber) Agrigentans. When the news of his arrival spread, the Palermitan forces returned to the capital and immediately dispatched an embassy to the new governor offering excuses for their battle with Agrigento. The Agrigentans in turn also sent their emissaries to complain of Palermo's abusive policies. Following these initial attempts to play off one against the another, which apparently did not succeed in bringing Abu al-'Abbas to one side or the other, the Sicilians (and here we are to assume both Palermitans and Agrigentans) united – for reasons never explained by the historians – and waged an attack against the newly arrived Aghlabid forces. The following month, September 900, the combined Sicilian militias were defeated after a series of bitterly fought land and sea battles, and Abu al-'Abbas took control of the capital first and then the rest of the Muslim-controlled areas of the island. The leaders of the army who led the revolt fled to Christian territories in the northeast of the island, Val Demone, with some going even as far as Constantinople. Once order was restored, Abu al-'Abbas headed in the direction of the northeast to continue the jihad.

In Ifriqiya, meanwhile, Ibrahim's erratic behaviour reached such a peak that the caliph in Baghdad, al-Mu'tadid, was called upon and implored to intervene. He sent orders in 902 for Ibrahim to abdicate the throne. As previously mentioned, the Ifriqiyan masses still regarded the caliphate in Baghdad as a higher religious and political authority despite Aghlabid autonomy, and these orders held powerful sway over local politics. Ibrahim complied and named his son, Abu al-'Abbas, as his successor. Father and son, in essence, exchanged jobs. In a public and ostentatious display of contrition and penance, Ibrahim donned the robes of a pious ascetic and holy warrior (*mujahid*) and set sail for Sicily to participate in the jihad, a response that echoed Ziyadat-allah's pomp-filled invasion to invade Sicily seventy-three years earlier. Ibrahim led an expedition across the Straits of Messina and died a martyr's death in Calabria that same year. The command of Sicily, meanwhile, had been bequeathed to Ibrahim's grandson, Abu Mudar Ziyadat-allah III. During his brief reign there, his own father had him arrested for drunkenness and abuse of office. In revenge, he conspired in the assassination of his father and ascended the throne upon his death in Ifriqiya. Although he remained committed to the Sicilian jihad, his patricidal legacy and his licentious ways had become targets for the mission of the Fatimid Mahdi and its anti-Aghlabid campaign. His escape to Egypt in 909 put an effective end to Aghlabid rule in Ifriqiya and its Sicilian province.

Fatimid Sicily (909–944)[9]

In the vast stretches of the Maghrib in the early years of the tenth century loomed the proselytizing mission (*daʻwa*) of the Fatimid Shiʻite missionary Abu ʻAbdallah (al-Shiʻi).[10] It was a time and place of widespread discontent, especially among the Berber populations who felt deprived of the privileges of Arab elitism. Some had found comfort and support in the fiery rhetoric of the Kharijite movement that not only denounced the immorality and illegitimacy of the Aghlabid rulers but proclaimed as well that any righteous Muslim could serve as the leader of the community. Others, especially Berbers of the Kutama tribal confederation, were at this time responding to the invitation of the Fatimid mission that was gaining ground in such a climate of discontent. The Fatimids, who claimed descent from Fatima, the daughter of the Prophet Muhammad and wife of the fourth caliph, ʻAli, were a branch of the Ismaʻili Shiʻites who were advancing a brand of popularist egalitarianism and calling for economic, social and religious reform, the headline of their campaign. They also addressed the widespread opposition to years of Aghlabid corruption and abuse of power, and their campaign succeeded in the end in muffling the Aghlabids' last desperate and half-hearted appeals at reformation. Ibrahim II's abdication and public display of holy contrition, and Abu al-ʻAbbas's promises of 'justice, moderation, and jihad' were insufficient to save the dynasty. Ziyadat-allah III was overthrown in 909 by the forces of Abu ʻAbdallah, and in the following year the Fatimid Mahdi, ʻUbayd Allah, entered Raqqada[11] in triumph. He wasted little time in erecting his official palaces, having his name read at the Friday prayer (*khutba*) and bestowing upon himself the title of Commander of the Faithful.

The success of the Mahdi and his mission in North Africa had repercussions in Sicily, obviously, given that the island continued to exist as a province to Ifriqiya whose native sons settled the newly conquered lands and produced successive generations of Sicilian-born Muslims. The Sicilian-Ifriqiyan relationship had also developed into one of mutual dependency. The Sicilian jihad movement, and those who depended upon it for their livelihood, continued to be heavily dependent upon constant reinforcements from Ifriqiya. These reinforcements not only included heavy doses of arms and other war materiel but manpower as well. For its part, the rulership in Ifriqiya depended on the spoils of war that filled its coffers, and it counted on Sicily as its base in the Mediterranean to protect its overseas interests. Also, the jihad machinery kept a restless and rebellion-prone army employed, while the aura of a ruler as 'defender of the faith' remained well burnished.

A quick stray from the chronicle path and a look at the contemporary Shi'ite literature sheds much light on how vital the Fatimid mission viewed Sicily, at least in the early years. The Fatimid Isma'ili jurist, political theorist and court historian, al-Qadi al-Nu'man (d.973),[12] arguably their most eminent and accomplished propagandist, served the first four Fatimid caliphs: 'Ubayd Allah (d.934), al-Qa'im (d.946), al-Mansur (d.953) and al-Mu'izz (d.976). His *Da'a'im al-islam* (the Pillars of Islam)[13] was the standard Isma'ili law text throughout the Fatimid empire. Among his many works, his *Iftitah al-da'wa* (the Initiation of the Mission),[14] a history of the Fatimid mission from its beginnings in Yemen to the Mahdi's triumphal entrance into Raqqada in 910, sheds precious light on how the new Fatimid rulers maintained – if not surpassed – the Aghlabid Sicilian jihad in its thrust and execution and how they manipulated it to serve their political interests and expansionist goals.

In the several passages addressed to the Muslims of Sicily, three major points of interest are worthy of note. Firstly, the Shi'ite Fatimids displayed cautious (if not feigned) deference to the Sunni caliph of Baghdad, crediting him, at the expense of the Aghlabids, with supplying much of the power that produced a Muslim victory in Sicily. This was clearly a case of treading lightly in an area dominated by Maliki Sunnism, and whose religious/scholarly leaders had been outspoken critics of Aghlabid abuses and champions of the cause of the urban working classes and the rural poor. Secondly, the Fatimid mission lavished praise on the Muslims of Sicily and promised its full support of their jihad movement.

> You, inhabitants of the island of Sicily, are most worthy of favors and special treatment, because you live so close to the polytheists and remain engaged in holy war against the wicked infidels; God willing, I will fill your island with horses and soldiers from among the faithful who will wage the most just of wars so that God will strengthen our religion and the Muslims through whom He will crush polytheism and polytheists. For all change and power is with Almighty God, upon whom we rely. He is indeed the Best One to rely on.[15]

Thirdly, the Fatimid appeal to the Sicilians and their jihad was built on an anti-Aghlabid campaign that was subtle in its beginning and unequivocally hostile by the end. It grudgingly paid homage to Ziyadat-allah I for his decision to launch the jihad against the enemy, albeit for self-serving reasons, and it urged the Muslims to obey the Aghlabid rulers especially while they were actively engaged in combat against the Christians. But the mission's frequent use of the word for enemy (*fasiq*: one who departs from the right way; disobedient; transgressor; sinful; wicked; immoral), which was 'mostly applied to one who has taken upon himself to observe what the law ordains, and has acknowledged its authority, and then fallen short of observance in respect of its ordinances',[16] offers a most interesting lexical alternative to the usual *kafir* (infidel), *mushrik* (polytheist), *'lj'* (pagan) or *'adu* (generic enemy) that are generally used by the Arab chroniclers – and poets – in referring to the Christian enemy. Given the accusations of corruption and immorality that the Fatimids hurled against the Aghlabids, one can comprehend the propaganda. Exhorting the Sicilians to carry on with their jihad against the enemy, the Mahdi raised the accusation of guilt by association through the manipulation of the term *fasiq* and, in so doing, redirected the holy war against the enemy within.

> Undertake jihad with your possessions and your souls, just as it has been prescribed to you; rid yourselves of your licentiousness and your sacrileges, lest you be led away from the rightful path of your religion; and defend it (religion) against anyone who would alter it; free yourselves from whomever would innovate or change it.[17]

The Fatimids, capitalizing on the deterioration of the Aghlabid dynasty by constantly reminding the public of its patricide, mass murder, corruption and moral depravation, interpolated these events and failures into their own vision and interpretation of jihad, projecting themselves as ruling in absolute adherence to both the scriptural and juridical precepts of righteousness, purity of heart and the legal authority of the ruler (*imam*) of the Muslim community to wage a holy war. In the process, they were also able to put forth the Shi'ite concept of caliphal legitimacy.

> Thanks be to God and His blessings. Since assuming my duty to serve His Truth, I have not ceased to defend His religion and seek justice for

His pious followers. I rule by His command, pray to Him for guidance, and prohibit that which He has prohibited. I warn that I will resurrect what the oppressors have destroyed in the way of the truth. I shall wage holy war against the heretic enemies of God who have usurped the right which belongs to the descendants of God's prophet. I reproach the Aghlabids and serve them notice that I will diminish their ranks and penetrate their cities in order to shame them into the truth, so that they may return to it, acknowledge it, and live under its banner. I will do this patiently, in the hopes of sparing Muslim lives. Yet, the more I try to be kind to them with every good intention, the more they persist in straying further from the truth, openly oppressing God's servants, sinning without hesitation, transgressing boldly, and usurping everything for themselves arrogantly. For indeed they have seized what belongs to God as their private property and His servants as their chattel, with no regard for righteous conduct, and with no respect for God's people and everything that is sacred.[18]

The first Fatimid caliph, 'Ubayd Allah, acted quickly in turning his attention to the affairs of Sicily, which he ruled through direct proxy. He did this first from his new capital in Raqqada and then from the newly built palatine town of al-Mahdiyya, and similar in fashion, one might add, to that of his Aghlabid predecessors. In order to secure control over the island's Muslim population, as well as the politically powerful and economically lucrative jihad campaign that had already made significant inroads into Southern Italy (especially in Calabria and Apulia), 'Ubayd Allah appointed trusted followers with proven military skills. As governor for Sicily, he chose al-Hasan ibn Ahmad ibn Abi Khinzir, a member of the Kutama Berber tribe, which was fiercely loyal to the Fatimids. Al-Hasan arrived at Mazara at the end of 902, along with Ishaq ibn al-Minhal who was appointed as chief judge of Sicily. Given the injustices inflicted upon Sicily by the last Aghlabid governor of Sicily, Abu Mudar Ziyadat-allah III, 'Ubayd Allah may well have been staging an attempt to redress Aghlabid injustices. In addition, he appointed al-Hasan's brother 'Ali as regional governor of Agrigento, the stronghold of the Sicilian Berber community. Amari observes that this separate appointment was not in existence under the Aghlabids, and he suggests that the Mahdi was trying to win favour with the Berbers and instigate tension between them and the Arab community.[19]

Little is reported in the sources on the immediate reaction of the Sicilian Muslims to the changing of the guard in North Africa. Although the master historian Ibn al-Athir (d.1233) reports widespread opposition in and around Qayrawan, nothing is mentioned of rampant disturbances in Sicily upon the arrival of Ibn Abi Khinzir.[20] Thus, it can be assumed that the Sicilians were at least cautious. It is interesting to note that one of the new governor's first public actions was to lead a raiding expedition in 910 into the Val Demone, 'pillaging, taking prisoners and burning the lands'. Once again, this may well be read as reinforcement of a clearly established pattern that an activist role in the jihad campaign was essential to legitimating and solidifying one's (right to) rule. However, not long after his return from this expedition, the Sicilians revolted against him and sent him and his brother back to Raqqada. The Fatimid palace responded by appointing 'Ali ibn 'Umar al-Balawi, but his tenure in Sicily was even shorter.

Despite Ibn Abi Khinzir's jihadish foray into enemy territory, neither he nor his successor apparently understood or mastered the art of ruling the island: the former was too harsh and the latter too weak, according to the Arab chroniclers. And the Sicilians, with an uncanny ability to come together when their collective interests were at stake, made their case to the Fatimid court in no unequivocal terms. The Mahdi could only acquiesce to their wishes and recall his first two Sicilian appointees. Acting upon the conviction that they knew best, and reverting to their old political habits, the Sicilians elected by acclamation one of their own, Ahmad ibn Qurhub, to assume the reins of power.

The curious case of Ahmad ibn Qurhub

The dynastic interregnum of Muslim Sicily (903–909), that is, the short period of the last years of Aghlabid decline and the consolidation of Fatimid rulers, had already witnessed, as we have seen, the murder of the Aghlabid leader Abu al-'Abbas, engineered by his own son, Abu Mudar Ziyadat-allah III. It also witnessed the killing of other prominent members of the ruling family. Abu Mudar had been deposed by his father, then Aghlabid emir in North Africa, from the governorship of Sicily, because of his corruption and addiction to alcohol. At that time of Abu Mudar's imprisonment, Abu al-'Abbas had appointed a certain Muhammad ibn al-Sarqusi (from Syracuse) as governor of Sicily. This period also saw the rule of Ahmad ibn Abi al-Husayn ibn Rabbah, of the Arab (Mudarite) aristocracy of Palermo (and grandson of Rabbah, the uncle of 'Abbas b. al-Fadl), whose family remained loyal relatives to the Aghlabids and distinguished for its leadership in Sicily. His rule was followed by the rule of 'Ali ibn Muhammad ibn Abi al-Fawaris, a local champion of the Fatimid cause.[21]

The relatively rapid succession of these rulers underscores the fact that Muslim Sicily had suffered from the political disruption caused by a combination of local squabbles and the disruption and chaos taking place within the ruling family in Ifriqiya. The election of the above-mentioned 'Ali ibn Muhammad ibn Abi al-Fawaris suggests that the island's (Sunni) Muslim population may not have been totally hostile to the (Shi'ite) Fatimids, at least in the beginning. But the failure of the first two Fatimid appointees in Sicily, Ibn Abi Khinzir and 'Ali ibn 'Umar al-Balawi, and the subsequent election by acclamation of Ahmad ibn Qurhub to power with a wide base of support (i.e. the backing of both Arab Palermo and Berber Agrigento) were undoubtedly an internal response to the rapid changes taking place in Ifriqiya. Most interestingly, Ibn Qurhub's initial reluctance to accept the mandate to rule the island adds confusion to the already chaotic and speculative accounts of events at this time. It was only after the Sicilians gave Ibn Qurhub their assurances of staunch support that he begrudgingly acquiesced. Amari sees his rise – 'prominent citizen, nobleman, orthodox, held in esteem by both the Aghlabids and the Sicilians' – as something of a compromise between two hostile factions within Sicily that emerged in confrontation during the interregnum between Aghlabid and Fatimid rule.[22]

Once Ibn Qurhub accepted to be governor of Sicily in 912, he set out, within what has now become a discernible pattern, on a raiding expedition into Christian territory. He crossed over into Calabria where his plundering yielded vast amounts of treasures and slaves. In the aftermath of this successful raid, he dispatched his son 'Ali in 913 to seize the Christian hill town of Taormina. His intention was to make it a personal fortress where his son could safeguard the family holdings in the event of any future Muslim Sicilian uprising. Three months into the siege, factions of the army revolted against 'Ali. They set fire to his tents with the intention to kill him, but a contingent of Arab troops (*al-'arab*) intervened on his behalf.²³

Back in Palermo, Ibn Qurhub announced his intention to pledge allegiance to the Abbasid caliph al-Muqtadir in Baghdad, amounting, in essence, to an open rebellion against the new Fatimid government in Ifriqiya. With popular consent, at least according to our admittedly Sunni chroniclers, he replaced the Mahdi's name with that of the Abbasid caliph at the Friday sermon and dispatched an emissary to Baghdad with Sicily's pledge of allegiance. In what may be considered a preemptive strike, Ibn Qurhub dispatched a flotilla to the Ifriqiyan coast where it was met by the Mahdi's naval forces commanded by Ibn Abi Khinzir, Sicily's first ousted Fatimid ruler. The reports of this battle waver between the bare essentials and the most gruesome of details. In sum, the Sicilian forces burnt the Mahdi's ships, killed Ibn Abi Khinzir and sent his severed head back to Ibn Qurhub in Palermo. Following this victory, the Sicilian navy headed south along the Tunisian coast, pillaged the city of Sfax and made their way towards Tripoli where they were stopped by a Fatimid naval force commanded by the Mahdi's son, al-Qa'im.

Back again in Palermo, when the robes of investiture arrived from Baghdad, Ibn Qurhub, predictably, dispatched a fresh battalion into Calabria. During its return, it was ambushed and soundly defeated by a flotilla of the Fatimid navy. This defeat signalled the end for Ibn Qurhub. The Agrigentans rebelled against him and sent word to the Mahdi that they were ready to recognize Fatimid authority. As more towns followed suit, the rebellion against Ibn Qurhub spread throughout all of Muslim Sicily, including Palermo. He was captured, taken prisoner and sent, along with members of his inner circle, to the Mahdi in Raqqada. When asked why he rebelled, Ibn Qurhub responded to the Mahdi that the Sicilians were prone to disobedience and rebellion against their leaders and that the only way to control them was with an iron fist. The Mahdi ordered Ibn Qurhub and his followers to be executed at the gravesite of Ibn Abi Khinzir. But the Mahdi did heed the advice of Ibn Qurhub. He immediately dispatched to Sicily a major battalion, commanded by Abu Sa'id Musa ibn Ahmad and manned with a large army of Kutama Berbers, to reassert his control. The Sicilians' reaction was to group together and launch a united military resistance, but as the Mahdi's forces proved to be too powerful, the Sicilians capitulated. Some factions requested safe passage, first the Palermitans and then the Agrigentans, with citizens from other towns following suit. Only the leaders of the revolt were executed, while a general amnesty was decreed by the Mahdi.

Modern historians have interpreted – subtly by Amari, openly by Aziz Ahmad (*A History of Muslim Sicily*, Edinburgh, 1975) – that Ibn Qurhub's rise to power was a reaction of Sunni Sicily against Fatimid Shi'ism. There is no doubt that Sicilian Islam, at least up until this point, was overwhelmingly Sunni. Yet this reason is, at best, secondary. The fact that Ibn Qurhub was deposed not long after his ascension to power undermines the explanation that Sunni reaction against Fatimid Shi'ism was the sole reason for Ibn Qurhub's acclamation as ruler by the Sicilian Muslims. Moreover, the Sicilian complaints against the first two Fatimid appointees based on ill treatment and weakness also suggest that Shi'ism may not have been the major bone of Sicilian contention with the Fatimids.

The Byzantine historian A. A. Vasiliev suggested that Ibn Qurhub was deposed by the Berbers.[24] Although the Berbers did initiate resistance to his ascent to power, they were not the only ones among the Sicilians to do so. The term *fear* used throughout the chronicles, if borne in mind in connection with Ibn Qurhub's remarks to the Mahdi concerning the recalcitrant nature of the Muslim Sicilians, provides us with at least a surface reason for Ibn Qurhub's tragic ending: the fact that he ruled Sicily with an iron hand was unacceptable to the Sicilians, regardless of whether he was a native son or appointed by North Africa. The references to 'the people', and then the emphasis of 'Agrigentans', and finally 'the inhabitants of the other towns' cancel out the Berbers or Shi'ism as being solely responsible for Ibn Qurhub's rise and fall.

What must be understood from these events, as well as from the ultimate fate of Ibn Qurhub, is something of a pro-North African versus anti-North African political divide among the Sicilian Muslims that often – but not always – ran perpendicular to Arab/Berber tensions. In Ibn Qurhub, Amari sees a Sicilian 'consciousness' and a struggle against North Africa.[25]

From the end of 913 until 925, scant information is provided as the chronicles thin out on the history of Muslim Sicily. Sometime around 917, the Mahdi appointed Salim ibn Rashid (r.917–37) as its governor. His first years in office coincided with renewed military aggressions against Byzantium in both Sicily and Southern Italy. His rule also overlapped with the death of the

Mahdi and the ascension of his son, al-Qa'im (r.934–46). This period saw a greater role for North African troops in these campaigns and the emergence of Slavs among them. The existence of a slav(e) quarter in Palermo, which the tenth-century Arab geographer and historian Ibn Hawqal would describe after a visit to Palermo some fifty years later, suggests their substantial numbers. The Mahdi also dispatched an expedition from Mahdiyya to pillage Genoa, and a flotilla even reached Sardinia where they were able to set fire to a number of ships along the coast.

The uprisings of 938: A united Sicilian front

In 937, the Muslims of Agrigento arose in revolt against their Fatimid governor, Salim ibn Rashid. He was able to put down the insurrection, and many of its participants were forced to flee the city when he set up a blockade around it. As a backup, he requested reinforcements from al-Qa'im, the new Fatimid caliph, who responded with a huge battalion under the command of Khalil ibn Ishaq.

The vacillation at this point in time between allegiance and rebellion on the part of the Sicilians – mainly the Arabs of Palermo and the Berbers of Agrigento – to their Fatimid-appointed governors, and by extension, the new Fatimid court in Mahdiyya itself, defies any clear-cut explanation. The heavy injections of Ifriqiyan and other foreign troops, iron-fist rule and economic exploitation all played a role in Sicilian discontent with North Africa in general, and Salim in particular, but, again, not enough to create a united Sicilian front with a clear and consistent articulation of grievances against the Fatimids. This time, resentment was, according to some accounts, aimed at Salim's repressive fiscal policies,[26] an issue that will be discussed in detail in Chapter 3. The influx of 'foreign troops' to assist in the jihad campaigns that had now been well underway in Calabria and Apulia undoubtedly raised the demand for increases in military salaries as well as parcels of land or other forms of booty to be distributed among the holy warriors. The insurrections in the cities and towns and their surrounding farm regions, meanwhile, wreaked havoc on the land and crops, pushing prices higher and forcing the local authorities to raise taxes on Muslims and non-Muslims alike.

When the Fatimid military commander Khalil ibn Ishaq arrived in Agrigento, the inhabitants came out to greet him en masse, as woman and children overwhelmed him with stories of atrocities perpetrated against them by their Fatimid governor, Salim. Citizens of other towns in Sicily followed suit. When many of them pledged allegiance to the Mahdi, Khalil was taken by surprise and offered his support to help them. Fearing for his position, Salim devised a scheme to pit the Sicilians against Khalil, calling attention to the huge army that accompanied Khalil to Sicily and convincing them that the Mahdi had sent Khalil to exact revenge for their uprising.

Salim's scheme succeeded in achieving more than its immediate goal of pitting the Sicilians against Khalil. The sight of a large battalion of newly dispatched Kutama Berbers from North Africa, compounded by the building of the new fortress city, frightened the Sicilians into, once again, uniting in armed revolt. With the odds overwhelmingly against them, the Sicilians dispatched an embassy to Constantinople seeking its assistance. Responding in kind, Khalil sought and received reinforcements from al-Qa'im. The next two years witnessed something of a civil war with broader 'superpower' dimensions, pitting Sicilian Muslims against their leaders in Ifriqiya and the Fatimids against the Byzantines. When the forces of Khalil prevailed, many Sicilians took refuge in Christian-held territories, while those who remained in the fortresses were granted amnesty on condition of their surrender.

Despite Khalil's success in putting an end to the insurrection in 941, Sicily in its aftermath suffered its many consequences. In addition to the obvious decrease in population due to death in battle, pillaging and the emigration of substantial numbers of Muslim citizens, residual animosity still smouldered in what had now become an even more brittle relationship between the island and its North African rulers. The fact that Sicilians could seek the military assistance of the Byzantine enemy against their own patrons and co-religionists must have had a severe impact on the fragile network of alliances and balances that kept the Muslims together. Also, the island suffered mass starvation in the years 940–2, in which the pillaging and burning of land and crops had undoubtedly played a role.[27]

The Fatimid court in Mahdiyya at this time was battling a serious threat to its government on its own turf with a rebellion, led by the Kharijite Abu

Yazid (Makhlad ibn Kaydad), which came to a head in the years 943–7. Simultaneously, the Fatimid forays into the lands of the east, towards which the court had always set its goals, were beginning to bear fruit. Their mission's successes in Egypt were redirecting their energies away from North Africa and Sicily. With an eye towards Baghdad, the Fatimids prepared the departure by breaking up their vast North African territories into smaller principalities to be ruled, separately, by loyal and trusted servants.

Kalbid Sicily (944–1044)

The family of the tribe of Kalb of the Bani Wabara[28] came to rule Sicily in the same way others before them had come to do: by way of services rendered to, and unflinching support for, the dominant rulers of North Africa. Just as the Aghlabid court chose family members and trusted generals to execute its military and administrative policies in Sicily, so too did the Fatimids continue in this practice of appointing loyal servants. Their Kalbid clients, however, would eventually evolve into their own dynasty, which succeeded in completing the jihad campaign in Sicily and provided a considerable degree of political stability and social cohesion among the Sicilian Muslim population. Their rule over the island also coincided with the early stages of the development of Arabic and Muslim civilian and scholarly institutions with a particular Sicilian flavour. This was as much due to their fortuitous timing, having come to power after a century of Arab settlement, as it was to their attention and cultivation of local talent, which they encouraged and patronized.

It should be recalled that the outbreak of the rebellions of 937 and mass starvation in Sicily, along with the intensity of Abu Yazid's anti-Fatimid campaign in North Africa that came to a climax in 947, helped bring the Kalbids to power in Sicily. They ruled the island at first under close scrutiny of the Mahdi but gradually came to enjoy a greater degree of freedom to rule. The Fatimid move to Cairo in 972, decreasing but not altogether eliminating Fatimid hegemony over Sicily, allowed for increasing Kalbid autonomy. 'Ali ibn Abi al-Husayn al-Kalbi (son-in-law of Salim ibn Rashid) died during the uprisings in Agrigento in 938, and his son, al-Hasan ibn 'Ali, who served both Mahdis, al-Qa'im and al-Mansur, proved himself in suppressing the Kharijite rebellion of Abu Yazid. His was rewarded with the governorship of Sicily, and through him, the line of Kalbid succession actually began.[29]

Other local factors contributed to al-Hasan's appointment to Sicily as well. A certain 'Attaf, who had been in charge of the island prior to al-Hasan, was viewed as so weak that the Christians saw no need to pay a tax stipulated by a treaty concluded with the Muslims. Also, there emerges in the chronicles during this time an influential clan, the Bani al-Tabari, whose strength was based upon a vast network of clientele. Their numbers and influence, testament to local powers and interests, had allowed them to form a solid front against 'Attaf. When the Palermitans joined forces with them in their rebellion against 'Attaf, he fled the island in 947, once again prompting the court at Mahdiyya to intervene. All of this, once again, reflects the close attention the rulership in North Africa paid to its vital interests in Sicily.

Once firmly ensconced at Palermo, al-Hasan resumed raiding expeditions against the Sicilian Christian strongholds in the northeast of the island and full-scale military attacks against the Byzantines in Calabria. At this time, Constantinople was renewing its reinforcements via Otranto, where the Byzantine forces had been previously defeated by Muslims forces dispatched directly from North Africa. But when al-Mansur died in 953 and his son al-Mu'izz (r.953–75) became Mahdi, al-Hasan was called back to the court in Mahdiyya. He left the duties of ruling Sicily to his son Ahmad, and it would be more correct to say that 'Kalbid' Sicily actually begins here. Whereas al-Hasan had always been closely connected to the Fatimid governments in North Africa and later in Cairo where the Fatimid caliphate and central government moved in 969, it was more accurately under Ahmad that Muslim Sicily gained a significant degree of autonomy. Al-Hasan's reappearance in Sicily at major battles, however, does point to a still-ongoing Fatimid involvement in Sicilian military affairs after the Fatimids' move to Egypt.

Muslim-Christian relations within and immediately around Sicily had become more varied and complex by this time. The number of treaties increased, as did the number of confrontations. Added to this richness and complexity was the Sicilian-Maghribi-Egyptian axis created by the newly established Fatimid dynasty of Egypt. At the heart of this axis lay a lucrative and bustling commerce that brought together Muslim, Christian and Jewish merchants, craftsmen, importers and exporters, shippers and soldiers of fortune from the

Mediterranean basin. Ibn Hawqal mentions the Jewish neighbourhood during his visit in 973, which he locates between the Bab al-Jadid and Ibn Saqlab Mosque quarters, two neighbourhoods of Palermo he cites as having the most markets.[30] Whenever hostilities did erupt, the historians speak of breaking treaties or violating conditions of truces. The fact that the fiercest of battles were fought by troops from North Africa and Constantinople, sent onto the Sicilian battlefield to assist their co-religionists, may in some way be related to Ibn Hawqal's disparaging remarks about the cowardly Sicilians who shirked their responsibilities in fighting the jihad.

As the Muslim, Christian and Jewish Sicilians cohabited the same land between the swells of war and peace, as well as within the capricious and unpredictable complex of Fatimid-Byzantine relations, other external factors began to emerge in and around Sicily. The Fatimids, as was mentioned, directed their efforts and energies towards the East, remaining on constant guard against their rivals in Baghdad, as Southern Italy and Sicily loomed increasingly in the eyes of ambitious rulers from the North. The capture of Taormina in 962, the last major Christian stronghold on the island, and the subsequent fall of Rometta, as well as the great naval victory for the Muslims fought at the Straits of Messina (*waqʿat al-majaz*: the Battle of the Straits) in 965 brought Fatimid-Byzantine hostilities to both a height and a halt.[31] The humiliating defeat at Messina suffered by Byzantium under the command of Manuel Phocas put an immediate halt to the tremendous momentum gained by his uncle, Nicephorus (Phocas) II, conqueror-turned-emperor, which had begun with the capture of Crete in 961 after 135 years of Muslim occupation.[32] In the aftermath, a new alliance between the Fatimids and Byzantium emerged through necessity. Although skirmishes between the two enemies would break out from time to time, they were not on a large scale. The pressure was coming from the North where the Emperor Otto I (r.936–73) cast his sights on Southern Italy, where both Byzantium and the Muslims had much to lose. In 982, the army of Otto II (r.973–83), comprised Saxons, Bavarians and other Germans, as well as Italians from the North and the Lombard provinces, was defeated in Calabria by joint Muslim-Byzantine forces.[33]

The three decades after the reign of Ahmad ibn al-Hasan (d.969) were relatively peaceful and prosperous ones for Sicily. With the exception of an outburst in 969 between rival Arab and Berber factions, between the clients (*mawali*) of the Kutama and the tribes (*al-qaba'il*), the chronicles make no mention of civil unrest. Those who occupied the government at Palermo, moreover, are reported as having been popular with Sicilians. The circumstances surrounding the outburst of hostilities in 969–70 are not clear, but they did occur during the brief reign of Ya'ish, a client of al-Hasan ibn 'Ali ibn Abi al-Husayn, who was appointed by the Mahdi, al-Mu'izz. When word of this reached al-Mu'izz, he had Ya'ish removed and appointed Abu al-Qasim ibn al-Hasan ibn 'Ali ibn Abi al-Husayn to replace his brother Ahmad, much to the satisfaction of the Sicilians.

Whatever the underlying reasons were for this outburst, for which it may be assumed that Ya'ish bore some responsibility, it is clear that the new quasi-autonomous ruling family of the Kalbids enjoyed the confidence of both the Fatimid Mahdi and the majority of the Sicilian Muslims. Their position strengthened when al-Mu'izz moved to Egypt, between 969–972, where he established the centre of his new caliphate. With the move to Cairo, al-Mu'izz left the province of Ifriqiya in the hands of Yusuf Bulukkin ibn Ziri, but he did not grant him control of Sicily, thus wrestling the island, for the first time, from under the control of al-Mahdiyya. In this reconfiguration of Fatimid-held lands in the Maghrib, Abu al-Qasim ibn al-Hasan was given an unprecedented degree of autonomy to rule Sicily.

Abu al-Qasim ruled Sicily for twelve years during which time he expended much energy and resources into military ventures in Christian territories of the northeast province of Val Demone and in Calabria of the Italian mainland. There seems to have been few troops dispatched onto the island from North Africa at this time, in sharp contrast to the days of Salim ibn Rashid and Khalil ibn Ishaq. Abu al-Qasim's death in 982 during the battle with Otto II's forces in Calabria prompted the Muslims to elect his son, Jabir. Jabir's decadent behaviour and poor administration, however, forced the Sicilians to remove him from office a year later. In his stead, they elected his cousin Ja'far, who had been a minister and boon companion to the Fatimid Mahdi al-'Aziz (r.973–96). His election proved wise, because he was able to restore the order that Abu al-Qasim had brought to the island. His death four years later was followed by his brother 'Abdallah's rule, who continued Ja'far's policies.

This period of internal stability came to a high point with the nine-year rule of Abu al-Futuh Yusuf ibn 'Abdallah, from 989 to 998. The chroniclers lavish high praise on him, and since little is recorded in the way of military encounters with the Christians or of internal factionalism among the Muslims, it is safe to assume that the island passed through one of its most peaceful and prosperous periods under his rule. Unfortunately, Thiqat al-Dawla (the confidence of the state), the name by which Yusuf was popularly known, suffered a stroke that left him partially paralysed in 998. He then transferred the affairs of state to his son, Ja'far (r.998–1019).

Concurrently, it is at this moment in Arabo-Sicilian history when the Arabic sources begin to yield rich information on the cultural and intellectual production of Muslim Sicilians. The entries of early biographers and chroniclers, echoed by and preserved in later medieval master histories and anthologies, attest to prodigious scholarship in the religious or Qur'anic sciences. Sicilian works of Islamic jurisprudence (*fiqh*), mainly written in the tradition of Maliki law, confirmed the island's scholarly connection to the motherland of North Africa where Maliki Sunnism survived and flourished even during the period of Fatimid Shi'ism. The study of law in Sicily, as elsewhere throughout the Islamic world, included its cognate disciplines of prophetic traditions (*hadith*), Quranic exegesis (*tafsir*) and speculative theology (*kalam*).

Secondly, particularly strong in Arabo-Sicilian scholarship was the study of the Arabic language (*lugha*) and its subfields. One could comfortably assume that the necessity of teaching Arabic to large segments of the Sicilian population whose native language was not Arabic broadened the depth and scope of language studies. The relatively scant information from the medieval Sicilian Arabic bio-bibliography nonetheless provides surprisingly copious works on grammar, syntax, poetry and prosody, prose composition, lexicography and literary criticism. These fields, perhaps the hallmark of Sicilian-Islamic culture, would reach their high points throughout the eleventh and early twelfth centuries, with eminent philologists such as Ibn al-Birr (d.1068), Ibn Makki (d.1107), Ibn Fahham (d.1112) and Ibn al-Qatta' (d.1121).[34]

Thirdly, the field of poetry, as a logical extension of and subfield to linguistic scholarship, and as a public and transposable commodity for the propagation of political legitimization and the advancement of high-court culture, came into full bloom at the Kalbid Court in the later decades of tenth-century Palermo. Sicilian poets, from the fully professional to the dilettante, came from different walks of life. Many of the philologists and grammarians, who read and researched the anthologies of the masters of classical Arabic poetry for imitable models of linguistic perfection, in turn tried their hand at poetic composition. There were also the royal princes and their protégés, some of whom were elevated to positions as high as governor (*amir*), who composed their own verses for sport as much as to display their erudition and elitist social stature. Finally, there were the court panegyrists, the hired guns of public opinion, who were called upon to enhance the image of the prince and his court, to sing his personal praises, to congratulate him on a military victory, or to offer condolences on the loss of a member of the royal family or of a loved one. Perhaps the best example of these was Abu al-Hasan 'Ali al-Rub'i, best known as Ibn al-Khayyat, whose career as a Kalbid panegyrist began sometime within the reign of Abu al-Futuh Yusuf (r.989–998) and extending into the reign of petty warlord Ibn al-Thumna, that is, from as early as 989 until possibly as late as 1050.[35]

Apogee and decline: The house of Abu al-Futuh Yusuf divided

Ja'far ibn Yusuf's ascendency to power over the Kalbid court upon his father's paralysis in 998 began with all the confidence and support the Sicilians had bestowed upon his father. However, c.1014, for reasons never made clear, his brother 'Ali rose up and rebelled against him with the support of Berbers and the slave corps. Ja'far dispatched an expedition against 'Ali from Palermo. The eight days of fighting, during which a large number of 'Ali's forces were killed, ended with 'Ali's capture and execution, the execution of the slaves and the expulsion of Berber forces from the island. As a precaution against further disturbances, Ja'far rebuilt his military forces, conscripting only 'Sicilian' troops. This may suggest that the Berbers who had supported his brother 'Ali's rebellion were those Kutama Berbers who had come to Sicily within the past few generations and not the native Sicilian Berbers who long inhabited Agrigento as well as other parts of the islands.

Other acts that contradict the earlier reports about Ja'far's reputation as a ruler surface in the chronicles and suggest that he had a change in policy towards ruling the island. His ill treatment of members of his own family, princes who themselves must have had their own entourages of wealthy and influential clients, eroded his base of support in Palermo. His regional representatives treated the populace and the elders of their communities with contempt, and they used oppressive measures in exacting a 10 per cent tax on agricultural products, a tax normally levied on non-Muslim subjects. In reaction to Ja'far's new tyranny, the Sicilians turned against him, dethroned him and demanded his execution.

The paralysed Abu al-Futuh Yusuf was brought out on a stretcher just in time to save his son's life. Still very much loved by the people, Yusuf was able to appease them by appointing his third son, Ahmad, known as al-Akhal (r.1019–1037), to govern Sicily. Yusuf then departed to Egypt with Ja'far, taking along with them exorbitant amounts of their wealth. The new governor wasted no time in setting out on raiding expeditions into enemy territory. During one of these raids his son, also named Ja'far, was placed in charge of the court during the father's absence and, opposing the conduct of his father, rebelled against him.

Tensions flared up once again, and the tenuous peace of Muslim Sicily was torn apart along pro-Sicilian and pro-North African lines. Al-Akhal summoned the Sicilians with a proposition: 'I will rid you of the North Africans with whom you have been cohabiting by expelling them altogether from the island.'[36] The Sicilians responded: 'We have united with them in marriage and we have become one people.' He dismissed them and proposed the same thing to the North Africans. When they responded favourably, he gathered the North Africans around him, placed protections on their property and imposed a tax on the Sicilians.

The series of disturbing and complicated events that follow the paralysis of Abu al-Futuh Yusuf were not lost on the insightful Ibn al-Athir who, writing two centuries later, saw a sudden sequence of rise and fall in the twisted and tortuous line of succession into which the sons of Yusuf fought their way to power. In fact, his entire narrative on the fall of Muslim Sicily, which he records in the events of 1091, the year in which the Normans in effect completed their conquest of the island, begins an entire century earlier where he sees the self-destructive rebellions, fratricide and disastrous attempts to pit the old-generation Sicilians and the more recently arrived North African Sicilians against each other as the real reasons for the breakdown of the jihad campaign and the consequent tearing of the political fabric of Muslim Sicily.

In 484 (1091) the Normans – may God damn them – occupied the entire island of Sicily. May God return it to Islam and the Muslims! The reason for this is as follows: In 388 (998) the ruler of Sicily, Abu al-Futuh Yusuf ibn ʿAbdallah ibn Abi al-Husayn, who had been appointed to the post by the Shiʿite ruler of Egypt and Ifriqiya, al-ʿAziz, suffered a stroke that paralyzed his right side and severely weakened the left. He appointed his son, Jaʿfar, to replace him. He assumed power and took full control of the country. He treated his subjects well until 405 (1014) when his own brother ʿAli rebelled against him.[37]

In Ifriqiya, meanwhile, the Zirid princes, by now well established through an orderly dynastic succession, took an aggressive interest in Sicilian affairs and sought to regain the Ifriqiyan role as major patrons for the bitterly divided and beleaguered Muslim population. In 1021, al-Muʿizz ibn Badis (r.1016–62) assembled a flotilla of four hundred ships and dispatched it to Sicily upon receiving news that the Byzantines had recaptured all the territories in Calabria that had been under Muslim control. Unfortunately, most of the navy perished during a storm at sea, somewhere off the coast of Pantellaria, between Tunis and Sicily.

The Fatimid presence in Egypt had still not resulted in severed relations altogether between its court in Cairo and that of the Kalbids in Sicily, but it did create a distance the Zirids sought to exploit. While Fatimid interests, energies and priorities lay in Egypt and pointed east, the newly assertive Zirid court in Mahdiyya succeeded in their goal of regaining influence over Sicily. Zirid political animosity towards their former Fatimid patrons culminated in Muʿizz ibn Badis's break with Cairo, and his symbolic pledge of allegiance to the Sunni caliphate in Baghdad, c.1044, brought them increased political leverage, especially among the Sunni majorities in Sicily and North Africa. It was from the Zirid court that the Sicilians sought assistance in 1036 in an attempt to protect their own interests in the face of al-Akhal's double dealing.[38] Al-Muʿizz was all too willing to accommodate them for a number of reasons. First, with the departure of the Fatimids, their North African territories were divided among a number of petty principalities whose rivalries often led to skirmishes and outright wars. A new Zirid hegemony over Sicily would enhance both the political and military prestige of its court in Mahdiyya. Secondly, the vast majority of Muslim Sicilians, Arabs and Berbers, traced their ancestry, from as recently as one generation to as many as six, to the province of Ifriqiya that provided the hundreds of thousands of soldiers who fought the jihad, settled the land and sired new generations of native-born Sicilians. It was proximity, a demographic continuum, and generations of coexistence and interdependence that preserved the bonds between the province and the motherland. And thirdly, the militarily powerful, politically prestigious and economically lucrative jihad machine provided wealth in the form of land, gold and silver, and slaves, stimulating an arms industry and providing new avenues for trade and the circulation of capital. How could the Zirid court refuse such an offer to the Sicilians when they sent messages asking for its help? In their plea to al-Mu'izz, they expressed their desire to remain as his subjects, but they made it clear to him as well that they would seek the assistance of the Byzantines if he failed to do so.

Al-Mu'izz ibn Badis responded to the Sicilian pleas with an army, this time commanded by his own son, 'Abdallah. When he reached Palermo and surrounded al-Akhal at the Fatimid al-Khalisa fortress, once again the Sicilian Muslims, true to form, divided in dispute. While some chose to remain with al-Akhal, others joined forces with 'Abdallah. When the two factions came face to face, a Sicilian loyal to al-Akhal asked a Sicilian loyal to al-Mu'izz: 'You have brought in foreigners to help you, and, by God, to what end?'[39] The Sicilians were quick to patch up their differences, at least for the moment, and in a surprise turn of events, they launched an attack against the Zirid army. With a loss of eight hundred men, 'Abdallah returned with his remaining troops to Ifriqiya.

In 1038, with al-Akhal dead, the Sicilians elected his brother, Hasan al-Samsam (r.1040–1053), the fourth of Abu al-Futuh's sons, as their governor. In spite of several successes in resisting new Byzantine offences, which included the recapture of some territories in Calabria and a handful of minor victories around Messina, al-Samsam's effective control was short-lived. Added to the rapid deterioration of Muslim unity and Byzantine counter offences was the expanding meddling of Northern armies in the affairs of Southern Italy and the Mediterranean. The Pisan and Genoese navies, and above all the Normans, whom the Arab Sicilians first encountered at Salerno in 1016, were progressing farther south. As early as 1034, the Muslim armies were very much on the defensive. The deposition of Hasan al-Samsam led to the fragmentation of the island, divided and ruled by a small number of warlords. ʿAbdallah ibn Mankut took Mazara and Trapani, ʿAli ibn Niʿma al-Hawwas held Castrogiovanni and Agrigento, and Ibn al-Thumna claimed Syracuse and Catania. The constant hostilities among the three give credence to Ibn al-Athir's assessment: 'The Sicilians then appointed Hasan al-Samsam, brother of al-Akhal, as their leader. But the situation deteriorated and power fell into the hands of the most despicable of men, each seizing independent control over a part of the island.'[40]

Ibn al-Thumna's overtures to the Normans, a promise of delivering the island to them in exchange for their assistance, evokes the memory of Euphemius two centuries earlier. The die was cast. The Norman entry into a precariously divided Arab Sicily and thirty-five years of relatively easy victories ended Muslim rule over the island. The Fatimids were focused on the lands of the east. The Zirids of North Africa, who themselves were facing tremendous political and social pressures from the onslaught of the Banu Hilal tribes and rival petty states in the Maghrib, offered assistance wherever they could. And despite the last-minute heroic resistance from the Muslim populations of Castrogiovanni, Agrigento and Noto, the Arabs had no choice but to step aside and let the Normans take their turn in the occupation of Sicily.

2

Treason as Historical Anecdote and Literary Trope in Narrating Muslim Sicily

Treason is a crime which has a vague circumference and more than one centre.

F. W. Maitland, 1905

Treason in Sicily's 'rise and fall': From Euphemius to Ibn al-Thumna

Acts of treason, deceit or betrayal surface often in the meta-narrative of Muslim Sicily. Whether committed by individuals or groups, they destabilize and often contradict the prevalent view, in the eyes of chroniclers and poets alike, of a united and politically and culturally coherent Islam in perpetual holy conflict with a monolithic Christian enemy. I read these acts of treason, 'touches of the real', as *petit récit* against the putative and dominant monolithic jihad as *grand récit*.

The word most often employed in the Arabic sources is *'khiyana'*, derived from the verb *'khana'*. According to Edward William Lane, the verb *'khana'* has several meanings and connotations:

> To be or act unfaithfully (to one's confidence or trust); to be or act perfidiously; to neglect or fail in the trust placed on someone; to act contrary to what is right; to break a contract or a covenant; to make someone suffer or lose, or to make something diminish.[1]

By the time a reconstructed history of Muslim Sicily takes its full form in Arabic historiography in the master chronicles of Ibn al-Athir (d.1233) and Ibn Khaldun (d.1406), as well as in Amari's *Storia dei Musulmani di*

Sicilia, 1872, a fully developed, discrete narrative with a beginning, middle and end had taken shape. To both the medieval and modern historians, the period of Arab rule over the island contained all the constituent parts and lessons of both history and literature – that is, what men did and why they did it. In plotting out a trajectory for the rise and fall of Muslim Sicily, and bearing in mind Ibn Khaldun's master thesis of the rise and fall of nations, the image of treasonous actions marking both its beginning and end stands in stark relief.

History and literature as modes of discourse share common features and often trespass each other's premises. Much of what has been written, and continues to be written, about Sicily straddles the dividing lines between fact and fiction. The fictional cosmos of many modern Sicilian stories, from those penned by Leonardo Sciascia, Gesualdo Buffalino and Giuseppe Buonaviri, for example, draw from the medieval Muslim era to narrate contemporary Sicily. They take liberties with chronology, personalities and historical facts – but they nonetheless help us to visualize and understand the continuities and ruptures of the island's past and present.

Hayden White's prolific studies about narrative in historiography and on the relation between, or progression from, chronicle to story to history are helpful guides in filling in the dots between history and literature. What interests us here of his massive opus are three points:

(i) Narrative is … a *form of discourse* which may … be used for the representation of historical events, depending upon whether the primary aim is to *describe* a situation, *analyze* an historical process, or *tell* a story.[2]
(ii) Every narrative combines two dimensions in various proportions, one **chronological** and the other **nonchronological**. The first may be called the **episodic** dimension, which characterizes the story made out of events. The second is the **configurational** dimension, according to which the plot construes significant wholes out of scattered events.[3]
(iii) That narrative in general, from folklore to the novel, from the annals to the fully realized 'history,' has to do with topics of law, legality, legitimacy, or, more generally, to authority.[4]

Perhaps there is no one figure in the epic of Muslim Sicily whose life sketches lend themselves more easily to the curious yet creative mixture of history (fact) and myth (fiction) than the Byzantine renegade general, Euphemius, especially given that his role in Sicilian history is based on treason. It should be recalled that the Sicily of Byzantine rule in the early decades of the ninth century was teetering on the brink of collapse with civil unrest and bitter divisions within the military ranks. Across the Mediterranean at a short distance southwest, the autonomous Aghlabid dynasty of Ifriqiya was facing its own existential threats with widespread discontent among the urban masses, supported and encouraged by hostile and critical clerics (*ulema*), a restless underemployed army and a militant insurrection by Kharijite Muslims.

A retelling of the Euphemius story at this time will provide a convincing illustration of history and myth's organic relationship: In 826, when the Sicilian-born Euphemius was appointed admiral of the Byzantine naval forces on the island, he proceeded to launch raids along the North African coast, kidnapping its merchants and plundering their wealth. The island's governor was ordered by the Imperial Court in Constantinople to arrest and punish Euphemius for these provocative and unlicensed actions, and the recalcitrant and independent-minded admiral rallied his forces and staged a mutiny. They sailed to Syracuse, at that time the Byzantine capital of the island, took control of it and chased the governor out pursuing him up along the eastern coast to Catania where they engaged him in battle and killed him.

Euphemius declared himself ruler of Sicily and appointed a certain P/Balata to govern another province of the island. P/Balata subsequently refused to take orders from Euphemius and, along with his cousin, Michael, governor of Palermo, combined their militias and attacked and defeated Euphemius, resulting in the restoration of Syracuse to Byzantine control. Euphemius rounded up what remained of his militia and sailed to Ifriqiya. Upon his arrival, he dispatched an emissary to Ziyadat-allah in Qayrawan and promised him sovereignty over Sicily upon the condition that he help defeat the Byzantines and declare him 'emperor' of Sicily. In return, Euphemius would pay an annual tribute tax to the Aghlabid court.

Ziyadat-allah's response to Euphemius's act of treason is the stuff of Muslim Sicilian lore. Faced with his own problems cited above, he found a 'domestic' solution in raising the spectre of a 'foreign' enemy. After much debate among his inner circle and high-ranking legal scholars, he accepted Euphemius's offer. He mobilized a massive army, described in the previous chapter, and launched an attack on Sicily with all the pomp and ceremony of a full-blown jihad.

When the Muslim forces landed at Mazara in June of 827, the commander, Asad Ibn al-Furat, sent an expedition to attack P/Balata but ordered Euphemius and his forces to remain behind. A turncoat of any colour, he must have thought, is still a turncoat. If this was the case, then Asad's instincts would serve him well. Euphemius's deception would not end with his breaking Byzantine ranks and joining forces with Islam. Taking pity on the town of al-Karrath that was about to surrender, at least ostensibly, to the invading Muslim army, Euphemius did an about-face and sent word to them to hold their ground and protect their land. The townspeople made a gesture to pay the protection tax (*jizya*) and pleaded their case to the Muslims to allow additional time before they entered the city. With this request granted, the citizens of al-Karrath fortified themselves and prepared to resist the invaders. Seeing this as a betrayal of the rules of safe passage (*aman*), the Muslims responded by taking the town by force. Euphemius would meet his fate later that year: he was assassinated by members of the imperial garrison at Castrogiovanni (now Enna), which had become the Byzantine military headquarters after the fall of Syracuse. The details of his execution vary in the sources.

The saga of Euphemius would not be complete without a romantic element, and like many of its kind in the history of medieval Mediterranean crossings, our archive does not disappoint. In contemporaneous Latin and Greek sources (albeit conspicuously absent in the more reliable Arabic sources), it was reported that Euphemius had kidnapped a beautiful novice from her cloistered monastery and fallen madly in love with her. When her brothers appealed to the emperor in Constantinople to intervene, Euphemius was ordered to return her. In an act of spite and revenge, he set sail to Ifriqiya and sought the aid of the Aghalbid Court.

What is of interest about the various and contradictory readings of Euphemius is found less in the medieval archives and more in modern historiography. The two dominant narratives, which can be classified as (i) the nativist Italian version and (ii) the European Byzantinist version, uncannily reflect the various visions of Sicily that may be grafted along geographical and culturally dividing lines.

Amari's magisterial *Storia dei Muslmani di Sicilia* (published in mid- to late nineteenth century) draws on just about all the extant sources available to him – Latin, Greek and Arabic – and he tells his story of Euphemius with measured objectivity.⁵ He sees Euphemius as a native Sicilian of Greek origin, formation and profession. And he reads his memorable actions – from military adventurism, piracy and insurrection, to his ultimate invitation to the Muslims of across the Sea to invade the island – as being compatible with Sicily's, as well as his own, best interests.

Amari begins his account of Euphemius by citing the Greek and Latin **configurational** accounts of his romantic story of falling in love with the young nun, stealing her away from her convent and defying imperial orders for her return. The bulk of his 'historical' account is drawn primarily for the chronologically ordered **episodic** accounts of the Arabic sources (Ibn al-Athir, al-Nuwayri and Ibn Khaldun). The mutiny against the Byzantine government in Sicily and the appeals to the Aghlabid Court 'south of the border' are presented by Amari as actions that fall within the interpretation that the rebellions of 825–8 stemmed from an indigenous movement to rid the island of 'foreign' rule.

Ferdinando Gabotto, the Torino-born Italian historian and former professor at the University of Messina (Sicily) took this reading a step further in the next generation. In his 1890 article, '*Eufemio e il movimento separatista nell'Italia bizantina*', he laments the fact that Euphemius is much maligned and insufficiently treated in the historical sources. He makes the claim that historians lack the understanding of what was happening in Sicily on the ground, and erroneously conclude that Euphemius's appeal to 'outsiders' – to Arabs no less – was nothing more than an act of treason. Gabotto, echoing Amari, reads the events of 825–8 as a national movement of resistance to Byzantine occupation and an attempt to make Sicily an independent state. He concludes that Euphemius was a national hero whose actions must be read in the context of this movement. His appeal to the Arabs, Gabotto asserts, does not take away Euphemius's passionate patriotism and the lofty ideals of his rebellion.⁶

The later alternate readings, proffered by two scholars with primary interest in and broad knowledge of the history of the Byzantine Empire, refute this view altogether.

Irishman John B. Bury (d.1927) dismisses any possibility of Euphemius as a national hero:

He was simply ... a successor of Mizizios, Sergius, and Elpidus, who had in the 7th and 8th centuries used a favorable occasion to set up a 'tyranny', and has no claim to be distinguished from other 'tyrants'.[7]

In *Byzance et les Arabes*, the Russian historian Alexander Vasiliev (d.1953) takes a more nuanced approach towards refuting the Siciulo-Italian narrative.[8] The scholarly value of Vasiliev's treatment of Euphemius rests in his ability to read and appreciate both the 'romantic' and 'historical' dimensions of the Euphemius saga, demonstrating what I argue in this chapter as the intertwining modes of fact and fiction, or, truth and lie, in reading Muslim Sicily. Vasiliev calls attention to the early Byzantine and Western (*occidentales*) accounts of the passionate love that prompted our romantic hero to snatch the young nun from her cloister, and in the vein of a good storyteller, he ends the affair with the execution of Euphemius in a version that contradicts other accounts. Following the recapture of Syracuse by Byzantine forces, Euphemius and his militia join forces with the Arabs and head inland where they eventually dismount in Castrogiovanni (Enna). When the Arabs sense his change of heart and his encouragement to his Sicilian compatriots to resist the Arabs, they lure him into a position and kill him from behind. Vasiliev then cites a Greek account whereby Euphemius is murdered by two brothers – and here we are led to believe that these were the brothers of the virginal object of his unbridled lust. In a scene with all the makings of a classical Greek drama, as Vasiliev observes, the brothers pretend to be bearing robes of investiture sent by Constantinople to ordain Euphemius as emperor of Sicily. As they stand before a genuflected and bowed-headed Euphemius, one brother takes hold of his hair and the other slices off his head.

As much as he appears swayed by this account, and even accepting the possibility that it may hold '*une certaine part de vérité*', Vasiliev argues for a political (read: historical) interpretation. Taking something of a medial position, he supports the thesis that the Sicilian revolt in the years 825–8 is the proper context in which we must read Euphemius's actions, but he cautions against the designation of a 'national hero'. Vasiliev dismisses Bury's argument that pure ambition and greed prompted such acts of treason, and he sees credence in the view that widespread local discontent was behind both the revolt and Euphemius's participation in it. But in the end, he concludes that insufficient historical evidence and discrepancies in the accounts do not justify that Siciulo-Italian claim that Euphemius was a national hero whose aim was not only to rid Sicily of foreign occupation, but also to restore the island and the Roman Empire.[9]

The closing chapters of Muslim rule in Sicily two centuries later end in a similar fashion. Following the deposition in 1044 of the last Kalbid prince, al-Hasan ibn al-Samsam, the island was carved up into petty kingdoms. Ibn al-Thumna, who had taken control of Syracuse and Catania, was married to the sister of Ibn al-Hawwas, warlord of Castrogiovanni and Agrigento. One night, following a heated argument, Ibn al-Thumna, in a drunken rage, had his wife's veins bled, and he left her to die. When her son found her, he summoned physicians who came in time to save her life. On the following morning, Ibn al-Thumna made his apologies, pleaded for her forgiveness and (at a time soon thereafter) granted her request to visit her brother. When she notified her brother of what had happened, Ibn Hawwas refused to return his sister to her husband, his rival warlord. The indignant husband set out to battle his revenging brother-in-law, but ended up defeated. With his army in disarray and his power base weakened, Ibn al-Thumna sought the assistance of the Norman army. In a near carbon copy of the act of treason Euphemius committed two hundred years earlier, Ibn al-Thumna paved the way for the Muslim defeat.

Once again, to the master Arab chroniclers, the history of Muslim Sicily must have read like a history in miniature – a complete story with beginning, middle and end – replete with classic themes of 'what goes around comes around', of turned tables, just deserts and revenge exacted. The 'thin description', to borrow from new historicist terminology, of these acts of treason perpetrated by both Muslim and Christian individuals or groups contrast sharply with the 'thick description' of universal Islamic jihad in all its claims to a world neatly divided between peoples of two distinct faiths. But the *jihadist* view of a divided world along religious or civilizational fault lines unfolded right before their eyes as they chronicled the particulars of Islamic history's 'Sicilian' chapter.

A society in flux: Marginalization and shifting loyalties

When the tenth-century Baghdad-born traveller and merchant Ibn Hawqal visited the island of Sicily in 973, he wrote an account of his journey that has come to enjoy a prominent – if not unique – place in the historiography of Muslim Sicily. Its curious mixture of precise scholarly observations, on the one hand, and its caustic, overstated judgements worthy of the ugly tourist, on the other, convey a tone of shock at what Ibn Hawqal was witnessing. My intention in this chapter is not another re-reading of his Sicilian observations in his *Surat al-ard* to affirm Islam's presence on the island, but rather to focus on those aspects of Sicilian Islam that our Muslim traveller from the east found so objectionable.

Ibn Hawqal was stunned by the large number of mosques and the Sicilians' obsession with owning their own private and exclusive places of worship. On the other hand, he expressed his disgust with people he referred to as riffraff and freeloaders, whom he described as congregating at the many fortified monasteries (*ribat*) that stretched along the Sicilian coastline, and whom he accused of stealing alms for the poor and defaming honourable women. He was appalled at the large number of teachers, castigating them for their arrogance and cowardice and for hiding under cover of their professions to shirk their responsibility to defend the faith and fight the jihad.

Ibn Hawqal's acerbic criticisms assume in some way the hallowed and heroic reputation Muslim Sicily enjoyed by its second century as a *thaghr* (frontier society) where Islam extended itself for protection against its enemies, trespassing the boundaries between the worlds of true faith and disbelief. The Muslim invasion of Sicily and its incorporation into *Dar al-Islam*, north of the Mediterranean divide and deep into enemy territory, must have indeed captured the imagination of the traveller-scholar from Baghdad, as it did no doubt that of Muslims throughout the lands of the east, and it raised all sorts of expectations for Ibn Hawqal, realistic or romanticized, at the time of his arrival. Any contradiction or violation of Sicily's picture-perfect image of a society perpetually at holy war with the infidel would need to be explained away or rationalized.

Ironically, Ibn Hawqal's visit came at a relatively stable moment in Muslim Sicily's war-riven history. The capture ten years earlier of the city of Taormina, the last serious Christian stronghold on the island, and the subsequent fall a mere three years later of the neighbouring fortress town of Rometta, secured Muslim sovereignty over the island and meant that any serious Byzantine challenge was successfully held off. More significantly, the Muslim victory at the Battle of the Straits (*waq'at al-majaz*) in 965 put Byzantium on the defensive and granted to the Muslims at least a semblance of peace and stability.

Ibn Hawqal's reactions and comments on what he judged to be the Sicilian Muslims' less-than-stellar performance in defence of the faith and their lacklustre observation of other religious duties clearly clashed with his expectations of finding a world neatly delineated between *Dar al-Islam* and *Dar al-Harb*. His was a world, real or imagined, in which jihad would remain the spiritual force, if not the legal and political instrument, that established and monitored the accepted (and acceptable) norms of cohabitation, whereby defining the self and regulating all relations with the other. However, his comments beg further interrogation into the porous and shifting boundaries that marked an island long accustomed to the tricky business of war and peace, of assimilation and dissimilation, where people's preoccupations, including by now those of his own co-religionists, were not always centred on engaging in battle against a monolithic (and here: Christian) enemy. Above all, he needed to make sense of the perennial internal skirmishes and rivalries that tore at the fabric of Muslim unity itself.

His comments, in sum, are crude reminders that something was rotten in the state of jihad. His observations led him to denounce all those who did not conform to his preconceived notions of the perfect community of *mujahidin*, men he describes as snobby elites, arrogant and cowardly teachers, freeloaders and riffraff who steal and seduce, and in later passages, men who marry Christian women and allow their daughters to be baptized, who fail to observe the rituals of purity prescribed by sacred law, and who neglect to give alms to the poor and perform the pilgrimage to Mecca (*Surat al-Ard*, 123). The tone of these passages hints at a sense of betrayal, not only to Islam, but to Ibn Hawqal personally. It disturbs his romanticized vision of a Muslim frontier society imbued with all the physical and spiritual attributes of the Islamic jihad. These were attributes prescribed and expounded upon in the *siyar* literature of the contemporaneous Muslim jurists, interpreted and manipulated by the Aghlabid princes of Qayrawan and their Fatimid successors in Mahdiyya in the execution of their Sicilian jihad and inscribed throughout subsequent centuries onto classical Arabic historiographical literature. The fact remains that any prescribed or theoretical notions of jihad's vision of *Dar al-Islam* and *Dar al-Harb* were often ignored, blurred, challenged or violated in practical historical circumstances, and Ibn Hawqal's caustic remarks are best read with this in mind.

***

In treating the theme of treason as historical anecdote and/or literary trope, I draw attention to two issues that open up to broader contexts for understanding the nature and reasons for these treacherous acts: (i) political and social marginalization and (ii) shifting or negotiable loyalties. From the onset, I readily concede that self-preservation, financial greed, craving for power or personal ambition, and other universal human weaknesses that cut across eras and cultures could well have played roles in the perpetration of these acts. But the specificities of time and space, from the immediate pre- to the immediate post-periods of Muslim Sicily warrant further investigation that will, among other things, debunk the myths and clarify some of the misunderstandings of historical jihad.

Muslim Sicily stood at the crossroads of Islam and Christendom, East and West, or what is now Europe and the Middle East, and much of what divides the two historically, politically, culturally, psychologically and aesthetically today indeed divided them in the tenth century. As a 'frontier', Sicily experienced a complex of cross-cultural conflict and exchange, offering porous borders that could be drawn and redrawn, penetrated and violated with relative ease. The Muslim invasion in 827 was yet one more in a long series of foreign invasions, and once again the battlefield became the foremost public sphere. With the capture of Palermo in 831, there gradually emerged a new Muslim urban centre onto the Sicilian landscape. The new central administration would oversee changes to the old Latin/Byzantine *latifunda* system, with landed estates being carved up and distributed to the victorious holy warriors. As the Muslims gradually settled, these new urban centres and the rich agricultural estates surrounding them formed a nexus that came to define the contours of the new society. The settled fortified towns and the adjacent rural landscapes gave rise to new spaces – public and private, military and civilian – that brought Muslims and non-Muslims into daily contact. In the nooks and crannies of these spaces, new identities shaped by both physical environment and historical circumstances came into existence. The Arab and Berber warriors brought with them a need for mosques and schools since, as a religious obligation, physical jihad could only find its completion in spiritual jihad. Ziyadat-allah, the Aghlabid prince of Ifriqiya, understood this when he appointed Asad ibn al-Furat, accomplished scholar of Maliki jurisprudence, to command the first Sicilian expedition, and when he dispatched scholars and men of religion to accompany the battalions. Consequently, in time, the Arabs introduced into Sicily factories, arsenals, mills, *funduqs*[10] (inns for travellers and merchants), *hammam*s (public baths) and *souk*s (open markets) where men and women of different religions, ethnicities, languages and professions mixed and mingled amid 'antagonism and a sharing of a common life'. Even in private homes, if we are to take Ibn Hawqal at his word, *Dar al-Islam* intercoursed with *Dar al-Harb* through marriage, concubinage and harems, and his image of a single family with Muslim sons and Christian daughters challenges the medieval (and modern) world view of two religions in perpetual, irreparable conflict.

Unlike the major Muslim centres of Qayrawan, Cairo, Damascus, Baghdad and Isfahan, where Muslim sovereignty was unquestionable, and where any minority 'other' was held in legal, social and religious check, the Palermo of Ibn Hawqal's encounter was still a frontier, still very much a '*ghazi*' society in which jihad was the dominant law and ideology but not the only social and political force which to contend. Conflict was the first order of business, but with colonization, urbanization and cohabitation it had to cede ground eventually to other professions and walks of life.

Once again, the specificities of Muslim Sicilian time and space generated on the island a significant degree of social marginalization. 'Medieval societies were far from stable spatially', writes Bronislaw Geremek. 'Great waves of migration and the colonization of new lands that from time to time put enormous masses of people into motion, together with the processes of urbanization, led to demographic imbalance as population flowed continually from rural areas to the city or from smaller towns to the larger cities.'[11] Such was the case of medieval Sicily, where migrations of people living life on the legal, social and political margins of society can be viewed from several perspectives. First, as the largest island in the Mediterranean, Sicily's strategic location rendered it an important trading centre attracting merchants from many lands, near and far. As a crossroads of civilization, Sicily had long been accustomed to hosting people whose different linguistic, religious and professional origins and backgrounds did not always stew in a monolithic Sicilian melting pot.

The Arabs did not invade and occupy a homogeneous island, and their very presence, in all its own tribal and ethnic diversity, added to the knots and gnarls of Sicilian heterogeneity.

Second, from a religious or legal perspective, Sicily was a natural landscape for exile. Since ancient Roman times, and reincorporated throughout medieval Christianity, any infraction of sacred law or the social code ended in banishment or excommunication which, Geremek reminds us, are 'typical processes of marginalization'.[12] Murderers, thieves, blasphemers, heretics, deserters and dissidents, vagabonds and unemployed, lepers and prostitutes, could find some space in the porous boundaries of Sicily.

Third, foreign domination and shifts in government enhanced marginalization as new political and economic powers privileged their own elites and their affiliated landed gentry at the expense of both the impoverished local population and the non-assimilated minority groups. And fourth, war itself contributed greatly to marginality. Geremek writes:

> [War] created possibilities for existence outside the normal life experience of peasants and artisans, first in regularly commanded companies and then in autonomous bands. The difference was not great between normal military service and brigandage, between an army company and a robber band.[13]

Which all brings us to the second issue of loyalty.

As people moved, individually or collectively, mobility and relocation led to a state of dislocation, both physically and psychologically. The various processes of resettlement, exile or banishment, capture, imprisonment or enslavement, elected or coerced conversion, assimilation or intermarriage, had serious implications for both 'acquired loyalties' and 'loyalties of category', defined by Roy Mottahedeh as loyalties 'forged through deliberate acts', and loyalties 'men felt they owed each other because of their common participation in some broader social grouping.'[14]

As a land frequently subjected to foreign invasion, the Sicilian landscape was drawn and redrawn to reflect historical circumstances, and its inhabitants, by force, were long accustomed to becoming different things to different people. Religious, ethnic, linguistic, political and cultural boundaries were reset, shifted, negotiated and at times compromised, to accommodate and concede to the powerful forces of history. Local populations, communities and subgroups must have 'felt pulled by the many horizontal and vertical ties of identity',[15] and allegiances to a king, a baron, a church, a language or culture, were always negotiable.

One wonders, then, who might have been all those freeloaders and draft dodgers who hung around the Sicilian *ribat* and who made Ibn Hawqal's blood boil. And who exactly were those '*musha'midhin*' he refers to who let their daughters grow up as Christians and who neglected to circumcise their sons and make the pilgrimage to Mecca? Was this in fact an observation on apostasy and dissimulation, or merely on lapses in religious observance?

A closer examination of all those who came to be considered 'citizens' of *Dar al-Islam* in Sicily reveals a great complexity and diversity that would test the limits of any society or political entity in commanding the same degree of allegiance from each and every member. It must be recalled that the Arab warriors were foreign invaders, and they brought with them a relentless zeal for their religion that was perceived by the island's inhabitants as inimical and antagonistic to their own religious values and creeds. Added to this is the fact that both the dominant Latin-speaking population and the Greek-speaking minority community were bound in allegiance to either the Roman or Byzantine churches, allegiances reinforced by assertive and competing monastic and clerical missions that dotted the Sicilian landscape.

Moreover, the Muslim armies brought to Sicily their own old tribal rivalries and divisions that traced their roots back to the Arabian Peninsula. Their Berber co-religionists also fell victim to their own tribal factions, and added to these were the perennial and persistent Arab–Berber tensions that punctuated Muslim Sicilian history. The chroniclers mention on occasion Persians and Africans among the Muslim armies, and, although they remain invisible and voiceless in much of the Siciulo-Arabic historical documentation, one must always wonder how their loyalties were obtained and maintained. Added to these ethnic and tribal divides were sectarian differences that always had the potential to flare up in civil strife. The court of Ziyadat-allah in Qayrawan, the motherland of the Sicilian jihad, was rife with sectarian squabbles, with the Sunni Hanafis bickering with the Malikis over the meaning of true orthodoxy, with adherents of Shi'ism and Mu'tazilism jockeying for political influence, not to mention the Kharijites who made deep inroads into the disenfranchised rural Berber population. All of whom were imported to Sicily as long as the jihad movement depended heavily on North African manpower.

The Islamic conquest of Sicily also reproduced other groups or categories of citizens that formed part of *Dar al-Islam*, but whose loyalties and allegiances proved to be even more fickle and unreliable than those of the conquering, male, Muslim, tribal Arabs and Berbers. For the sake of expediency, these can be grouped as (i) *mawali* (Muslim and non-Muslim clients of the wealthy and powerful) and (ii) slaves, both military and civil/domestic. Fortunately for these groups, the sources do provide some voice.

The *mawali* of Muslim Sicily may have included converts to Islam, freed slaves or Christians and Jews who, through acceptance of paying the poll tax (*jizya*), were given legal status and 'state' protection (as *dhimma*). Their designation as *mawla* (a term which, incidentally, designates both the client and the patron) was predicated on the formal and legally recognized relation of *wala'*, which Patricia Crone defines as 'a tie of dependence which derives its efficacy from the fact that the client is detached from his natal group without acquiring full membership of another'.[16] Throughout the Muslim Empire the conquest of new territories and the subjugation of large numbers of non-Arab and non-Muslim populations increased the numbers of those who sought or accepted *wala'* as a means of survival, accommodation or even advancement in the new world order. Crone furthermore makes the point that although non-Arab Muslims initially made their careers in the service of their patrons, their education, skills and sheer numbers quickly opened positions of influence. She cites as examples labourers, craftsmen, traders, shopkeepers and bureaucrats (scribes), and she astutely observes that scholarship in its many various disciplines opened the doors of advancement to members of the *mawali* classes. For those with high levels of literacy and education, opportunities to tutor the children of the rich and powerful abounded.[17] One cannot help but wonder, with this in mind, if the large numbers of 'freeloading' teachers who congregated at the mosques and were derided by Ibn Hawqal may be no more than unemployed *mawali* whose ranks glutted the market and whose supply exceeded the demand.

The second group, the slaves, also formed a significant portion of the Sicilian Muslim *jihadist* demography. As long as the Muslim armies settled along the frontiers and engaged in battle, the taking of prisoners and their incorporation into society created a range of legal and social statuses and functions that allowed for various degrees of penetration and manoeuvrability within *Dar al-Islam*. Military slaves were more often than not men captured in battles whose sons and grandsons inherited similar positions that passed down through generations. The soldier-slave could serve an individual or clan as a bodyguard or a backup in battle, or could become part of a privately owned and controlled militia. He could also be conscripted into the collective or royal forces, or at times serve as a palace guard. A freed slave could conceivably continue in a military role or assume some other function within a *wala'* relationship.

Ibn al-Athir provides us with a snapshot of how this relationship worked. In his account on an early Norman incursion into Sicily in 981, he reports that a Norman general, one Barduwil, was fighting during an assault on the Muslim fortress town of Miletto in the northeast province of the island. He was accompanied by a Jewish horseman who rode as a backup to his patron in battle. After Barduwil's horse was killed underneath him, the Jewish client offered his patron his own horse in an act of fealty, pleading with him at that very moment that the general assume legal guardianship of his son in the event of the Jew's death in battle. Ibn al-Athir reports that the Jew did succumb and that Barduwil survived, but nothing more is said, leaving the reader of the report to make his own assumptions.[18] The anecdote, despite the fact that it deals with a Christian and a Jew, nevertheless illustrates one kind of strand in the web of cross-religious relationships that informed the medieval Sicilian landscape. It furthermore underscores the reality that the lines dividing medieval Muslim, Christian and Jewish interactions were not as clear-cut as often imagined.

Whether a convert to Islam, a legally recognized *dhimmi*, a client through manumission (*mawla al-'itq*), or simply a soldier-slave, the client maintained his loyalty to his patron but not without extracting some benefit in return. It was an unequal relationship in any case, no doubt, but one where there was a clear recognition of mutual rights and obligations. The irreproachable act of loyalty enshrined in Ibn al-Athir's anecdote cited above contrasts with other examples that abound in the sources, suggesting once again that loyalties and allegiances could be kept and broken, bought and sold, at any time. Apart from the obvious cases of Euphemius and Ibn al-Thumna, many acts of treason were committed by men in (military) uniform. The earliest reports of acts of betrayal within the Muslim ranks in Sicily, in fact, came at the hands of members of the slave corps who murdered both Khafaja ibn Sufyan in 869 and his son and successor Muhammad in 871. Beneath the scant information on these murders provided in the chronicles lies a vast subtext of possibilities, especially given that both assassinations ended with successful escapes by the culprits.

Indeed, the silences in the chronicles lead one to speculate on the possible reasons why these assassinations took place at these times. It is possible that the perpetrators of these 'treasonous' acts were soldier-slaves who were 'native' Sicilians captured during the Muslim conquests, or sons of men captured and who inherited this status. Although fully integrated into the Muslim military establishment, these men may have still harboured loyalties to Roman or Byzantine authorities. Another possibility is that these acts were forms of revolt against a system that was inequitable or abusive, given that slaves, many of who had their manhood severed from their bodies, were performing equal fighting but not receiving an equal share of the spoils of war. A third possibility lies in the recent chink in the chain of command within the Sicilian jihad. With the death in 850 of Muhammad ibn al-Aghlab, the handpicked cousin of the emir in Qayrawan, the Sicilian forces elected their own popular general, 'Abbas ibn al-Fadl, who took command before receiving Qayrawan's consent. This scenario was repeated again in 861 following 'Abbas's death when the Sicilians elected his son, Muhammad. This time, Qayrawan rejected the election and dispatched Khafaja to rule Sicily. The assassinations of both Khafaja and his son, also named Muhammad, the first reported only as having been perpetrated by a Muslim soldier, and the second by a personal eunuch slave, could well be viewed within the context of a growing rift between the 'Sicilian' Muslim forces and their commanders from North Africa. Although it would be too early and much too speculative to speak of any desire on the part of the Muslim soldiers on the ground in Sicily for autonomy from the 'mainland', it does suggest differences of opinion on how and by whom the jihad should be commandeered. These divergent opinions open yet another front for dissent, division and shifting loyalties that could lead to acts of treason and betrayal.

In 1006, the slave corps was once again implicated, this time along with the Berbers, in a rebellion against the governor in Palermo, Ja'far, which was supported – if not engineered – by the prince's own brother, 'Ali. In the aftermath of the rebellion, the Berbers were expelled and the slave soldiers put to death, an act so drastic that it suggests the rulers' fears of either their growing power or their dangerously unpredictable shifts in loyalty.

On the domestic front, slaves also had a visible presence in Muslim Sicilian society. With the Islamic prohibition of killing women and children in battle, large numbers of them grew up to be incorporated into the system in various capacities upon capture. Prepubescent boys could anticipate a military assignment, but also a civilian one as well, functioning as messengers, personal aides or some type of domestic servant. Women and girls were brought into the multi-layered world of domesticity, and again with the possibility of a wide range of functions. The ninth-century Baghdadi polymath al-Jahiz (d.869) provides five terms for women servants in his *Epistle on Singing Girls* (*Risalat al-Qiyan*), and although not all of these terms appear in the extant Siciulo-Arabic lexicon, they do nonetheless broaden our scope on the multi-layeredness of slavery in medieval Muslim society. Incidentally, the works of al-Jahiz appear in some of the biographies of fourth- and fifth-century Sicilian philologists, and so it is within the realm of possibility that this particular work was known in Arabo-Sicilian academic circles. But I cite it here less for its potential textual circulation than for its description of how foreign women trespassed, penetrated and even broadened the linguistic, social, legal and artistic boundaries across medieval Muslim domestic life.

Al-Jahiz's five terms – *raqiq, wasifa, ama, jariya* and *qayna*[19] – conspicuously omit the most familiar and widely used term, *'abd*. Although all five words carry the basic meaning of slave(girl), the enumeration and sequencing of the terms very possibly suggest a hierarchy, beginning with the bottom rung, and indicating differences in function. The first (*raqiq*) is simply a generic term for any slave, male or female, who has not been granted any modicum of freedom. On the other hand, the last (*qayna*) has come to mean quite specifically a singing girl of high calibre, one fully educated and cultivated, and whose duty is to 'entertain' her patron and his guests with poetry and music, not unlike the Japanese geisha.

The second term (*wasifa*) is a servant, and we can assume that she was a domestic servant in charge of menial household tasks, such as serving food and drink or cleaning. The third or middle term *ama* most likely was used for one discharged with the duties of caring for children, a nanny of sorts, or a servant with higher domestic responsibilities. The fourth, the most generic and complex, is the *jariya*, the most often cited term in both historical and literary sources. She is often viewed in the company of the patron and her functions range from those of a handmaiden to a sexual consort.

Once again, the Siciulo-Arabic sources provide us with glimpses of how these women functioned in society. The Sicilian poet Ibn Hamdis (d.1033) composed three elegiac pieces (one extant only in fragment) on the occasion of the drowning of his *jariya*, Jawhara, giving us an unambiguous image, albeit terse and opaque, of a master-slave relationship. It must be remembered that all slaves were forced – more often than not, violently – into this status, and they were acquired and distributed through the division of booty, purchase or as gifts. A slave-girl such as Jawhara, whom Ibn Hamdis alludes to as having purchased in one of his poems,[20] most probably had witnessed the murder of a father, brother or even husband, at the time of capture. And although neither literary nor historical medieval Arabic writing provides the deluge of graphic images of chains and whips that accentuate much of the early modern European and American narratives of slavery, we are to assume that life could be extremely difficult for a slave. On the other hand, Islamic law and medieval Muslim culture stipulate benign treatment of slaves – that they be fed and clothed, attended to when ill and that they be set free at the time of the patron's death. Furthermore, much of Arabic literature – and here, Ibn Hamdis's elegies to Jawhara are to be included – provides examples of slaves who were fully integrated into the social structures, and even at times, elevated to powerful positions, public and private.

A chronology of Ibn Hamdis's life in exile can be reconstructed through a careful and literal reading of many of his verses. For, in between the lines of his highly mannered and, at times, heavy-handed reworkings of the idioms, images and motifs of classical Arabic poetry emerge snippets of information, allusions and vivid accounts of real historical people and events that give his poetry extraordinary historiographical value. We can thus surmise that Jawhara perished at sea, in a journey that preceded him, and one very likely that followed his second exile from the city of Seville in 1091 when the Almoravids sacked the town and imprisoned his friend and patron, al-Muʿtamid Ibn ʿAbbad.

The two fully extant elegies differ slightly in stylistics: the first is a short piece of thirteen lines with short metres and a quick-paced rhyme scheme, suggesting that it was composed, possibly extemporaneously, soon after the poet heard the news of her death; the second is a long poem of twenty-nine lines, with a longer metre and a more brooding, philosophical and reflective tone, suggesting a composition later in the poet's life. Once again, to those familiar with the poetry of Ibn Hamdis, the Jawhara elegies strike two familiar chords: First, they are composed along the literary conventions and strictures of the classical Arabic elegiac poem for women and children, with its gnomic introduction, emphasis on the physical attributes and innocence of the deceased and the agony (*tafajju'*) of loss; and second, these poems share the language, images, themes and moods that inform what has now been widely accepted as his *siqilliyat* – that is, those handful of poems in which Ibn Hamdis remembers, laments and eulogizes the loss of his beloved homeland of Sicily.

The fact that the poet could inscribe his relationship and loss of his slave-girl onto the most sacred ground of his poetic universe suggests a relationship far deeper than one of master and slave(girl). More than a precious commodity, Jawhara was a companion in life and in exile, being in essence an integral part of both his private and public worlds. Important to him was her youth and beauty, but also her companionship and loyalty, and we see this in the following verses:

> 22- O link to my world, you have disappeared from my sight;
>   my heart reads your tender companionship on the pages of misery.
> 23- Had I found you not so distant from me,
>   the Master of my soul would see it as a reflection of you.
> 24- If he was compelled to submit to a fate that delivered you to [the sea],
>   he did not do so out of betrayal or deceit.
> 25- Was he not [like you] drowning with one hand raised?
>   Whoever ordered your death deprived [me] of the same cup to drink.
> ("Elegy to a slave Girl *(Jawhara)* Who Drowned at Sea;" *Diwan*, #1)

In articulating his personal agony of loss, the poet questions his own loyalty (l. 24), since he allowed her to separate from him and travel at a different time. Explicit in his questioning is her own unquestionable loyalty to him, as exemplified in the fact that she gave up her life in his service. The line explodes in irony on several fronts. First, as a slave, as a female and as a non-Arab, being most likely a Christian captive or an African slave, Jawhara was forced into her status, and to ascribe to her such a noble quality as loyalty, one that was more often than not evoked in the medieval world to male bonding, elevates her rank considerably. Secondly, it debunks the myth of pure 'Arab' origins as vital to true nobility, one that Ibn Hamdis often used in his panegyrics to the many princes who sought political and personal legitimation to their ascension to power. Read against his hollow praises to the Berber Zirid warlords of North Africa, the elegies to Jawhara stand in stark contrast. Thirdly, that a non-Arab, female slave stood by the perennially banished, exilic poet during his darkest hours, while fellow Muslims and Arabs sat passively and allowed his beloved homeland Sicily, and his adopted country Seville, to fall into the clutches of the Christian armies gives the elegy its most poignant meanings. For, the *petit récit* of Jawhara's loyalty disturbs and violates the *grand récit* of the Islamic jihad, drawing attention to the fact that Seville was being torn apart by the re-conquest of Alfonse VI from one side and the invasion of the fundamentalist Muslim Berber Almoravid warlords on the other. At the same time, petty Muslim warlords of Sicily were battling one another for control of the island, effectively allowing for a relatively easy Norman conquest.

The elegies to Jawhara and Ibn al-Athir's anecdote of the Jewish horseman illustrate first and foremost how the quality of loyalty was so powerfully valorized in the societies of the Middle Ages. They are also small but illuminating examples of how (some) marginal people lived and died, functioned and survived, within the clashing worlds of medieval Islam and Christendom. Both of these pétit-protagonists, along with the many Muslims and Christians who 'jumped ship', shifted allegiances, converted, sold out or committed acts of treason for personal benefit or merely to survive, are pieces in the vast network of contexts and subtexts to treasonous acts. Sicily, the consummate pawn in a world of religious and political conflict, was a natural landscape for cross-cultural conflict and exchange, and all that transpired in between. Moreover, it was negotiable terrain, as I have been arguing, where the power and limitations of *Dar al-Islam* and *Dar al-Harb* were constantly tested.

***

Muslim frontier societies like Sicily and al-Andalus were inhabited by significant numbers of people living on the margins, from indigenous populations to men and women in transit, from clients (*mawali*), slaves, travelling merchants, scholars, and pilgrims and soldiers of fortune, to political and religious discontents, whose loyalties were fickle and negotiable. As power and power centres shifted from place to place, sultan to sultan, and from Islam to Christianity or vice versa, acts of treason and betrayal often occurred as a means of survival or advancement. It is worth reiterating that the complex politics of war and peace also gave way to these shifting boundaries. Above all, the nearly constant state of military confrontation, which resulted not only in the capture of slaves and the occasional shifts to the enemy side, had deleterious effects on the economy, especially in the destruction of the enemy's farmlands, the pillaging of natural resources, and the confiscation of private and public property. All of these, not to mention the occurrence of natural disasters such as earthquakes, droughts and floods, created waves of impoverishment for many sectors of society. Poverty and desperation also bred treasonous acts. Given all these factors, we may broaden our definition: 'Invoking the term *treason*', writes N. Ben-Yehuda, 'elicits a set of concepts associated with it, such as revolt, sedition, insurrection, disobedience, mutiny, uprising and subversion. Similar terms are associated with other forms of betrayal, such as treachery, deception, trickery, perfidy and infidelity.'[21]

The role of espionage also had its place in Muslim frontier societies. Whether in the form of individuals or, to use a modern neologism, a fifth column,[22] spying on the enemy was an effective means of maintaining and controlling power balances in 'international' relations. In a rare but insightful study of treason and war written between the war years of the mid-twentieth century, Hans Speier notes that 'throughout history fifth columns have made their appearance in civil and religious wars, when the enemies were separated not by geographical boundaries but by hostile loyalties.'[23] Speier includes in his study a distinction between the 'spy' and the 'fifth columnist', although many of their functions are the same: the spy, for which he cites four categories: (i) the common spy; (ii) the spy of consequence; (iii) the double spy; and (iv) the forced spy who 'belongs to the past era of the national sovereign state …

operating in an international system in which power was so distributed as to insure a more or less precarious balance', while the fifth columnist works for a new era of hegemony in world politics. His emphasis on espionage as 'indispensable when relations between states were based on the public recognition and secret distrust of the principle of sovereignty' puts its finger on the pulse of the state of affairs between the Islamic and Christian states of the middle and western Mediterranean basins throughout much of the Middle Ages. Declarations of war and cessation of hostilities were bound – at least nominally – by treaties that specified rights and obligations, establishing a de facto recognition of the other. One need only recall Aghlabid-Byzantine relations at the time of the Muslim conquest of Sicily in 827 to understand this. Ziyadat-allah, in search of a foreign venture to divert attention away from his many domestic problems, was determined to invade Sicily, but he was bound to a peace treaty with its Byzantine governors, we may recall, that had been concluded by his successor and was still in effect. The debates that ensued between his two chief judges, Abu Muhriz, a powerful voice in the Qayrawani *ulema* who counselled caution and pleaded for a wait-and-see strategy, and Asad ibn al-Furat, maverick scholar and Aghlabid loyalist, who took the opposite position after learning from spies that the Byzantines were holding Muslim prisoners in violation of the treaty, underscore the legal limitations of making war and peace. Obviously, the more powerful of the two parties was in a position to dictate terms favourable to it and to execute the treaty in ways and by means most advantageous to it.

To the later Arab historians and chroniclers reading and reconstructing the events of Muslim Sicily, and upon whom, once again, we depend almost entirely for our information, the Arabo-Sicilian 'narrative', as we have shown, began with an act of espionage. Most likely the renegade captain, Euphemius, was himself the *spy of consequence*, whom Speier describes as 'rich and expensive', motivated by his own disobedience and personal ambition, the treasonous villain to this story who remained in distrust by both his Muslim contacts and his own subjects to the very end.

If the likes of Euphemius appear in various ways throughout medieval Muslim frontier history, we may also add to them more organized forms of espionage, in groups or 'fifth columns', which operated within the complex world of Muslim-Christian relations. A graphic example is provided by the fifteenth-century geographer-historian, al-Himyari, in his account of the events leading up to and including the battle of Zallaqa in 1186, between the armies of King Alfonse VI of Castile and the combined Muslim armies under the command of Prince al-Mu'tamid ibn 'Abbad of Seville. Al-Himyari begins with the eruption of tensions between the Muslims and Christians resulting from al-Mu'tamid's failure to pay his tribute tax to Alfonse. He reports that al-Mu'tamid was facing cash-flow problems stemming from his expenses in fighting a Muslim arch-rival. The account also details al-Mu'tamid's invitation to the Berber Almoravid warlord, Yusuf Tashufin, to participate in his jihad against the Christians, much to the dismay of most of the Muslim governors of the Andalusian princedoms who feared the fundamentalist appeal of Islam the Almoravids were brandishing in their climb to power. The following passage sheds precious light on the eve of the battle:

> When [Alfonse] Ibn Ferdinand received confirmation of Yusuf [Ibn Tashufin]'s crossing [the Straits], he mobilized all the troops of his territories as well as those from adjacent regions. The priests, monks, and bishops formed in procession with hoisted crosses and raised Bibles, and vast numbers of Galicians and Catalans answered his call. He monitored closely the reports of the Muslims' movements, seething with anger at [al-Mu'tamid] Ibn 'Abbad, holding him responsible [for the outburst of hostilities], and issuing threats of dire consequences. At the same time spies from both camps were teeming about.[24]

This passage emphasizes three critical points: first, the treaty that existed between Alfonse and al-Mu'tamid was clearly lopsided, favouring the Christians who now held the upper hand in the middle Iberian Peninsula; second, the existence of warfare and disagreements among the Muslims triangulated the network of power struggles, thus complicating Muslim resistance to the Christian re-conquest; and third, both sides were equally engaged in and subjected to espionage, most likely perpetrated by members of their own confessions.

Concerning a fourth and related point, al-Al-Himyari describes the crossing of the Almoravid troops onto Iberian soil and how the peasants, townsfolk and mercenaries lined up to greet the soldiers. In his account, we see the setting up of makeshift towns, brimming with markets, prayer pavilions, and stalls for providing (re: selling) food and water, teeming with merchants selling wares to the soldiers and poor folk lining up to join the holy army in order to earn a living. These scenes, along with the several mentions of monks, bishops and court physicians of Castille instigating Alfonse to trespass Muslim sacred spaces, resonate strongly with Hans Speier's analysis of modern warfare that 'modern warfare is waged by the whole of society rather than by the armed forces alone'.[25] Such was the case in the medieval world as well, as the planning and execution of war employed large numbers of people, military and civilian, who had political and financial stakes in its outcome. As a dynamic, lucrative and multifaceted enterprise, war – especially in the frontier zones – was a wide-open arena for new opportunities and a site for negotiating new loyalties and allegiances, providing men and women living on the margins to find their own entries or exits from one system to another.

Towards a poetics of treason: Treason as moral depravity

The conquest of the well-fortified Byzantine fortress town of Castrogiovanni at the end of 858 was launched from Palermo, Muslim Sicily's 'capital city' since 831. The emir, 'Abbas ibn al-Fadl, dispatched an exploratory expedition to attack and plunder Castrogiovanni. The expedition captured several prisoners, including a high-ranking Byzantine officer who was brought back to the court in Palermo. When 'Abbas ordered this Byzantine prisoner to be executed, he bargained for his life with vital information that would secure Muslim entry into Castrogiovanni.

According to the officer, the Byzantines were convinced that severe winter weather would prevent the Muslims from attacking them, so they let their guard down. 'Abbas thereupon dispatched a thousand elite troops under the command of his uncle Rabbah to launch a full-scale invasion. Rabbah handcuffed the captured Byzantine officer to himself as he and several of his men made their first foray under the dark of night. His mistrust of the Christian traitor is reminiscent of the Muslims' treatment of Euphemius thirty years earlier.

The Muslims erected a stairway up the side of a steep hill and climbed to the walls of Castrogiovanni. They reached it just before dawn while the guards were still asleep. They entered through a small gate where there was running water and where they dumped the night soil. Then they killed the guards and opened all the town gates. ʿAbbas and the remainder of the forces joined Rabbah at the time of morning prayers on 23 January 859. ʿAbbas erected a prayer hall and installed a minaret. On the following day, he delivered the Friday sermon. Then the Muslims killed as many Byzantine soldiers they could find and seized the sons and daughters of the commanders and senior officers.

Ibn al-Athir's depiction of this event, as a self-contained narrative unit, incorporates a curious mixture of the sacred and the profane that touch upon the very act of treason: the Muslim army enters the city through a cesspool; they execute sleeping soldiers; ʿAbbas builds a mosque, installs a minaret, and leads the Friday prayers and sermon. More killing follows, and the capture and molestation of young woman and boys lead to committing acts which the historian cryptically and ambiguously notes as being too horrific to describe. Both the prescriptions of ritual purity (*tahara*) and the ideals of the spiritual or greater jihad clash with the images of impurity (*najasa*) – of human faeces, violence and possibly sodomy. The historian's inability – or refusal – to elaborate on the particular details of this significant historical event implies a betrayal of the righteous values that jihad discourse constantly strives to uphold. Since the narrative begins with and is sustained by an act of treason, one must consider the possibility that Ibn al-Athir's reconstruction of the battle scene reflects the army's betrayal of the *jihadist* ideals.

Treason or deception, and here I refer specifically to the term *khiyana* as a recurring trope in the Siciulo-Islamic narrative, often enjoins the physical realm of political disunity and human weaknesses to the spiritual realm of moral corruption and religious decay. The following lines by Sicilian poet al-Samantari capture the sentiments:

> Civil strife approaches and people are unaware;
> and time lays an assault on humanity
> They lay listless to it and heed not its end;
> what prevails among them is corruption and sin.
> O, you betrayer whose sole concern is vice,
> and whose gain is what is unlawful, what do you say?
> You sold eternal life for a mere pittance,
> for a life that is about to unfold.
> – Abu Bakr ʿAtiq al-Samantari (d.464/1071); *Muʿjam* #75: 73–4

Indeed, these sentiments of mixing treason with moral decay are often evoked throughout the poetry of Ibn Hamdis: the year 1091 was indeed a momentous one in his life. Once again, his world was caving in, this time due to the invasion and capture of the kingdom of Seville by the fanatic Almoravid warlords. His patron and friend al-Mu'tamid was banished to a prison in the Maghribi desert town of Aghmat, and the court poet found himself embarking on a second exile. His arrival at the Zirid court of al-Mahdiyya compounded Ibn Hamdis's angst and despair as he was drawn closer to the events of his homeland. And in 1091, the Muslim stronghold of Noto also fell, securing a decisive victory and completion to the Norman conquest of Sicily.

Not long after his return to Ifriqiya, Ibn Hamdis composed a panegyric to his new patron, the Zirid prince Tamim ibn al-Mu'izz (r.1062–1108). For our purposes here and now, I cite several verses to illustrate how Ibn Hamdis manipulates the trope of treason into his panegyric. A foreshadowing of how Ibn Hamdis will accomplish this is set (line 11) where the poet injects personal experience within the traditional remembrance function of the *atlal*:

> 11- You think that I have forgotten, but I still remember
>   the treason of my time and the treason of my companion.

Later in the poem, during the praise segment proper, Ibn Hamdis interjects what I refer to as a 'Sicilian' interlude, in which he distracts his audience's attention away from whatever praise or appeal he intends for his patron to remind them of what is happening to his beloved homeland:

> 36- If my country were free I would go to it with a resolve
>   that considers separation a constant affliction.
> 37- But my country, how can it be ransomed for me from captivity,
>   while it sits in the clutches of the usurping infidels?
> 38- These dogs have prevailed by consuming my lands,
>   and after a lull they lunged for the veins.
> 39- Before my eyes my compatriots perished by obeying civil strife,
>   in which every woodsman lit a bonfire.
> 40- And their desires for it became such that they conducted themselves
>   in ways contrary to our faith.
> 41- Kinfolk showed no mercy to their own people,
>   as swords were dripping with the blood of kin.

42- Like the joints of the fingers that have been ripped apart,
   that were once held together by the flesh of the hand.

The Sicilian interlude of lines 36–42, some of the verses that are most often cited by modern critics, articulates unequivocally the personal anguish of the Sicilian poet-in-exile. His abrupt interjection of Muslim backbiting and political divisiveness, an otherwise uncharacteristic practice in medieval Arabic panegyrics, carries an important function not only in its stark and honest realism, but also in its exact – and, I argue, highly strategic – location within the poem. The images of Sicilians setting fires against themselves, acting in ways that violate religious laws and committing acts of murder against one another, reaffirm the dyptich image of treason and moral depravity. In the expressions of loss and separation that follow, the poem posits to Tamim the qualities of hospitality (*al-diyafa*) and protection (*al-ijara*) that are the true values of Arabness.[26] Its stark and bleak messages are clearly targeted as much to the masses of the Ifriqiyan populace and the throngs of recent emigrés from Sicily as they are to the Zirid princes, and they pose a challenge to Tamim as 'defender of the faith', the most crucial attribute to Arabo-Islamic political legitimacy, to do his political – and religious – duty.

In this regard, the trope of treason/deception in Ibn Hamdis's 'Tamim panegyric' can be read against three historical contexts: First, still traumatized by his Seville experience, Ibn Hamdis may see the treacherous invasion of the Almoravid warlords against the kingdom of Seville as a betrayal of the inclusiveness and tolerance for which the 'Abbadid court was renowned. Secondly, the trope addresses the political fragmentation of Ibn Hamdis's native homeland; the failure of the Muslims to defend themselves against the Normans; and most likely a veiled reference to Ibn al-Thumna's treason in colluding with the enemy. Thirdly, it is the betrayal of the spirit of the Islamic jihad itself, addressed to all Muslims who stood or stand by helplessly as the *umma* disintegrates.

Turncoats in a new world order

In his study of treason, Robert King examines the nature of treason and the responses it elicits in modern times. He poses such questions as 'What makes people betray their country? When is treason justified? What is treason?' And, most importantly, 'What are the limits of the claim the state is entitled to make on a citizen's allegiance?'[27] For the study of medieval societies, especially those engaged at once in domestic and external struggles, these questions are equally valid. Tenth- to twelfth-century Sicily, the site of perennial Muslim-Christian contestation, was plagued by treasonous acts committed on many fronts and in different ways: *on se trahit entre groupes, entre institutions, entre états. On trahit soi-meme.*[28] This protracted period of contestation, with its rapid movement of peoples and the constant – and at times, abrupt – shifts in political leadership, cultivated Sicily as a fertile ground for shifting allegiances. And, in spite of the institution of *dhimma* (protection to 'peoples of the book', i.e. Christians and Jews) and other Muslim legal practices and prescriptions that favoured benign treatment to non-Muslims – practices, it could be justifiably argued, that by comparison may be considered as being more tolerant than those of Christendom at that time – the fact remained that many people were brought into *Dar al-Islam* against their will. People did not freely elect to be captives in war, political prisoners or slaves.

Emerging from the pages of medieval Sicilian historiography is a rogues' gallery of mutinous generals and greedy rulers, ready and willing to cross enemy lines to further their own causes. We also see prisoners of war offering information against their own people in order to save their lives, actions all understandable as part of the human will to succeed or to survive. But in addressing the question concerning the limits of the claim the state is entitled to make on a citizen's allegiance, we can open up the full gamut of treasonous actions and their equivalents to a richer and more nuanced understanding of medieval Sicilian societies. Various actions call into question the state's ability to command the allegiance of its citizens, for example eunuch soldiers' assassination with impunity of their commanders during the siege of Castrogiovanni; the rallying around Ahmad ibn Qurhub by Palermitans in their rebellion against the early Fatimid governors, followed by their inexplicable turning against him; and the rebellions against Salim ibn Rashid and subsequent mass defections by Sicilian Muslims to Byzantine territory in 941. Ibn Qurhub understood only too well the tenuous and fickle nature of his countrymen's allegiance when, as he stood before the Fatimid Caliph al-Qa'im in Mahdiyya in 914 to face charges of sedition, he warned his North African nemesis of the treachery of his fellow Sicilians. And the Kalbid prince al-Akhal, in pitting the older generations of Sicilian Muslims against the newer

North African arrivals in 1020, directly tested the question of allegiance to the state before his citizens. The results – fratricide, mass executions and internal divisions – were disastrous for him and for the brittle *Dar al-Islam* on the island. The combination of these actions contributed to the end of nearly two centuries since the establishment of Palermo as 'capital city', while the Muslims of Sicily were groping with the essential questions of trust, loyalty, deception and betrayal.

With this in mind, I return to those vitriolic verses of the Sicilian exile poets who castigated their compatriots and cursed their enemies, evoking the evils of treacherous and deceitful behaviour. Given the span and nature of the treasonous acts discussed above, we come one step further in parsing the historical contexts and actual intentions of these actions. Again, given Muslim Sicily's time and place, with mass movements of people and political, economic and religious competition for power, it now seems even more natural that loyalties and allegiances would remain unstable. But the *traitor*, broadly defined, emerges as three types:

First, there is the victim of circumstance or the haphazard bystander, a captured soldier or innocent merchant or wayfarer, caught in the crossfire between enemy forces, ready or willing to save his neck at the cost of betraying his social, political or religious group.

Secondly, there are the traitors of discontent, individual or groups who defy, disobey, rebel or crossover to enemy lines, at times greedy for power and wealth but more often due to political or religious differences, or in response to some form of injustice or oppression. One must imagine the eunuch soldiers who murdered their officers as victims of severe bodily damage and sustained inferior treatment in an army that privileged race, class and physical manliness; or the Muslim defectors from Palermo and Agrigento who rebelled against their governors due to excessive, illegal, taxation and property confiscations. These include the more familiar traitors, such as Euphemius and Ibn al-Thumna, whose reaching out to the enemy may well have extended beyond the desire for personal ambition. Might Amari's reading of Euphemius as a Sicilian nationalist, leading a revolt against the (foreign) Byzantine occupation of the homeland, lead us to think more creatively about the nature of treason within the Sicilian context?

Thirdly, there are the traitors who defect, those whom I suggest were the real targets of the Sicilian poets' scathing verses. For, as much as we bear in mind the internal squabbles, sectarian rivalries and political infighting that plagued Muslim Sicilian history in its rise and fall, and as much as we read how Ibn Hamdis took every occasion in his poetry to reprimand this behaviour and cast blame on it for Sicily's loss to the Norman conquest, we must consider the generations of Muslim Sicilians who remained, out of necessity or choice, in their homeland, surviving, contributing to and flourishing in the new Norman kingdom. It was a betrayal that stung Arabo-Islamic sensibilities no doubt, but one that was not altogether unfamiliar to the Sicilian landscape.

The reign of Roger II in Sicily (c.1105–54), like many before it, was built upon the judicious use of local resources in what we today would refer to as state building. Just as Latin- and Greek-speaking Sicilians eventually join the ranks of a new Muslim government and its burgeoning civil institutions, so too did the Arabic speakers of eleventh-century Palermo and other urban centres contribute to Norman society. The fact that Roger could boast a chorus of Arabic court panegyrists, as we shall see in more detail in Chapter 5, who extolled his virtues, heaped praises on his buildings, and composed eulogies on the death of his loved ones bears witness to the cultural diversity and social interaction of medieval frontier politics. And while Ibn Hamdis and his exiled compatriots, scattered throughout the petty statelets of North Africa, cheered on the Muslim armies to liberate the homeland from the usurping infidels, the Norman princes succeeded in attracting Muslim scholars and scientists to grace their courts.

A most dramatic example of the traitor of complete defection to have flashed on the medieval Sicilian landscape may be seen in the figure of George of Antioch, whose entry from al-Maqrızi's (d.1442) biographical dictionary[29] has been recently deconstructed, magnificently, by Jeremy Johns.[30] By examining the broad strokes of George's life, we can define more precisely the role Sicily played in what we may now euphemistically call 'EastWest' relations. More significantly, we can see how men on the margins straddled the precarious dividing lines between empires, even climbing to the pinnacle of power.

George, son of Michael of Antioch, as the name suggests, was born to a Christian family in the Levant in the later decades of the eleventh century, most likely being a very young man at the time the first Crusade was getting under way. He and other members of his family served in the Byzantine court, but the king expelled him and his entire family on an unspecified charge. They eventually made their way to Ifriqiya where they found acceptance, favour and position at the court of the Zirid prince, Tamim. A specialist in accounting (finance), George was given a high position within the government. Once again, George and his family found themselves in trouble with the authorities, this time with Tamim's son, Yahya, who was angered by George's brother Simon, who spied on him and reported back to Tamim on his mischievous ways. Fearing for their lives, George dispatched an appeal to the Normans of Sicily for help in exchange for pledges of loyal service. A Norman vessel arrived, and George and his family, disguised as Zirid sailors, escaped safely during Friday prayers. With his accounting experience, mastery of Arabic and Greek (and possibly Latin), not to mention his native intelligence and the massive information undoubtedly accrued as a high functionary within the Zirid government, George found himself rising steadily up the ranks of the increasingly powerful Norman court.

Fast forwarding to 1123, we see the figures of Ibn Hamdis and George of Antioch intersecting at a significant historical event: the Battle of Dimas, fought over an ancient castle on a small island off the coast of Tunisia where the Christian Norman forces, under the command of George of Antioch, fought their Muslim Zirid enemies in the latest round of competition for control over the middle Mediterranean. The fierce battle ended, surprisingly, with a Muslim victory, and on that happy occasion, Ibn Hamdis, as Zirid court poet, was called upon to deliver a celebratory ode.

The lives of Ibn Hamdis and George of Antioch were similar in many ways. Born into privilege but in precarious political times, both spent their formative years achieving professional success but were forced into an exile more than once. Both had strong connections to Sicily: the one as a native son-émigré, forced to witness the downfall of a homeland; the other as an adventuring immigrant, climbing to the pinnacle of power at the dawn of a new era. Both poet and accountant, highly bi-cultured, traversed the wide expanses of the medieval Mediterranean landscape, carving out their living by serving kings and kinglets, manoeuvring in and out of religious and political circles, reaping the benefits of cross-cultural exchange and falling victim to cross-cultural conflict, deftly walking the tightrope that connected Islam and Christendom. Both were men of strong convictions and fierce loyalties, up to a point. They were the products of their time and place, and their connectedness to Sicily was sustained by their ability to survive, succeed, flourish and adapt and change, when necessary.

With this in mind, I return to the meanings(s) of *khiyana* in Ibn Hamdis's verses, and in the verses of other Sicilian poets in exile, and in the narratives of the later Arab chroniclers in their attempts to reconstruct and make sense of the rise and fall of Muslim Sicily. Less the target of condemnation, I would argue, are the treasonous actions of frightened captured soldiers, of disgruntled slaves, of starving or oppressed masses or even of the greedy petty princes competing for power that Ibn Hamdis decried. It was more the likes of George of Antioch whom the poets and historians had in mind. Although he was not a Muslim, he was raised in the Muslim east, educated in Arabic, and, above all, given refuge, protection and high rank at a Muslim court. It was George's betrayal of Arab hospitality and protection, in jumping onto the Norman ship, and his violation of the spirit of coexistence that Ibn Hamdis vilified in his verses bemoaning the fate of his beloved homeland. Above all, George of Antioch, like the modern fifth columnist, was a crude reminder of a new hegemony in world politics, as were those many Muslims who remained in Sicily, long after Islam's defeat, to survive, flourish and remain Sicilians.

In sum, my examination of treason as historical anecdote and literary trope leads to two overarching conclusions:

First, that the history of Muslim Sicily is frequently punctuated with acts of treason committed by men and groups that cut across religious, ethnic, political and professional lines.

And second, that the historiographical and literary reconstructions of these acts – and here I am not as much concerned with the '*logos*' of history as I am with the '*muthos*' of historiography – operate at both literal and metaphorical levels:

On the literal level, the Arab historians and poets recognized the processes of human history and the psychology of men living in difficult times. They saw in the actions of Euphemius and Ibn al-Thumna the realities of human flaws and the greed for power. They understood that poverty, war and oppression led the Agrigentans to revolt against their Fatimid governor Salim ibn Rashid in 938, and they saw in the Muslim Sicilian defections across enemy lines in 941 acts of treasonous desperation for which the autonomous author of the *Chronicle of Cambridge* offered a chilling description: 'There was so much starvation at the time, in Palermo as well as in the countryside, that parents began to eat their children.'

Finally, Arab poets and chroniclers recognized that Islamic history as played out in Sicily assumed that life was lived on the margins of society and that loyalties shifted and men crossed boundaries in circumstances and settings unfamiliar to, or beyond the reach of, the centres of power. By the time George of Antioch makes his appearance onto the pages of the *Biblioteca arabo-sicula*, his life story fitted neatly into the folds of Muslim Sicilian history, with his abilities to deceive, betray, shift and negotiate loyalties, and to straddle with relative ease the religious, linguistic and geographical dividing lines between Islam and Christendom.

Metaphorically, 'treason' as historical anecdote and literary trope in narrating Muslim Sicily contests, challenges, disturbs and contradicts the medieval Islamic discourse of jihad, which denotes a world clearly divided between Muslims and non-Muslims. These anecdotes expose Islamic and Sicilian history to the realities of cross-cultural conflict as well as to cross-cultural contact, to what Americo Castro describes for medieval al-Andalus, 'a constant oscillation between antagonism and the sharing of a common life between the Christian and the Muslim peoples'.

3

Land, Law and Jihad: Al-Dawudi's Anti-Fatimid Polemics

The life and times of an alienated scholar

Towards the end of the tenth century, an eminent but controversial North African legal scholar, Abu Ja'far al-Dawudi, acted upon an Islamic legal principle that was known among the legal community but infrequently practised, which allowed a pious Muslim to reject the legitimacy of a current government, excommunicate himself from the realm and take up residence elsewhere. This action was deemed the lesser of two evils, because Islamic scriptures uniformly condemned the use of violence as a means of changing the political order. The presence of an unjust ruler or illegitimate government, it was believed, was better than total chaos (*fawda*) and anarchy, and it was incumbent upon the community of believers to work within the system to effect change. The principle was known as *al-takfir wa al-hijra*, literally 'accusing of disbelief and exile'. The term ironically resurfaced in the modern political lexicon in the 1970s when a group (or groups) of Islamic militants adopted it as a name for their movement. Ironic in that in 1981, for example, these militants declared Egyptian president Anwar Sadat an infidel (*kafir*), but instead of taking up residence elsewhere as a sign of their opposition, they chose to massacre him and others during a public parade orchestrated by the Sadat regime to commemorate the Egyptian military victory of crossing Israel's Bar Lev line in the war of 1973.

Abu Ja'far Ahmad ibn Nasr al-Dawudi al-Asadi was born either in the city of al-Masila or Biskra (both in modern Algeria).[1] He was raised, educated and spent most of his professional life in Tripoli (western Libya), and died in the city of Tlemcen (in western Algeria near the border with Morocco). None of the biographical sources report the year of his birth or his age when he died. We only know that he spent the greater part of his life in Tripoli and that he died in Tlemcen in the year 1011 (402 AH). We can only approximate that his exile occurred in the later years of his life, since nothing of his curriculum vitae can be traced to his Tlemcen years. The scant information culled from the classical bio-biography attests to two undisputed facts: first, that he was a productive and influential scholar and lawyer in the Maliki school of Sunni Islam; and, second, that he lived all of his life during the period of Shi'ite Fatimid political sovereignty in North Africa (Ifriqiya).

Al-Dawudi was a self-taught scholar, thoroughly grounding himself in Qur'anic studies, prophetic *hadith*, and theoretical and practical jurisprudence, all in accordance with the principles and precepts of Malik ibn Anas (d.796) and his disciples. His biographers note that, in addition to his scholarship, al-Dawudi taught, issued *fatwa*s (legal opinions) and engaged in public debating (*munazara*) on legal issues. He was among the first to write commentaries on al-Bukhari's *Sahih*[2] and Malik's *Muwatta'*, two monumental canonical works on *hadith* and Maliki jurisprudence, respectively. He was lauded as a reflective, critical reader (*naqid mutabassir*), a talented legal scholar (*faqih bari'*), a skilled debater (*munazir thaqib*) and an assiduous writer (*mu'allif mujtahid*). Word of his vast knowledge, the clarity of his writing and his independent thinking (*ijtihad*), an attribute not commonly associated with the usually tradition-oriented Malikis, had become so widespread that law students throughout North Africa and al-Andalus came to study with him. He is reported to have written eight major works: five are lost, one exists in a single but poorly preserved manuscript, and two have survived in two manuscripts.[3]

The span of al-Dawudi's life, and certainly the years of his education, profession, and exile, as previously mentioned, all occurred within Fatimid rule (909–1171) in North Africa. The Shi'ite Mahdis rose to prominence and power by taking control, firstly over Ifriqiya proper, and eventually over vast stretches of land both to its east and west, including the island of Sicily. Recall that even after the Fatimid caliph al-Mu'zz li-din Allah conquered Egypt and moved the Fatimid capital to Cairo in the period 967–972, most of the Fatimid lands in North Africa remained for some time under their sovereignty through proxy governors. As a staunch Sunni Maliki loyalist, al-Dawudi categorically rejected their legitimacy, but his strong vocal opposition was no match for the complacency and acquiescence of many Maliki *ulema* who found some form of justification to work – and at times flourish – within the Fatimid system. Snippets of information suggest that al-Dawudi directed his wrath more at his Maliki colleagues than at the despised Shi'ite enemies.[4]

By the time al-Dawudi died in self-imposed exile in the western Maghrib city of Tlemcen (beyond the borders of Fatimid rule) in 1011, a century of Fatimid ascendancy had already passed, including their conquest of Egypt, where they established the centre of their new government, and the installation of the Zirid princes (973–1152) as their proxy governors of Ifriqiya. The members of this clan ascended the political ladder via military service. Ziri ibn Manad (935–71), a Kutama Berber and loyal military general, assisted the Fatimids in suppressing the Kharijite rebellion of Abu Yazid (943–947). When the Fatimid caliph moved to Cairo, he appointed Ziri's son, Buluggin, as governor of Ifriqiya, who in turn put into place a dynastic government through his son and grandsons that would continue until 1152. Sadly for al-Dawudi, he didn't live long enough to see al-Mu'izz ibn Badis al-Ziri (1015–1062) break with the Fatimids in 1048 and restore to Ifriqiya Sunni Islam and allegiance to the Abbasid caliphate in Baghdad, actions that would have certainly vindicated the recalcitrant Maliki disciple and advocate.

Al-Dawudi's *Kitab al-Amwal* (*Treatise on Finance*), by virtue of its mere survival in two manuscripts (Rabat and Madrid), undoubtedly remains his most important and influential work. It has been recently edited twice: first, with an introduction and critical notes by Ridha Shahada; and second, with an introduction and critical notes by Muhammad Hasan al-Shalabi.[5] The fact that it is one of its kind within the Maliki school enhances its importance. Above all, and for the purposes of our concern here, its meticulous attention to thorny legal questions pertaining to the conquest and administration of Sicily in its Muslim period lends itself as a unique prism through which the triangular relationship among the Maliki establishment, the (Sunni) Sicilian populace and the Shi'ite Fatimid leadership comes into focus. Central to understanding al-Dawudi's *responsa* to Sicilian issues are the tensions and ambiguities that arose from the exercise of *ijtihad* in drawing legal conclusions: on the one hand, the progression of Islamic thinking on jihad issues, as reflected in the proliferation of legal texts and treatises, gradually granted to the *imam* (leader) of the *umma* greater degrees of discretion in matters of fiscal management and public administration; on the other hand, the Fatimid caliphs, as they became more and more ensconced in power (including their success in appeasing at least some constituents within the Sunni establishment), were only too willing to take full advantage of these discretionary powers. How, then, could al-Dawudi reconcile his abhorrence for the Fatimid government to his commitment to these legal principles and practices?

Al-Dawudi's chapter, 'North Africa, Spain and Sicily'[6] deals primarily with Sicily. And in what follows, I propose a new reading of it against two contexts: the broad context of the lines of development and expansion in jihad literature, with special reference to the role of the *imam*, and the more local context of Sicilian Muslim history, with special reference to the rise of Fatimid sovereignty over the island and the Sicilian anti-Fatimid revolts of 938. The series of questions posed and responded to in the chapter call attention to the still debatable or unresolved issues regarding land distribution, private versus public ownership of property, the legal status and rights of Muslims and non-Muslims, and the role of political legitimacy in the management of a jihadist socio-economy. And perhaps in more immediate and exciting ways, these questions shed new light on the inner workings of Sicilian Muslim society in the tenth century.

Al-Dawudi's questions include the following:

- What is the status of land[s] and property granted to a group of Berber soldiers who requested them instead of their legal share of the booty, and who were later expelled from these lands by a new ruler?
- Why did Sahnun ibn Sa'id say that of all the lands conquered by Islam Sicily was the most unlawful?
- What is the status of property [land] abandoned by [non-Muslim] Sicilians who had made peace treaties with the Muslims when they were conquered? And the status on selling land or property after the Muslim conquest?
- What is the status of property that was unequally [sic: unjustly] distributed by the commander of the Muslims to his own troops who may not have distinguished themselves in battle, depriving those who did of their rightful share?
- What are the rights of an individual [Muslim] who restored an abandoned or unaccounted for house [or fallow land] who attained it by purchase, as a gift, or as his share in the spoils of war?

- May the produce of a farm be consumed by Muslims, with or without the permission of the current legal or illegal owner?
- Does the [Muslim] owner of a land or property who was forced to inhabit it have sole and absolute right to do with it as he pleases?
- May a land or property designated for public use (a well, mosque, etc.), but then reclaimed by the state via eminent domain, be inhabited or eaten from?
- What is the status of land seized without the ruler's permission? What rights do Muslims have when their lands are seized by other Muslims supported by the ruler? Can they be forced to cut down their trees by order of the ruler for wood to make ships for a holy war?
- How does one arbitrate between a Muslim who came upon fallow land or abandoned property and restored it, and then years later the original owner returns to reclaim it?
- What is the status of the property of someone who dies after being expelled [justly or unjustly] by the ruler and who left no legal heirs?
- May an outsider (specifically a Muslim North African) legally take possession of a piece of land and cultivate it with or without the permission of the ruler?
- May the poor inhabit the land or property of an abandoned fortified town and drink from its wells and plant on its soil? Must the wealthy inhabit it if forced to do so by the ruler? And, may its produce be purchased, and its ports used to dock and load ships with produce to be sold?

***

The questions listed above, with the second one concerning Sahnun's condemnation of the Islamic conquest of Sicily sticking out like a sore thumb, echo in many ways the divergence of opinions concerning jihad and the settling of conquered territories that divided the early Muslim leaders and political theorists. M. J. Kister convincingly illustrates that the issues of rights of ownership of conquered land, obligations to till its soil, distribution of its revenues, and the very aims and purposes of jihad itself were at the centre of the political maelstrom as early as the years of the wars of conquest, especially during the caliphates of ʿUmar ibn al-Khattab (634–44) and ʿUthman ibn ʿAffan (634–56).[7] In many ways similar to the Bedouin armies – organized in tribal units, storming across the lush fertile lands of Mesopotamia (al-Sawad) in the first years of the Islamic conquest – the North African holy warriors of the Aghlabid princes entered the island of Sicily in 827. A major point of disagreement in these early debates was 'Umar's decision that the conquered lands of the Sawad not be divided as the spoils of war among the troops but remain as property of the state, whereby the original owners would continue to till the soil and provide the Muslim community with lucrative land (*kharaj*) and poll (*jizya*) taxes that would enrich the Muslim treasury. His successor 'Uthman's concession to practical politics by meting out much of these lands to powerful members of his own clan enacted a diametrically opposite policy to his predecessor's that would divide Muslim rulers and jurists for centuries. Sahnun's condemnation of land distribution in Sicily, as well as al-Dawudi's evocation of 'Umar's policies in al-Sawad, as will be seen further down, may very well be read as his adhering to orthodox ideas and practices that grew out of these early experiences, giving further credence to Kister's suggestion that all subsequent legal thinking on these issues is attributable to the early days of Islam.[8]

The literature of Islamic jihad

The problems and challenges facing the political and military leadership in the post-Islamic conquests have been assiduously recorded and documented in a wide range of writing. Whatever issues of immediate concern the Qur'an did not specify were often cited and expounded upon through Prophetic words and deeds (*hadith*) and other contemporaneous historical sources. How the new Islamic *umma* was to govern both conquerors and conquered, Muslims and non-Muslims, in a new society became the focus of *sira* (biography) and *maghazi* (battle accounts) literature. By the middle of the second Islamic century, Islamic legal writings and jurisprudence (*fiqh*) had branched out to address matters of public administration, financial and fiscal policies, and relations among the various religious, ethnic and social groups who came to comprise *Dar al-Islam*. When al-Dawudi set out to compose his treatise, *Kitab al-Amwal*, he enjoyed access to a vast library of two centuries covering collections of scriptural citations and traditions (*athar*), legal responses, (*fatawa*), disputations (*munazarat*), handbooks on international relations (*siyar*), and theoretical and practical treatises that treated a staggering array of questions, big and small. Only a couple of generations away from al-Mawardi's (d.1058) *magnum opus, al-Ahkam al-Sultaniyya*,⁹ considered the high point in the literature of medieval Muslim public law, al-Dawudi's treatise falls well within the period of maturation in classical Muslim legal literature.

A brief look at several texts that predate al-Dawudi's reveals a positionality that is informed by his own personal, political and legal stances on questions of immediate concern to the times and places in which he lived. Firstly and secondly, Malik ibn Anas's *al-Muwatta'* and Sahnun ibn Sa'id's *al-Mudawwana*, the two master canons of western Maghribi Maliki law and practice, incorporate the essentials of Maliki Sunni orthodoxy as interpreted and practised throughout the first centuries of Maghribi Islam. Thirdly, Abu Yusuf's *Kitab al-Kharaj*, a mid-third-century Hanafi masterpiece of public administration and finance, commissioned by the caliph, Harun al-Rashid, is perhaps the most important work of its kind. The Hanafis were the first to break new ground on many legal questions, and the Hanafi school of Sunni Islam, especially its embracing of the Mu'tazilite movement popular among legal intellectuals and their Aghlabid patrons, was still in operation in Qayrawan by the middle of the third century. And finally, al-Qadi al-Nu'man's legal treatise, *al-Da'a'im al-Islam*, represents the new Shi'ite legal opinions at a time of Fatimid sovereignty.¹⁰

Malik ibn Anas (d.796) treats in his chapter on jihad (*Muwatta'*)¹¹ four areas: personal conduct and piety, the distribution of the spoils of war, martyrs and martyrdom, and rights of owners of conquered lands. On the matter of the first, Malik draws heavily from both the Prophet and Abu Bakr (r.32–4), the first patriarchal caliph.¹² He reiterates the 'orthodox' positions against taking the Qur'an into enemy territory; killing women, children and the elderly; destroying fruit, especially palm trees, and inhabited places; killing animals (except for food); stealing from the spoils of war; and cowardice in the face of the enemy. On the question of the spoils of war, he takes the position that only free men who actually participated in a battle have a legal share of its booty. He addresses questions of what need not be divided into fifths, the consumption of food at the time of conquest, the seizing of the slain enemy's possessions and the distribution of the surviving enemy's possessions. In this category, Malik concedes to the commander of the Muslims (*al-imam*) discretionary authority in distributing contested property and in granting bonuses (*al-nafal*) as he sees fit. Also, Malik defines a martyr as one who dies in battle serving God (*fi sabil allah*). His body may not be washed or prayed over, and he should be buried at the exact spot where he died. It is permissible to bury more than one martyr in a single grave, he affirms, as long as the elder faces the direction of Mecca. Finally, Malik reiterates that all conquered peoples must be treated according to the treaties or terms they accepted with the Muslims.

Sahnun ibn Sa'id's (d.854) *al-Mudawwana* expands only slightly in his chapter of jihad from that in Malik's *Muwatta'*. One noticeable difference from the onset is the distinction he makes among the different modes of jihad, mentioned previously in the Introduction to this volume: jihad of the heart (*al-qalb*) which is the struggle against immorality; jihad of the tongue (*al-lisan*), which is the fight against insults and lies; jihad of the hand (*al-yad*), which combats physical abuses such as wine and fornication; and jihad of the sword (*al-sayf*), which is the fight (war) against the enemy. He reiterates the injunctions against violence towards women and children and the rules and regulations of treating prisoners and distributing the booty. He takes up the complex questions of escaping in battle when outnumbered and comportment in enemy territory when engaged in commerce. He expands the boundaries of social authority in ruling that both a son and a slave must have a father's or owner's permission before participating in battle. Sahnun puts forth six conditions for fighting in a jihad. One must be: born Muslim or converted to Islam, the age of puberty, of free status, male, of sound mind and in good health and financial stability. He discusses the different juridical positions on the ways and means of distributing the spoils of war and managing public finances, the rights of the Christians to Muslim property, and the proper care of fortresses (*ribat*), animals and conquered lands. Finally, he emphasizes the obligation of securing safe passage (*aman*) to slaves, women and children.[13]

Ya'qub b. Ibrahim Abu Yusuf (731–798),[14] prominent disciple of Abu Hanifa and a chief architect of the Hanafi school of Islamic jurisprudence, was commissioned by the caliph Harun al-Rashid (r.786–809) to compose his magnum opus on public finance and government administration. His *Kitab al-Kharaj* is available in several printed versions and constitutes a quantum leap forward in the expansion of a broadly defined jihad literature.[15] Completed by the middle of the third Islamic century, this work relies less on Prophetic *hadith* – as is the case of Malik's *Muwatta'* – and less on the authority of a prior prominent scholar, as in the case where Sahnun's *Mudawwana* elevates Malik as a primary legal authority. Abu Yusuf relies more on juristic principles of logical analysis (*ra'y*) and reasoning by analogy (*qiyas*).[16]

Abu Yusuf's *Kitab al-Kharaj* collates, classifies and analyses many of the familiar themes and issues that have come to comprise the jihad chapters (*abwab*) in medieval Muslim literature. He documents what is clearly stated in the Qur'an and the Prophetic *hadith* and offers various points of view that have coalesced around the major issues. He treats the division of booty of which, according to Qur'an 8:41, one-fifth belongs to God (i.e. that which goes into the state treasury) for the use of the Prophet (and by extension for the use of any leader of the *umma* (*imam*) to follow him), the members of the Prophet's family, and orphans, poor people and wayfarers. Also, the role of the *imam* in the execution of jihad as perceived, understood and prescribed by Abu Yusuf draws as much from Islamic Scriptures, the deeds of the early companions and caliphs (*athar*), Arab customs ('*urf*), as it does from the practical politics of this time. The custom of allotting to the *imam* the choicest parts of the booty (*safiya*) most assuredly has its roots in ancient Arabian tribal society and was carried over into Islamic polity, and it maintained its strength and significance in the ninth century. In grey areas, matters of divergence of opinion or, in cases with no immediate precedents, the discretion of the *imam* to act independently comes to the fore. This was customary in the time of the Prophet and his immediate successors, and their judgement calls became matters of public record. In time, Muslim scholars such as Abu Yusuf and al-Dawud came to recognize the discretionary powers of the *imam* as having significant legal and political force. As long as legal questions remained highly debatable, the *imam* was granted the power to arbitrate: how to divide equitably and allot bonuses for extraordinary feats of bravery or to curry political favour or alliances; when and if to kill enemy prisoners or release them by exacting a price; whether to cut down fruit trees in enemy territory; what to do with Muslim horses or camels if they could not be brought back to safe ground, etc.

The limits to which the ruler would use his own personal discretion and break with tradition – be it in the form of Scriptures or legal scholarship, tribal praxis or political precedents – were dramatically exceeded when 'Umar ibn al-Khattab (r.634–44) made the decision not to divide the lands of al-Sawad (Mesopotamia) among the participants in its conquest. Ignoring highly publicized appeals and dire warnings from his own senior officers, it should be recalled, 'Umar opted to leave the lands to their original owners and charge them the lucrative 20 per cent land tax (*kharaj*) in order to (i) pay the wages and pensions of government servants and (ii) to leave those lands for future generations of Muslims.[17] The division of any land to the holy warriors would have altered its status to the 10 per cent Muslim land (*'ushr*) tax, depriving the state of half the potential revenue. Both Abu Yusuf and al-Dawudi saw the rationale and potential benefits of this ruling and drew heavily on the Sawad case in their own writings.

'Umar's *Sawad* ruling had far-ranging implications for Muslim land and tax policy. First, it was a clear victory for the discretionary power of the ruler. It lent strength and valorization to sound political and economic judgement over the heretofore sacred precedent and over popular consensus. It also opened the way for more creative forms of taxation, that is, proportional taxation (*muqasama*) that benefited the state without causing undue hardship to the less wealthy.[18] In addition, it secured jurisdiction of the state over dead lands (*mawat*), that is, land that had been abandoned, undocumented, ownerless or heirless, fallow, or in any degree of disrepair, and lands that would include ancient ruins, cemeteries, meadows, forests, swamps or public grazing grounds. And above all, the immobilization of the *Sawad* reaffirmed 'Umar and his successors' right to grant fiefs from ownerless or heirless properties once owned by the Persian Sassanian kings and members of the royal family. This prerogative was compatible with the *fiqh* ideal (in spirit if not in letter) to grant a reward (*al-nafal*) to those who make a substantial contribution to Islam. In a sense, this discretionary power comes with the de jure obligation to make the right political decision. Even in cases where the *imam* is unequivocally forbidden to grant fiefs, such as from properties in which Muslims or confederates (*al-mu'ahadin*) have legal rights to ownership, Abu Yusuf inserts a loophole that allows the *imam* to reverse the treaty if he deems this abrogation in the best interests of the state.[19]

Abu Yusuf's careful scrutiny and in-depth study of the *Sawad*, as reflected in the special chapter he devoted to it in his textbook, inscribed these discretionary powers and the rights of 'eminent domain' as much to emulate and legislate the

Prophet and his successors' actions as legal principles as to illustrate the benefits of sound legal judgement and judicious political and economic manoeuvring. The elevation of 'Umar as a kind of 'Solomon the Wise' for Islamic land policies, whose bold and stubborn refusal to yield to 'the law' in what he, and he alone, deemed to be in the best interest of the Muslim community, was a brilliant political tour de force that opens the flood gates to future rulers allowing them to act independently in the interests of government. Abu Yusuf must have undoubtedly realized the extraordinary power this could wield in the hands of any mortal ruler as well as the inherent dangers in exercising such power in the hands of someone lacking sound political judgement. His well-known advice to Harun al-Rashid to hold sessions at the Court of Grievances (*mahkamat al-mazalim*) on a monthly basis was clearly a reminder of the potential for injustices and disaster inherent in this power.

***

The ascendance of the Shi'ite Fatimids to political power in Ifriqiya in 909 brought significant but not radical changes to the region. It failed to put an end to the dominance of Sunni Islam, but it temporarily slowed the momentum engineered by Sahnun ibn Sa'id and his son Muhammad (d.860) to elevate the Maliki school as the sole Sunni *madhhab*, especially in its fierce rivalry with the Hanafi school, which at the time was still the *madhhab* of choice for many of the old Qayrawan elite. Also, the Kharijite rebellion, which was led by Abu Yazid Makhlad b. Kayrad against the new Fatimid state and which reached its peak in the rebels' capture of Qayrawan in 944, created a second front that compelled the Shi'ite Fatimids to be more conciliatory towards the Sunni mainstream. The creation of a two-tiered chief judgeship, one for Sunnis and one for Shi'ites, is but one of other illustrations of Fatimid acquiescence to local loyalties and concerns.[20] The rise of the Fatimids brought more Berbers (especially from the Kutama tribe) into public life, especially in military and political positions, and it undoubtedly curtailed the inordinate power and influence of the old Arab urban elite. Moreover, it curtailed ties with Baghdad and other points of the Muslim east, at least at the ambassadorial level, as the new Fatimid governors turned their immediate attention to local and adjacent areas.

In contrast to accounts in pro-Sunni historiography concerning Fatimid abuses and forced conversions to their mission against the Sunnis of Ifriqiya, we also read about intense efforts to win over public opinion. Farhat Dachraoui draws our attention to the late afternoon prayer classes (*durus al-hikma*) and the evening debates (*majalis al-hikma*) that were institutionalized in order to spread Isma'ili learning.[21] The public disputations between Muhammad Abu al-'Abbas, the erudite older brother of the Mahdi, 'Ubayd Allah, and Abu 'Uthman Sa'id b. Muhammad, premier Qayrawani Maliki scholar, however contentious they may have been, nonetheless underscore some degree of dialogue at the early stages of Fatimid rule.[22] One is again reminded of al-Dawudi's outbursts against fellow Maliki scholars who worked within the system, and one can only estimate how many Qayrawani Hanafis, arguably less hostile to Shi'ite theology than their Maliki nemeses, were brought into the new Isma'ili religious and educational institutions.

As a satellite state to Ifriqiya, the island of Sicily was no less affected by the new Fatimid government, and the Fatimids were quick to seize the opportunity to ride on the crest of what was their Aghlabid predecessors' greatest accomplishment in the Sicilian jihad. As Amari has observed, discernible patterns in jihad policy, both on the military and ambassadorial fronts, continued on the same trajectory during this transition of power. Fatimid appeal to the Muslims of Sicily was launched, as previously discussed, on two levels: strong anti-Aghlabid rhetoric, enumerating their many political and moral lapses; and strong commitment, financial and military, to the Sicilian jihad.

Muhammad b. Mansur Al-Qadi al-Nu'man (d.974) was the son of a scholarly family long ensconced in North Africa. He served the first three Fatimid caliphs and rose to the office of chief judge under the fourth, al-Mu'izz al-din Allah (r.953–75), becoming the chief propagandist for Isma'ili theology. His nickname (*kunya*) of 'Abu Hanifa' strongly suggests his Sunni roots among the Qayrawan Hanafis. His monumental – officially government-sanctioned – history of the rise of the Fatimids, *Iftitah al-Da'wa*, includes correspondence with the Sicilians, as alluded to above.[23]

His textbook on Islamic law, *al-Da'a'im al-Islam*, and its chapter on jihad (*Bab al-Jihad*) lay out systematically the Isma'ili Shi'ite positions at the middle of the tenth century.[24] Written no earlier than one or two generations before al-Dawudi's *Kitab al-Amwal*, this work was undoubtedly well known throughout North African legal circles. The jihad chapter consists of twenty-nine items that may be grouped into four broad categories: (i) the sanctity and spiritual rewards of engaging in jihad; (ii) the role of the *imam* in jihad; (iii) the rules and regulations of physical jihad – including launching war, making peace treaties, safe passage, the treatment of prisoners and the division of the spoils of war; and (iv) fighting tyrants and other sinful Muslims (*ahl al-baghiy*).

The first and third categories reiterate many of the themes and regulations we find in earlier texts. In fact, reading them reveals no appreciable divergence of opinion from the Sunni manuals. Items in the first category here include personal conduct, beginning with who may or may not participate, proper preparation for travel, treatment of the Qur'an in enemy territory, and the proper care of horses. In the third category, we again see many of the familiar guidelines but here prescribed with stronger appeals to pious conduct. The insistence on inviting the enemy (*da'wa*) to join Islam or to accept a peace treaty and pay the poll tax precedes the rules of an attack. Injunctions against killing women, children and the infirm; committing acts of mutilation, theft or deception; needlessly cutting down fruit trees; abandoning war materiel in enemy territory; abusing prisoners and conquered peoples; and violating commitments and treaties are all in accordance with mainstream Islamic jihad literature.

Al-Qadi al-Nu'man's second and fourth categories reflect significant expansions in Islamic legal writing concerning jihad in theory and in practice. With the consolidation of Muslim military power against the Muslims' non-Muslim neighbours, and with the increasingly bitter rivalries for political legitimacy among Muslims themselves, jihadist discourse, broadly defined, became more directed internally. Once again, the increasing power of Muslim sultans to act independently of the local *ulema* or of public opinion can be read into Al-Qadi al-Nu'man's second and fourth categories, as can the loopholes in Islamic law that allow the sultans discretionary powers.

The recognition of the power of authority is fronted in the first item of the second category: there is a chain of command in the execution of a holy war, and the commander must obey the *imam*. Having confirmed this basic principle, the new Fatimid manual outlines the proper rules governing the conduct of the *imam*: he may not act arrogantly; he must know his limits and capabilities; he must keep track of what he's doing; he must seek the advice of elders more experienced than he; he must be fair in his treatment of all those he governs; he must tend to the needs of his soldiers; he must choose wisely his senior military officers, judges, scribes, government workers and tax collectors, landowners, merchants and artisans. These strictures or guidelines, while recognizing the power of the *imam*, placed limits on his sovereignty by holding him accountable to God and the *umma*. They addressed the potential for greed among the wealthy and powerful and the necessity of establishing a cohesive paradigm for a more perfect society that includes all its members. The *imam* must also tend to the poor and downtrodden, and he must conduct himself with good behaviour (*husn al-sira*).

By the mid-tenth century, any lingering idea that the sword of jihad was exclusively pointed against the non-Muslim infidel could be seriously called to question in reading the fourth category. This section on (Muslim) evildoers is not new to Islamic literature. Abu Yusuf's *Kitab al-Amwal*, for example, ends with a chapter on how to deal with all sorts of social profligates from fornicators, thieves, criminals and drunkards, to army deserters, spies, apostates and polytheists.[25] What is significant here is the legislating, into the jihad chapter, of waging a (holy) war against a Muslim political opponent who conducts himself in ways contrary to Islam. Al-Qadi al-Nuʿman prefaces this section for a plea to arbitration in the case where two Muslim factions are at odds. But in eschewing direct calls for open rebellion against a Muslim ruler, he nonetheless casts the oppressors (read: opponents) in specifically anti-Muslim terms, such as tyrants (*ahl al-baghiy*) or polytheists (*mushrikin*). He evokes those early opponents of ʿAli as examples of those to whom a jihad could and should have been justifiably launched. And, in terms similar to dealing with the normative (i.e. non-Muslim) infidels, he cautions against killing the wives and children of tyrants and against seizing their property without legal division according to Islamic law. He finishes this section on familiar legal ground with justification for killing a Muslim in self-defence or punishment by death of Muslims who commit grave offences against Islam, such as apostasy or conversion to another religion.

***

With the broad strokes delineated above, we can agree that al-Dawudi's *Kitab al-Amwal* is situated well within the period of maturation in classical Islamic legal literature. It is among the last of its genre to carry that title, and it departs from the traditional *hadith* format and its use of *isnad* (chain of transmission) in forming arguments. It is based more on the *fatwa* format of questions and responses, reflecting the shift from *hadith* to *fiqh*. The work remains strongly Sunni orthodox in both the spirit and letter of the law, and well within the Maliki tradition, as reflected in its references to 'Umar's historic ruling on the Sawad, as well as in the frequent quotations from and evocations of Sahnun ibn Sa'id. As much as he wears the turban of the Sunni Maliki apologist, al-Dawudi also dons the robes of an independent thinker, using *ijtihad* (independent thinking) and *qiyas* (reasoning by analogy) in formulating opinions. He recognizes grey areas in the law, the processes of history (change), the validity of contrary opinions, and the realities and practicalities of contemporary politics. His work follows the line of progression within jihad literature that acknowledges the increasing power and discretion of the ruler in the administration of all matters, military and civilian, pertaining to jihad, and in it we see his support for the principles of '*masalih mursala*', the idea that a ruler may govern in accordance with what is in the best interests of the community at a given time. The issues of political legitimacy, judicious government, and moral conduct, and the emphasis on the religious aspects of wealth and elaboration on the just and ascetic practices of the Prophet Muhammad, are all inscribed in al-Dawudi's responses and weaved into his polemical opposition against the Fatimid government. How this opposition plays out in Muslim Sicily of the tenth and eleventh centuries constitutes one of the most complex and colourful themes in the Arabic writing on Sicilian Islam.

Jihad on the ground: Mapping new legal territory

A close reading of Sicilian Muslim annalist history from the Fatimid rise to power in Ifriqiya (909), continuing with the wide-scale Sicilian revolts against their Fatimid governors roughly from 937 until 945 and ending with the brief period of Kalbid peace and prosperity, provides an intriguing but fuddled context for reading al-Dawudi's Sicilian passages. Having now sketched an outline of the major themes and issues in the jihad chapters of Islamic legal writing, I proceed with some basic assumptions that open up to broader historical and social contexts for reading al-Dawudi's chapter, especially given the importance of land in his criticisms of Fatimid legal, fiscal and administrative policies.

The Arab invasion and settlement of Sicily in the early decades of the ninth century are best viewed within the dialectic of disruption and continuity that was a hallmark of medieval Mediterranean history. As we have seen in the previous chapter, Sicily in this period was at the crossroads of east and west, and as such carried both Western Latin and Eastern Byzantine features. As Amari has so thoroughly demonstrated, one of the major changes on the Sicilian landscape in the post-Muslim conquest period was the shift in agrarian policies and structures that reduced the size and scope of the imperial Roman *latifundia*, or large landed estate, that had survived the collapse of the western Roman Empire only to re-emerge in late antiquity with, as Averil Cameron writes, 'the growth of an immensely rich and powerful class of senatorial landowners'.[26] Also, the evolution of Palermo, Agrigento and Syracuse as major urban centres, and their codependence with adjacent small towns and rural areas, maintained the – if somewhat altered – balance of centre and periphery that was crucial to the economy, both in late antique and in Islamic times. The dependence on slave or tenant labour to work the vast farmlands in Sicily's dominant agrarian society carried over from Roman to Muslim rule, and late antique practices of forced labour recruitment and land grants for military services continued well into the ninth and tenth centuries, albeit resurfacing along Islamic laws and Arabo-Berber customs.[27]

Muslim Sicily, especially in its first century, resembled more the Byzantine east than the Latin west in its relatively higher degree of urban development, its more equitable distribution of wealth, and its willingness and ability to build upon and draw from preexisting peoples and institutions. However, with passing of land into Muslim hands, the veterans of the first waves of the Sicilian jihad came to either constitute a new landed gentry or form a new class of *curiales* in the urban centres. Eventually, the inevitable tensions between urban and rural, empowered and disempowered, and rich and poor resurfaced, and the succession of new governments, Aghlabid and Fatimid alike, came to encounter many of the problems that rulers faced in dealing with property disputes, economic disparities, power struggles, mismanagement and heavy-handed taxation. One dominant feature of late antique Sicily that survived and flourished in Muslim Sicily was the caricature of the much-hated and feared tax collector.

***

On the death of Ziyadat-Allah II, Aghlabid prince of Ifriqiya, and the ascension to power of his brother Abu 'Affan in 837, Ibn al-Athir writes of the new ruler:

> He displayed generosity to the army, eliminated many unjust practices, increased the salaries of the tax collectors so that they would keep their hands off the citizens, and emptied Qayrawan of wine and other spirits. Then, the following year, he dispatched an expedition to Sicily.[28]

This report, penned by the authoritative Muslim historian, encapsulates the values and standards set forth in classical Muslim writing on government, and it underscores the historical realities and challenges that governors faced. That a ruler oversee the defence of the community, provide adequate, if not generous, support to his soldiers, supervise the fair and judicious collection of taxes, and safeguard public morality are all the stuff of the expanded chapters on jihad, as elaborated on above. The quotation, above all, delineates a common ground of agreement, an accepted narrative of sorts, shared by the Isma'ili jurist, al-Qadi al-Nu'man and his would-be nemesis, Sunni jurist al-Dawudi. The agreement takes into account the interconnectedness of theory and practice (i.e. the interplay of legal speculations and historical processes), providing convincing evidence that Islamic legal literature followed social practice as much as social practice was guided by Islamic law.

The previous chapters called ample attention to the complications and contradictions that arose in Sicily during the transition of power from the Sunni Aghlabids to the Shi'ite Fatimids. The regional leaders from the power centres of predominantly Arab Palermo and predominantly Berber Agrigento, it has been shown, vacillated between support for and opposition to the new rulers of Ifriqiya. Undoubtedly there was opposition from the Sunni Maliki *ulema* against the Isma'ili usurpers to the throne but not enough to prevent the Sicilians, Arabs and Berbers alike from eventually finding ways of coexistence with their new benefactors. After all, the island was still in a state of jihad and its economy depended heavily on its success. And, as more and more Sicilian

Muslims retired from the battlefield and settled into the comforts of their landed estates or pursued careers in their new urban professions, there was the incessant need for massive infusions of manpower and financial support from North Africa to keep the engines of the Sicilian jihad running. The 'rise and fall' of Ibn Qurhub perhaps best illustrates the fickle and unpredictable nature of Sicilian politics and the ways and means by which Sicilian Muslims negotiated and manoeuvred to preserve and protect their own interests.

As much as the fault lines between Arabs and Berbers, Sunnis and Shi'ites, and eventually 'Sicilians' and 'North Africans' crisscrossed the Muslim Sicilian landscape, heavily impacting the island's politics as well as its relations with North Africa, economic and fiscal issues lay at the heart of many Sicilian tensions, internally and externally. The control and distribution over the vast amounts of wealth and property the war project generated were the prerogatives, at least in theory, of the legitimately recognized ruler. But in reality this could only be maintained and executed through the appointment of regional agents and tax collectors ('amil pl. 'ummal) whose power on the ground often exceeded their legally prescribed authority. In fact, Sicilian Muslim history, like the history of its motherland, Ifriqiya, is punctuated with cases of local uprisings against the abusive and illegal practices of these local agents. That these uprisings occurred against Aghlabid and Fatimid governments alike poses a challenge to al-Dawudi's anti-Fatimid polemics.

An incident that occurred in the early years of Fatimid rule, anecdotally provided by the historian al-Nuwayri, graphically illustrates the hand of tax collectors in the complex of relations between Sicilian Muslims and their North African patrons:

> Ibn Abi al-Fawaris wrote to the mahdi, ruler of Ifriqiya after the Aghlabids, asking permission to come to Ifriqiya. He was granted an audience, and when he arrived [the mahdi] had him imprisoned in Raqqada ... He had [earlier] been appointed governor [of Sicily] by the mahdi and arrived in Sicily in the 10th of Dhi al-Hijja, 297 [909–10]. The Palermitans revolted against him and deposed him the following year. The reason was that his agents/tax collectors had been mistreating the people. To amend, he organized a banquet and invited the local leaders. When they arrived, one of them claimed to have seen some of his slave guards with drawn swords. In a panic, they opened the windows of the dining hall and called out for arms. The

...ponded and surrounded the house, setting fire to the doors. [Ibn Abi al-Fawaris] then had his guests escorted out, disclaiming any intention to harm them. But the people, not accepting this, denounced him. He then fled his house and broke his leg while running toward a neighbor's house. [In response], the mahdi had him removed and pardoned the Sicilians. Khalil, *Sahib al-khums*, (minister of the booty), restored order to the city, after which the mahdi appointed 'Ali ibn 'Umar al-Balawi as governor.[29]

This colourful snapshot of a scene in Muslim Palermo during the grey period between Aghlabid and Fatimid rule confirms several important facts essential to Muslim Sicilian history: (i) the locally appointed agent to the central governor, or more precisely, the tax collector, often served as a catalyst for local dissent against the central government; (ii) the Palermitans, like the Agrigentans, as will be shown below, possessed their own militias whose allegiances were first and foremost to local authority; and (iii) the majority of Sicilians, who were to the best of our knowledge Sunni Muslims, were not altogether hostile to the new Fatimid rulers. They indeed realized that as a province engaged in jihad against a larger Byzantine Christian enemy, they were still beholden, as I have been arguing, to North African military, financial and human power without which they would not survive. They did, however, have local interests that were gradually but markedly diverging from those of the motherland, and they did not hesitate to use whatever means possible to protect those interests. The new Fatimid government from Raqqada, at least from the ways it responded to Sicilian uprisings, seems to have recognized and accepted these local interests and sensitivities. The Mahdi's appointment of one Khalil, the minister of booty, to restore order in the city, underscores the paramount importance which the jihad continued to play in the nexus of politics and economics.

***

As the dust settled from the chaos of the transition from Aghlabid to Fatimid rule by the second decade of the tenth century, the Sicilian Muslims abandoned, at least publicly, their pro-Baghdad loyalties and declared fealty to their new patrons from Ifriqiya. Political stability was restored, and the business of jihad got back on track. The completion of the conquest of the last Sicilian towns under Christian Byzantine sovereignty, mostly in the northeast corner of the island (Val Demone), and the lucrative raiding expeditions into Calabria and Puglia on the Italian mainland united the Muslims in common cause.

However, some thirty years later, the image of the tax collector once again reared its ugly head. This time, the rebellion began when the Muslims removed a regional agent/tax collector in protest against the abuses of the Fatimid government of Salim ibn Rashid who resided in Palermo. Although the incident began in Agrigento, it eventually spread to Palermo, Mazara and Platano, as well as other small towns in Muslim-controlled Sicily. Salim ibn Rashid's army, comprised both 'Sicilians' and 'North Africans' (the later suggesting newly arrived Kutama Berbers and the mainstay of the Fatimid army), was attacked and initially defeated by the Agrigentan militia. The details of the revolt – including Salim's call for reinforcements from North Africa, the Sicilians pitting Salim against the newly dispatched naval commander, Khalil ibn Ishaq, and Khalil's project to build the fortress town of *al-Khalisa* from demolished materials from Old Palermo – have been outlined in Chapter 1. This rebellion, which ends with al-Mahdiyya's success in putting down the rebellions and Sicilians' eventual acquiescence to Fatimid sovereignty, is richly significant to Muslim Sicilian history in that, in its aftermath, some Sicilian Muslim factions appealed to Constantinople for assistance against their co-religionist Fatimid governors, while others sought refuge in Christian-controlled areas of the island during the final stages of the revolts.

As shocking and abhorrent this must have seemed to large swathes of Muslim Sicilian society, still highly engaged in the holy jihad against the Christian enemy, it was a familiar episode in the complex dynamics of medieval Muslim-Christian relations. Islamic law, in fact, allowed for a degree of flexibility in its stance towards reaching out to non-Muslims in dire circumstances. It allowed, for example, for cases where polytheists (read: Christians) could be utilized in battle: destroying enemy fortresses, firing catapults and acting as servants on the battleground (collecting weapons, removing wounded or dead bodies, providing arms or other means of assistance).[30] The question of seeking non-Muslim military assistance was yet another grey area in the law, and the actual space to manoeuvre granted to a ruler or commander to make a spot decision in the best interests of the *umma* fell within the discretionary powers in areas where the law was vague. In the context of Sunni-Shi'ite contestation for religious and political authority and ni Sicilians' reaching out to the enemy against the Shi'ite nment could find at least a modicum of justification.

ᴊɪ events that make up the narrative of the Sicilian revolt ..gainst their Fatimid governors draw attention, once again, to several important factors particular to Sicilian Muslim history and which could offer themselves as interesting subtexts for reading al-Dawudi's Sicilian chapter. The narrative, both as discrete text and as a chapter of sorts to the larger Muslim Sicilian story, clearly illustrates that both Palermo and Agrigento maintained their own provincial interests by forming and maintaining local militias. The early successes of the Agrigentan forces against Salim's powerful battalions suggest that these local militias were loyal, united, well armed and well trained. Also, the dismissal of the tax collector mentioned at the beginning of the historical reports suggests that fiscal issues were very likely the bone of contention. Secondly, the anti-Fatimid revolts of 937 continue to illustrate the very complex relationship between Sicily as province and North Africa as motherland. The Sicilians wanted and needed North African support but on their own terms. If and when they sensed any threat against their own interests, they didn't hesitate to respond. The uprisings of 937 fit well within a long series of similar actions that erupted in conflict and ended in resolution, again, underscoring a mutual recognition of interdependence.

Finally, the story of the 937 revolts helped to alter the balance in the Sicilian-North African relationship with the Muslim breaking of ranks. The heavy-handed response of the Fatimids, the deep seeds of mistrust planted in the Salim ibn Rashid versus Khalil ibn Ishaq divide, and the Fatimid dismantling of large parts of Old Palermo to build the new fortified port city of al-Khalisa, which was undoubtedly at great expense to the old Sunni Arab elite and their cherished institutions, all added further pressures to the ongoing brittle relationship between empire and province. The Sicilian appeal for help from Constantinople and the flight of Muslims to Christian territories carries with it echoes of al-Dawudi's *takfir wa al-hijra* position. The abuses of power, lapses in judgement, and suggestions of negligence and bad government on the part of the Fatimid government that reverberate throughout al-Dawudi's chapter find concrete examples in the annals of Sicilian Muslim history. If al-Dawudi failed to diminish Fatimid power, he could at least cast a dark shadow of suspicion over their legitimacy to rule.

In the hundred years since the establishment of Palermo as the capital of Muslim Sicily, much of the Muslim population, scions of the first generation of holy warriors and recipients of the spoils of war, of rich farmlands, mines, industries and other kinds of property, were by now comfortably settled, especially in the urban centres and landed estates of the western and southern regions of the island. A good number of the most powerful and wealthy were undoubtedly family members, clients and supporters of the former Aghlabid regime. The arrival of the Fatimids and the legions of Kutama Berbers and other supporters who joined their ranks, with equal expectations of booty and wealth to which they could stake a rightful claim as *mujahidin*, generated new energies and opportunities on the one hand, but presented, on the other hand, new challenges and a significant degree of destabilization in the acquisition of power and wealth enjoyed by the old-guard elites.

Wherein lie the growing rifts within Muslim Sicily along 'Sicilian' versus 'North African' binary oppositional lines, as clearly reflected in the vocabulary of the chronicles, eclipsing earlier 'Arab versus Berber' and 'Sunni versus Shi'a' divides. The constant migration of North Africans into Sicily, soldiers and civilians, assuredly added pressures to the limited resources the island could offer to the many seekers of its fortunes. Land, land distribution, taxes and fiscal management undoubtedly tested the limits of political power and legitimacy.

Wherein lies the thrust of al-Dawudi's anti-Fatimid polemic. His Sicilian chapters contest Fatimid legitimacy on historical and legalist ground. Above and beyond the theological debates between the Fatimid and Maliki jurists, as illustrated in the Muhammad Abu al-'Abbas and Abu 'Uthman Sa'id ibn Muhammad disputations in Qayrawan in the early years of the Fatimid revolution, arguing differences of opinions on prophethood, the superiority of 'Ali ibn Abu Talib's knowledge, and qualifications over the first three patriarchal caliphs, approaches to legal methodology (*usul al-fiqh*), and liturgical practices, al-Dawudi registers his dissent through a series of questions and answers pertaining to the history and current state of jihad, the raison d'être of Sicilian Islam.

In bequeathing an historical document for the reconstruction of Muslim Sicilian history, al-Dawudi, like other Muslim jurists, 'co-opted, constructed, and reconstructed doctrinal and historical precedents' to borrow Khaled Abou El Fadl's phrase.[31] His quotations from the revered Maliki jurist, Sahnun ibn Sa'id, as well as his evocation of 'Umar ibn al-Khattab's *Sawad* policies in early Islamic history allowed him to anchor his chapter on solid legal precedence. Also, his reports of the Andalusian privateers who landed in Sicily during the first stages of the Aghlabid conquest in 827 and their subsequent squabbles over land rights, as well as incidents revolving around the anti-Fatimid revolts in 938, including the burning of the Department of Land Division and Taxes, all reflect al-Dawudi's careful consideration of historical processes in the ongoing debates on jihad.

Al-Dawudi's anti-Fatimid polemics, it must be emphasized, did not advocate rebellion in any way. Well within the mainstream of Muslim juristic thinking, he remained loyal to the sanctity of preserving law and order, and he advocated patience and consensus in dealing with what he judged to be infractions of the law. He recognized that rulers could be tyrants who use various means of oppression or injustice to maintain or increase their power. His statements to that effect are the bases on which he constructed his anti-Fatimid discourse.

Al-Dawudi's Sicilian chapter bears historical evidence that theological, juridical, military and socio-economic approaches to the Sicilian jihad did not diverge appreciably, again as Amari had long ago observed, from the Sunni Aghlabid to the Shi'ite Fatimid periods. However, this chapter is best read and best understood, bearing in mind that he was condemning not so much what the Fatimids were doing on the ground in Sicily – their Aghlabid Sunni predecessors having done much the same – as much as their legitimate right to do it. The importance of Sicily as a testing ground – a laboratory of sorts in which a plethora of questions straddling the theoretical and practical divide were being tried and tested against the universal recognition and acceptance of the discretionary powers of the legitimate ruler of the *umma* in areas lacking clear rulings – was not lost on the self-imposed exiled jurist. His polemics, above all, reflected his contempt for the fact that these discretionary powers had fallen into the wrong hands. His chapter does not reflect a shift 'from the absolute realm of political idealism to an absolute realm of political realism',[32] but rather a crafty reconciliation of the two.

Sahnun's jihads

Sahnun ibn Sa'id (d.854), like his older rival and nemesis Asad ibn al-Furat (d.828), was a product of his time and place. Both were the sons of men from the *Bilad al-Sham* (Syria) who came to North Africa as soldiers in the army of the Islamic conquest and settled in Ifriqiya. Unlike their respective fathers, each chose a different path of jihad, opting to pursue a scholarly career instead of a military one. As much as the North African littoral of the third Islamic century remained a frontier province of *Dar al-Islam* in its skirmishes with the Byzantine navy over control of the central Mediterranean, so too were its urban centres continuing to grow as sites of culture and learning ever since the Umayyad caliph, 'Umar ibn 'Abd al-'Aziz (r.717–720), sent ten scholars a century ago to teach Islam in the 'west'. With the founding of the Sidi 'Uqba Mosque in Qayrawan and the proliferation of Qur'an schools (*kuttab* pl. *katatib*) throughout the adjacent regions, opportunities in religious and legal scholarship abounded.[33]

The lives and careers of Asad ibn al-Furat and Sahnun ran along parallel and perpendicular lines. Having completed their early education in the Qur'anic sciences, including *fiqh* and *hadith*, with the foremost scholars of Ifriqiya, each man embarked at the age of eighteen on their 'study abroad' (*rihla*) to Egypt and the Hijaz to sit at the feet of the grand masters. Both men remained loyal to orthodox Islam (*sunna*), especially in their quest to reach preeminence (*riyasa*) in the Maliki school (*madhhab*), and both men completed the final phase of their *rihla* having studied under 'Abd al-Rahman ibn al-Qasim (d.806), considered by many at the time to be the leading scholar of Maliki law. Each man returned to Ifriqiya with drafts of what they intended to be the authoritative textbook for Maliki jurisprudence bearing the blessings and imprimatur of Ibn al-Qasim.

Where the two men differed, above and beyond their rivalry for Ibn al-Qasim's affections, was in the stance they took towards the disputes that were raging among scholars and jurists of their time. And at the heart of these disputes was the Aghlabid Court, which added flames to the fire. Asad's appointment by Ziyadat-Allah II as (second) chief judge of Qayrawan and his subsequent acceptance to command the Sicilian jihad, which the Aghlabid prince waged against the approval of many Maliki jurists, placed him on one side of the divide. Sahnun's reluctance and later acquiescence to accept the chief judge post at the age of seventy-four, and only on condition that he have a free hand to prosecute members of the royal family, placed him on the other. True to his word, Sahnun's first action as chief judge was to cleanse the mosques of Kharijites, Mu'tazilites and other groups he deemed as free thinkers.[34]

Once this was achieved, he began his purge of government officials. Most prominent among them was chief judge Ibn Abi al-Jawad who was accused of embezzlement. Denying the charge and claiming to have no money to make restitution, Sahnun had al-Jawad imprisoned and flogged repeatedly. Ibn Abi al-Jawad, who happened to be Asad ibn al-Furat's son-in-law, subsequently died from his lashes.[35]

Al-Dawudi, it should be recalled, cites Sahnun on several occasions as the authority on the question of the Muslim (read: Aghlabid) conquest of Sicily. He quotes Sahnun as having stated that in his examination of the conquest he found 'no documented proof' concerning the (legal) acquisition of land. He also quotes Sahnun as having pronounced: 'Of all the lands which the Muslims conquered, none were more unlawful than Sicily.' Al-Dawudi interprets Sahnun's remarks as meaning that (i) the Muslims entered Sicily illegally, thus the illegal status of the lands; (ii) the land was not divided legally, nor was it distributed to the soldiers in accordance with Islamic legal precepts; and (iii) there was no land held in trust for future generations of Muslims, as 'Umar had done in the lands of Mesopotamia (al-Sawad) in the early years of the Islamic conquest.

In attempting to understand Sahnun's comment on 'no documentary proof', I refer to Alex Metcalfe who has shed precious light on the state of the Sicilian archive of the pre- and post-periods of Muslim Sicily. He observes that the extreme document loss for the Byzantine and Islamic periods can be explained by the 'historical exigencies of conquest and colonial governance' and that 'Muslim Sicily's administration was a late developer whose existence was cut short by civil strife and war'. Metcalfe concludes that 'for the Islamic period in Sicily, we can at best infer the existence of state records for landed property, perhaps with lists of provincial officials, landholders, and presumably some estimate of land tax revenue', but that there are 'no records relating to coastal defences (*ribats*); church holdings, pious endowments (*awqaf* of *ahbas*) of landed property made to mosques and so on'.[36]

Concerning Sahnun's claim that the soldiers were not given land for their military service along prescribed Islamic legal practices, Metcalfe offers the explanation that the Fatimid/Kalbids 'were garrisoned in and around Palermo, and were not settled on the land. Indeed, they were enfeoffed with land for which they gave service, but derived incomes from salaries, booty and gifts'.[37] Finally, Metcalfe's thesis of a disjuncture of the 'written land registry tradition between Islamic and Norman Sicily' speaks to the historical archival problem that Sahnun had first raised in his criticism of the Islamic conquest of Sicily.

On the surface, Sahnun's critiques are grounded in the bedrock of orthodox Sunni juridical thinking to whose rulings he staunchly adhered via his rigorous and uncompromising commitment to and ultimate domination of the Maliki school (*madhhab*) of Islamic jurisprudence. The reference to 'Umar's actions in the Sawad, now a sacred model for land policies, not to mention the evolving rules and regulations that came to form the chapters on jihad in the legal manuals, gave Sahnun the legal *auctoritas* when he pronounced his judgement on the illegal invasion of Sicily. But in recalling the debates that took place at the Aghlabid Court of Ziyadat-allah on whether or not to launch the invasion, we may very well consider ulterior reasons for Sahnun's condemnation.

The issue of Muslim prisoners held by the Byzantines – information, it should be recalled, provided by the renegade Euphemius – was central to the debate in that it raised the possibility of a Byzantine violation of a treaty that was still in effect between the governments in Sicily and Ifriqiya. In which case, the Muslims would be well within their rights to invade the island with the assumed goal of liberating their soldiers. The fact that historians never mentioned or confirmed the existence of such soldiers held in captivity nor any attempts by the invading Muslim soldiers to liberate them begs the question concerning the reliability of Euphemius's claim. Be that as it may, the issue was argued by the two chief judges of Qayrawan, Abu Muhriz and Asad ibn al-Furat. The former, it should be recalled, was a traditional jurist who was well respected among the Qayrawani legal elite, while Asad ibn al-Furat was a maverick jurist who straddled the Maliki-Hanafi divide.[38] Were Sahnun's objections to the Sicilian jihad based on false information or on his rivalry with Asad? It should be recalled that Asad embarked on an academic journey (*rihla*), first to Hijaz, where he studied under Malik ibn Anas (d.795), then to Iraq, where he enrolled in the classes of Muhammad al-Shaybani (d.805), disciple of Abu Hanifa, and thirdly to Egypt, where he finally settled down to study with Ibn al-Qasim, the preeminent Maliki scholar of *hadith*. By the time he returned to Qayrawan, as mentioned above, Asad had under his belt a near-complete draft of his compendium of law, known as *al-Asadiyya*, which circulated widely to popular acclaim. His meteoric rise to the office of chief judgeship, it should be recalled, was no doubt due to a number of factors: his standing as a legal scholar, his backing of Aghlabid policies, his successful negotiations with the rebellious Ibn al-Tunbudhi and his unequivocal support for the invasion of Sicily. The result was his appointment to command the Aghlabid forces that were conscripted and mobilized to launch the jihad on Sicily, while at the same time maintaining his post as chief judge of Qayrawan.

Sahnun's condemnation of the Sicilian jihad is therefore best read on several levels – legal, personal and political. As a staunch devotee to orthodox Islam, Sahnun's life-long campaign to install the Maliki *madhhab* throughout the Muslim Maghreb was based on literal readings of all aspects of law and public life, as well as on imitation of the *sunna* of Malik ibn Anas and his disciples in Medina. His abhorrence to what he considered to be heretical innovations (*bid'a*) in legal practices, particularly those adopted by Mu'tazilizm, was the hallmark of his public persona and the weapon he used in his rivalry with and condemnation of the Qayrawani scholarly elite, many of whom embraced the Hanafi *madhhab*. Both the preference for the Hanafis and the acceptance of certain Mu'tazili doctrines, it should be recalled, were promoted by the Aghlabid Court in emulation of practices of the 'Abbasid Court in Baghdad at the time.

On a personal level, Sahnun's own rivalry with Asad ibn al-Furat is well documented in the biographical literature. Asad's compendium of law, *al-Asadiyya*, mentioned above, was the textual rival to his own compendium, *al-Mudawwana*, which would eventually become the standard textbook for Maliki law throughout western Islam for centuries to come. The fact that Asad studied directly under Malik ibn Anas, which Sahnun did not, may well have ignited a spark of jealousy on Sahnun's part. However, Asad's lessons with the Hanafi al-Shaybani in Iraq were the more likely cause for Sahnun's deep suspicions of Asad whose compendium accepted and embraced the legitimate differences that existed among jurists of the time. Linking Asad to the Hanafi *madhhab*, which embraced, or at least were not hostile to, Mu'tazili doctrines Sahnun judged as heretical, must be borne in mind in attempting to understand Sahnun's condemnation of the Sicilian jihad.

Most compelling was the political context of Sahnun's condemnation of the Sicilian jihad, precisely because it was initiated and executed by the highly unpopular Aghlabid government whose ruler was viewed as arrogant, corrupt and licentious, especially among the urban poor and disenfranchised Berber population. In response Sahnun spearheaded a movement under the Maliki banner of a righteous, moral and legitimate dissent that enjoyed widespread popular support. Since the launching of the Sicilian jihad had become the panacea for the Aghlabid government's domestic and external problems, it is only natural that Sahnun would condemn it.

In addition to the political, military and scholarly characters who played a major role in the two-century story of the Sicilian jihad, there were tens – or even hundreds – of thousands of men and women, free and unfree, whose lives were shaped or impacted by this historical phenomenon. As we saw in the previous chapter, these were people of many ilks and persuasions, drawn into the physical jihad at their own free will or against it. Above all, there were those who happily heeded the call of Ziyadat-allah to join the jihad that was launched on that June morning of 827. Many, no doubt, were imbued with deep religious fervour and committed to the struggle '*fi sabil allah*'. Whatever modern historians may interpret of the political or economic motives that lay at the heart of the decision to launch, the notion of jihad as a religious duty incumbent upon every healthy Muslim man was a powerful incentive and a noble cause. Whether inscribed in his writings or executed in his policies to rid Islam of heretical practices, Sahnun understood only too well the impact of jihad's spiritual (greater) and physical (lesser) force.

The chroniclers, historians, geographers and poets, however, tell us varying and at times disparate stories that undermine, as I have been arguing, a monolithic Sicilian jihad that was absolute in its conception, implementation and consequences. From the debates among Ziyadat-allah's council of ministers on the legality to launch an attack to the many contestations of command, as well as breaking of ranks and defections on the battlefields throughout the first century of conquest on the island, we see that the lines of the Sicilian jihad trajectory were crooked ones. The many verses penned by Sicilian poets, in situ or in exile, bemoaning the divisions among the Muslim community and their acts of treason, often drowned out their invectives against the usurping infidel enemy. And in connecting the dots between Ibn Hawqal's scathing criticism of Palermitan Muslims who marry Christian women and live their lives with one foot in *Dar al-Islam* and the other in *Dar al-Harb*, and the mid-eleventh-century collapse of the Kalbid government and ultimate division of the island into three petty chiefdoms, we see clearly the lines that blurred any absolute mapping of two distinctly separate and separated civilizations. And if these were not enough, one should recall the flight of Sicilian Muslims into Christian territory and contacts with the Byzantine government in seeking refuge in the aftermath of the widespread revolts against the new Fatimid government on the island. All of which puts to rest any idea of a clearly divided Muslim world and Christian world that constituted separate, internally coherent entities with neatly drawn boundaries and contours. This was the flesh and blood of jihad on the ground. As much as Muslim scholars and historians stubbornly adhered to a narrative of an idealized jihad, the texts and contexts of al-Dawudi's as well as al-Qadi al-Nu'man's chapters tell us alternative versions of the story of the Sicilian jihad.

Finally, the stories of the Sicilian jihad are not only culled from the political and military annals, nor do they draw exclusively from the anecdotes of contemporary chronicles or later universal histories. They take their substance and form as much from the descriptions of geographers and the invectives of poets as they do from the expanding and evolving body of jurisprudential literature. In reading the jihad chapters of al-Qadi al-Nu'man (d.974) and al-Dawudi (d.1011) in juxtaposition, and as sites of mutual contestation, we see in them the many historical, social and political dimensions and tensions of jihad as a dynamic process of lived experience. These chapters are best read, as I stated from the outset, along the horizontal and vertical lines of Islamic jurisprudence and real-life history. Or, in other words, these chapters are best understood as responses to the tensions that lay between the aspirations of Muslim jurists to create an abstraction of the ideal jihad as both spiritual (individual) and physical (collective) duty for devout Muslims, and between vernacular Muslim practices (individually and collectively) that evolved out of the realities and necessities of daily life and interactions with non-Muslims.

The legitimacy of the Sicilian jihad, which Sahnun refuted, undoubtedly haunts al-Qadi al-Nu'man's second chapter and its emphasis on the role of the *imam* as commander of jihad and leader of the community. His prescriptions concerning all aspects of conduct resonate loudly with (Sunni) Aghlabid malpractices, political and moral. And his fourth chapter concerning profligate and corrupt Muslims as enemies of Islam, and, thus, against those whom a jihad may be legitimately waged, empowers and legitimizes his (Shi'ite) Fatimid patrons in their own struggle against their predecessors.

Al-Dawudi's rejection of Fatimid rule, along with his decision to self-imposed exile, is best read as act of political resistance to the new Shi'ite government. His *Sicilian* chapter does not expose any serious juridical differences with al-Qadi al-Nuʿman. What one sees in both their jihad chapters is the question of political legitimacy, and any discernible differences that exist between them are based on questions of governance. More significantly, these chapters disclose an acknowledgement that jihad was more than just a set of scriptural precepts and laws. Rather, it was a dynamic process that was taking and retaking shape as actions and changes unfolded on new ground and that the *umma* and its leadership were in a position to steer its direction. The debates back at the Aghlabid court a century earlier drew attention to the varying legal and political opinions concerning the launching of the jihad, and these opinions were as much shaped by historical circumstances as they were by legal rules and regulations. The importance of Sicily as jihad testing ground undoubtedly prompted al-Dawudi to devote most of his jihad chapter to it. The crossing of social and religious boundaries by Sicilian Muslims living their lives alongside non-Muslims challenged al-Dawudi to tell a story of cross-cultural conflict and coexistence that was unfolding along the frontiers of the medieval Mediterranean.

4

Of Minarets and Shipwrecks: Ibn Hamdis and the *Poetics of Jihad*

White minarets of Gammarth, the noble remains of Carthage, it is in their shade that oblivion awaits me, and it is towards them that my life is drifting after so many shipwrecks. The sack of Rome after the chastisement of Cairo, the fire of Timbuktu after the fall of Granada. Is it misfortune which calls out to me, or do I call out to misfortune?

Once more, my son, I am borne along by the sea, the witness of all my wanderings, and which is now taking you towards your first exile. In Rome, you were the 'son of the Rumi'. Wherever you are, some will want to ask questions about your skin or your prayers. Beware of gratifying their instincts, my son, beware of bending before the multitude! Muslim, Jew or Christian, they must take you as you are, or lose you. When men's minds seem narrow to you, tell yourself that the land of God is broad; broad His hands and broad His heart. Never hesitate to go far away, beyond all seas, all frontiers, all countries, all beliefs.

Leo Africanus (Amin Maalouf: 360)

Like many a poet of the classical Arabic *qasida*, the contemporary Lebanese (exiled) novelist Amin Maalouf ends his *Leo Africanus*[1] with a supplication (*du'a'*) the protagonist addresses to his son. The novel recounts the life of a man in exile, wandering from country to country, as the rapid twists of fate, the fall of empires, sudden shifts in political and religious allegiances and radical transformations of identity force him to seek safe ground. The message of the plea, in so many words, is to be aware, to have faith and to survive the odds.

The real life and times of 'Abd al-Jabbar ibn Hamdis is not unlike that of the fictional (or factual) Leo Africanus. He was born in the year 1055 in Syracuse, in the province of Val di Noto, Sicily, during the island's period of Muslim rule. As a young boy, he hearkened to the rumblings of the impending Norman invasions, particularly dangerous given the internal political fragmentation of Muslim Sicily at the time. Being the scion of a family that had settled in Sicily for generations, and one that traced its origins to the Arabian tribe of al-Azd, we can safely surmise that the young ʿAbd al-Jabbar lived his early years in the lap of luxury, a life of the warrior Arab aristocracy who, through the spoils of war, political patronage, lucrative trade and Sicily's highly developed agriculture and industry (textiles, arms, shipping), reaped the benefits of living life in the crossroads of civilizations. The many recollections throughout his poetry of hunting outings and nocturnal gatherings of wine, women and song, if read literally, celebrate a privileged life of ease.

But the warring factions in his beloved homeland paved the way for an easy victory to the armies of Robert Guiscard, and Ibn Hamdis set sail toward the shores of Ifriqiya where he hoped to make his fame and fortune as a court poet. Following a brief sojourn in the city of Safaqus (modern Sfax) where many of his extended family then resided, he embarked on his first journey in crossing the North African desert, ending with his arrival in 1078 in Seville (al-Andalus), at the court of the petty prince, al-Muʿtamid ibn ʿAbbad (r.1061–91).[2] It was here where Ibn Hamdis would hone his poetic skills and taste the life of a highly prized royal panegyrist. But again, the hand of fate would wreak havoc on the poet's comfort and security. In 1086, the forces of Alfonse VI launched an attack against the emirate of Seville, forcing al-Muʿtamid to seek the help of the Berber warlord, Yusuf Tashufin, whose fundamentalist forces (*al-murabitun*/ Almoravids) had already seized control of much of the Maghreb. Although al-Muʿtamid won the battle (al-Zallaqa, 1086) against Alfonse, he lost the war when Yusuf returned as invading enemy in 1091 and banished al-Muʿtamid to a prison in Aghmat (modern Morocco) where he eventually died in 1095. Ibn Hamdis found himself on the road again, and, after a short visit to his former patron and friend in prison, he headed back eastward, along the North African littoral, proffering his poetic goods to whichever petty prince purchased his services.

Ibn Hamdis settled in the province of Ifriqiya where he spent the second half of his long life shuffling to and from the Zirid court at al-Mahdiyya (modern Tunisia). These were difficult times for the princes who faced the lingering hostility of their former patrons, the Fatimids of Egypt, the onslaught of the Bani Hilal migrants from the Arabian Peninsula, and the threat of the Norman invasions of Southern Italy and Sicily. Ibn Hamdis would never find the white minarets and comforting shade he selectively remembered of his youthful Sicily, as one shipwreck after another jostled his mind and bruised his heart. Until his last poetic breath, at the ripe age of eighty-something, Ibn Hamdis remained Muslim Sicily's premier exile, its most prolific panegyrist and its most eloquent wandering minstrel.

Ibn Hamdis bequeathed to Arabic literature a complete *diwan* (anthology) containing 370 pieces (amounting to well over 6,000 verses), ranging from two-line poems to full-length *qasidas* as long as eighty lines. The survival of this *diwan*, as opposed to the much shorter one of his compatriot, Abu al-Hasan 'Ali al-Ballanubi,[3] and the hundreds of fragments of poetry by Arab Sicilian poets that survived in larger anthologies,[4] has bestowed on Ibn Hamdis enduring fame and unique literary stature in both classical Arabic literature and in Muslim Sicilian history. The sheer size of the *diwan* attests to his long and prolific career. The diversity of its genres – panegyric (*madih*), elegy (*ritha'*), love poem (*ghazal*), devotional poem (*zuhdiyya*), wine song (*khamriyya*) and description (*wasf*) – underscores his artistic versatility. And the preponderance of the panegyric, from his earlier days at the 'Abbadid court in Seville to his twilight years at the Zirid court at al-Mahdiyya, calls attention to a career intrinsically tied to and financially and professional dependent upon the political whims and winds of his time.

However, above and beyond the size and condition of the *diwan* and its uniqueness in the literary history of Muslim Sicily, Ibn Hamdis's poetry scintillates in its power to capture the historical moment, when the politics, culture, aesthetics, and states of mind and emotion are brought to light through his particular vision of the world. If rearranged chronologically, Ibn Hamdis's *diwan* could be read as a 'diary in verse' in which the intimate details of his life and his emotional stances toward the people and events that shaped it give voice to those precarious and unpredictable times in which he lived. In fact, a chronology of Ibn Hamdis's life experiences has been as much a subject of scholarly inquiry as has been his poetic *oeuvre*: curious, given the fact that so little of his life has been recorded in the conventional sources of the Arabic archive, biographical dictionaries, anthologies and *adab* (belles lettrist) writings. Yet the snippets of information in his poetry, allusions to actual events and descriptions of real people and places, pieced together, have bequeathed to us a life-sized story that scholars have read, and at times perhaps hyper-read, with gullible fascination.

Ibn Hamdis and his modern critics

Much as he saw in the Euphemius of two centuries earlier, Michele Amari sees Ibn Hamdis as a native son of Sicily forced into exile by dire political circumstances resulting from foreign occupation of the homeland. To recall, Amari was born in 1802 to a prominent family from Palermo. At an early age, his father, a government functionary, was imprisoned for anti-government activities, and the young Amari was forced to earn a living for himself and his family. His early education lured him, first, into the volatile politics of popular resistance to the Spanish Bourbon rule and aspirations for Sicilian autonomy, and, later, into a national movement of Italian reunification that would culminate in the Risorgimento of 1860. His banishment from Sicily (and Italy) and his long period of exile led him to Paris, where he made the acquaintance of the eminent Arabists and historians, Reinhard Dozy and Levi-Provencal, learned Arabic, and embarked upon a life-long project to study Sicilian history in both the Muslim and Norman periods.[5]

Amari is the first of modern historians and critics to read Ibn Hamdis's poetry, to which he was first introduced by Dozy,[6] primarily through the prism of the biographical detail, read, extracted or understood from any given *qasida*. In Amari's case, his own nationalist agenda and his political and ideological conflicts drew him to situate Ibn Hamdis within the uninterrupted continuum of Sicilian history shaped by the perpetual conflict with the island's foreign invaders and occupiers. This led Amari to read Ibn Hamdis in a highly literal fashion, setting a paradigm for future scholars by which both meaning and intent of the poem are determined by and remain strictly within the confines of the historical moment.[7] It is here where the *diwan* of Ibn Hamdis takes on the unusual importance as a major source for the reconstruction of Muslim Sicilian history.

In 1897, Celestino Schiaparelli, a disciple of Amari, published the first modern edition of the *diwan* and followed it soon thereafter with an Italian translation. The edition was based primarily on the two extant manuscripts, one at the Vatican and the other at St. Petersburg, but it incorporated materials and fragments collated from other sources available to him at the time.[8]

Half a century later, Francesco Gabrieli (d.1991), premier Italian Orientalist best known for his work on early Islamic history, *adab*, and Kharijite poetry, published a full work on Ibn Hamdis (Mazara, 1948), drawing on the poetry as a reflection of his life and times. Gabrieli brings 'Ibn Hamdis studies' into a (more) modern phase of criticism and analysis, having himself been exposed to, and been a participant in, the remarkable advances in Arabic and Islamic scholarship of the twentieth century. The discovery of new material, the growing sophistication of manuscript editing, and the impact on modern humanities and social sciences on what had prior been a field of pure philological endeavour allowed Gabrieli to gently loosen the grip on Ibn Hamdis from Amari's nationalist agenda and recast him in broader historical and literary contexts.[9]

The *Diwan* of Ibn Hamdis as an anthology of poetry and as a docu-biography of the poet's life and times has also had similar treatment in modern scholarship in the Arab world. The Tunisian Zin al-'Abidin al-Sanusi (d.1965) published two books on Ibn Hamdis in the early 1950s, both conceived and drafted during his own exile in Italy in the years 1943–5. Both the first, *Patriotism in the Poetry of Ibn Hamdis* (1950), and the second, *'Abd al-Jabbar ibn Hamdis: His Life and Work* (1953), delve into the biographical detail and draw from the political ideology that fared prominently in Amari's treatment.[10] In the introductory remarks, as well as throughout his discussion of the poems, al-Sanusi makes unequivocal references to those very aspects of the poetry that piqued Amari's interest. What was intriguing about the *diwan* to both Amari and al-Sanusi was a political poetics that was at once cross-cultural and nationalistic, that it somehow articulated a consciousness of a unity within Mediterranean history and culture that is shared by its many people(s), that this unity is constantly threatened and challenged by outside forces, and that exile is the consequence of that demolished unity.

Al-Sanusi was a prominent figure among the intellectual elite of the 1930s–1940s generation, architects of modern Arabic literature and culture in Tunisia, who were dedicated to the dual task of liberating Tunisia from the fetters of French colonialism and forging a modern, popular, indigenous literature and culture. Much of this task included unearthing, re-reading and re-appropriating the classical Arabic literary heritage (*turath*) to proclaim Tunisia's indigenous Arab identity, and to construct (or even to imagine) a historical continuum and an aesthetic symbiosis between tradition and modernity (i.e. between Tunisia's pre-colonial past and its future). Ibn Hamdis's many *qasidas,* composed on Tunisian soil, in which he laments the fall of (Muslim) Sicily, lavishes praise on its freedom fighters and powerful benefactors and patrons, and hurls invectives against foreign invaders and occupiers, resonated strongly with al-Sanusi's anti-imperial sensitivities and strong nationalist proclivities, just as they had done with Amari a century before. Once again, for both Amari and al-Sanusi, the meaning of the poem was most compelling in the literal reading, where the same historical processes that shaped Ibn Hamdis's life and work were still operating in nineteenth-century Sicily and twentieth-century Tunisia.

Other works in Arabic have attempted to reconstruct the life of Ibn Hamdis through his poetry, but the work of Ihsan 'Abbas is the most noteworthy.[11] His publication of *The History of the Arabs in Sicily* (Cairo, 1959) drew new and wide attention to Ibn Hamdis as central to Islamic Sicily, and his literary analyses reflected the advances in both modern literary criticism and the study of Arabic literary and intellectual history.[12] Additionally, it brought 'Abbas to produce a new and updated edition of the *Diwan*, adding newly discovered materials and making significant editorial changes and deletions where needed.

Neoclassicism as 'form'; Sicily as 'meaning'

Both Gabrieli and 'Abbas correctly place Ibn Hamdis within the 'school' of neoclassicism that came to the fore in Arabic poetry in the tenth century and prevailed throughout the twelfth century. Readers of Ibn Hamdis will immediately recognize the pronounced influences on his work of poetic giants, such as Abu Tammam (d.846) and al-Mutanabbi (d.965). As stated previously, Ibn Hamdis's *diwan* include a number of sub-genres (panegyric, elegy, love poem, devotional poem, wine song and description poem), but it is the preponderance of the panegyric that is worthy of note. As a full-time professional poet, unlike many in the classical period who composed verse as a pastime or a second occupation, Ibn Hamdis depended upon both a wealthy, influential patron and a public audience to survive. As a perpetual exile, the course of his wanderings and the progression of his profession were subjected to a fickle market vulnerable to political upheavals and petty rivalries among a surplus of poets looking for work. Both his decision to leave Sicily during its slow and painful fall to the Normans and his resolution never to return as long as it was ruled by 'foreign invaders' were based, once again, on the harsh realities of the times in which he lived.

Thus, the panegyric, the centuries-old literary genre and a dominant theme of the classical Arabic *qasida*, came to play the major role in Ibn Hamdis's *oeuvre*, and both his *qasida* and his panegyric are immediately recognizable in their reworkings of the language, stock phrases, imagery, themes and motifs that are the stuff of the poetic canons established by the masters of *Jahiliyya* (pre-Islamic) poetry.[13] His neoclassicism is recognized in his conscious tampering with the tripartite structure of the *qasida* of the pre-and early Islamic periods (i.e. elegiac prelude/desert crossing/boast (*nasib/rahil/fakhr*)), and even in his tampering with the later Abbasid bipartite structure of elegiac prelude/boast (*atlal/fakhr*). His excessive use of archaic and low-frequency vocabulary, his forging of new meanings to words and phrases, and his playful manipulation of the rhetorical devices of the new poetry (*badi'*), that is, of punning (*jinas*) and antithesis (*tibaq*), brought to a peak of sophistication with Abu Tammam more than two centuries earlier, also accentuate his neoclassicism. And finally, Ibn Hamdis's neoclassicism is reflected in the pure historicism of his poem, the revamping of the (old) form to convey the (new) meaning that opens up the poem to a wider range of readings and significations. As Jaroslav Stetkevych astutely observes, 'The framework and the idiom of the traditional mold are used to contain and express or to comment on an immediately contemporary historical event.'[14] To Ibn Hamdis, the canonical panegyric was the mould, and Sicily would often provide, explicitly of implicitly, the contemporary historical event.

The theme of nostalgia for homeland (*hanin ila al-watan*) for Sicily that permeates the *diwan* has dominated just about all of the scholarship, critical and historical, on Ibn Hamdis in modern times. This theme cuts across genres, especially the panegyric, elegy and wine song, and it finds expression in a variety of familiar *topoi*, such as the vicissitudes of time, growing old, recollections of youth, praying for rain and even in poems of correspondence with family members. It often surfaces in contrasting images and themes within a single poem.¹⁵

To illustrate how Ibn Hamdis fashioned 'Sicily' as current event in the traditional mould of the *qasida*, I cite here a short poem, apparently composed at an early stage of his career, and at a time soon after he departed from Sicily in 1078. The poem has only nine lines, and it can be divided into three sections: lines 1–4 may be read as an amatory preface (*nasib*) or as a love poem (*ghazal*), lines 5–7 as a desert crossing (*rahil*), and lines 8–9 as a supplication (*du'a'*) that evokes a panegyric yet to be composed. Although the poem does not mention Sicily explicitly, a close reading of it, I argue, reveals its presence in several ways.

Leaving Sicily and Travelling to Ifrıqiya
Dıwan #98: 167–8

1- When she approaches at night *[sarat]* I extend my cheek in joy,
   and I greet her with a kiss on the hand.

2- I enjoin my affections to her soul,
   so that they may cool the burning of a broken heart.

3- She strokes my face with the palm of her hand like an enchantress,
   and her veil is like a bouquet of sweet-scented flowers moistened with dew.

4- I recognize her approach *[masra-ha]* by the whiff of her sweet aromas,
   just as a patient recognizes a physician among his visitors.

5- What is it with me that I endure a long estrangement from my homeland?
   Have I been born fated to live in exile?

6- Forever shall I squander my resolve in a distant land,
   for a hope only to be dispersed in faraway places?

7- How many a hostile terrain will I cross on the back of a sturdy she-camel,
   bleeding at the hooves and foaming at the nostrils?

8- May abundance preserve for her the most glorious of praise,
   binding her to all the camels that traversed the wastelands,

9- [and to my] camel which, in the company of noblemen, breaks untrodden ground,
   with a sword of water sheathed in her bowels.

In the first section (lines 1–4), several motifs of the amatory preface/*ghazal* come together: the affection and joy of proximity and the anguish of separation, the sickness of the separated lover, the magic spell of love, the intoxication of the scent of flowers and the terrain as green pastures. The choice of the verb *sarat* in line 1, which denotes 'to travel by night', adds an element of secrecy, a common motif in classical Arabic love poetry. The shift from the motion verb (*sarat*) of line 1 to its corresponding (fixed) verbal noun (*masra-ha*) in line 4 allows the poet to complete the section and to contrast the motion of departure (his) with the immutability of the beloved (i.e. Sicily). This section also confuses the sense of direction, since it is 'she' who moves by night, and it is he/the poet who greets (*qabul*) her with a kiss (*taqbil*). The confusing or disguising of identity is also a common motif in love poetry. The tension between proximity and distance – 'she is so close that I can touch, feel, smell and see her' – is dramatized when carried over into the next section, lines 5–7.

Here the tripartite *qasida*'s medial segment of desert crossing (*rahil*) is reworked, but in a most unusual way. The poet begins by questioning his fate, and the desert crossing is one that may or may not take place in future time, possibly a crossing that will last forever. The evocation of faraway places, of untrodden (unknown) terrain and the *Jahili* (pre-Islamic) images of the exhausted she-camel replete with bleeding hooves and foaming nostrils illustrate quite clearly J. Stetkevych's 'idiom of the traditional mold', and the poet's immediate and rather prescient fears of leaving Sicily forever express 'an immediate contemporary historical event'.

To reinforce the non-ending to the desert crossing (i.e. Ibn Hamdis's departure from Sicily and what would become his long life of wandering and exile), the poet repeats its imagery and articulates his emotional stance towards it in the third and last section of the poem. This is the customary supplication that intimates the theme of panegyric. Line 8 makes it absolutely clear what Ibn Hamdis is trying to convey: that Sicily becomes the object of praise (*mamduh*) of which the poet pleads for abundance. And equally Sicily, with her tantalizing proximity, intoxicating smells and lush gardens, becomes the abandoned encampment, departed from, separated from and longed for in the desert crossing. As she was the object of his affections in the amatory preface, so too does Sicily remain the prayed-for object of praise with which he hopes to fulfil his ambitions throughout his life and work.

Panegyric between poetic and political legitimacy

My intention henceforth is to look closely at the panegyric – and its relation to other components of Ibn Hamdis's *qasida* – to investigate some of the broader geopolitical and cross-cultural issues that form many of the contexts, subtexts and meta-texts to Ibn Hamdis's verses. Because panegyrics were composed for prominent figures such as kings and princes, ministers and high-ranking military officers, and because they were delivered, or performed, on momentous historical occasions such as military victories, ascensions to thrones (power) and public holidays, they convey much of what Ibn Hamdis chose for us (the patron, the audience, the reader) to know about his life and times. To be more precise, I am interested in how Ibn Hamdis understood political legitimacy and the ways in which he fashioned a poetics that straddled the sacred and the profane to launch his own 'jihad of the tongue'.

The connection between the traditional genre as form of the *qasida* and the contemporary historical event as content has been a major theme in Suzanne Stetkevych's work. In *Poetics of Islamic Legitimacy* (2002), Stetkevych draws a number of conclusions that help in reading and decoding the many possible meanings of the panegyric. I cite some of these as validly relevant to Ibn Hamdis's poetry in order to shed light on the literary–political implications of his artistic choices. Among her conclusions are the following:

i. The classical Arabic *qasida* created, encoded and promulgated a myth and ideology of legitimate Arabo-Islamic rule.
ii. The poet uses the panegyric to express the legitimate authority of the patron.
iii. The *qasida* is able to impose form and meaning on changing human and societal relationships.
iv. The continuity of the *qasida* genre encodes and transmits an ideology of empire, or 'Arabo-Islamic rule'.
v. The genre-determined poetic components – such as the departed mistress, the abandoned campsites and the desert journey – are powerful and evocative bearers of political and religious legitimacy.
vi. The panegyric ode allows Arabo-Islamic culture to interpret contemporary events and absorb them into a larger myth of cultural identity.

vii. The *qasida* form in itself creates a 'mythic concordance' between the Islamic present and the pre-Islamic Arab golden or heroic age, drawing on the qualities of the *Jahili* warrior aristocrat, especially might and magnanimity.
viii. The panegyric is supplicatory and appeals to leaders' *diyafa* (taking in; feeding and sheltering the guest, refugee or the destitute) and *ijara* (raw might and the nobility of character to provide and protect).[16]

These observations enable us to understand in a far more nuanced way the significance, the vitality and even the inventiveness of Ibn Hamdis's verses and to call into question what some modern critics have called Ibn Hamdis's rigorous traditionalism and mere imitation of neoclassicism. His staunch faith in and loyalty to the canons of Arabic poetry, of the form, rhyme, metres, language, stock phrases, themes and imagery of the *Jahiliyya* and earlier Islamic high periods were intentionally connected to his bigger project to assign to Sicily – and to himself – a prominent place in poetic perpetuity. His *diwan* recasts Sicily as sacred space, the abandoned abode of lovers, the place–time of youthful bliss and reverie, the 'covert for gazelles' and a 'thicket for lions', the pleasure garden replete with rich, flowing wine and ample-bosomed, slim-waisted maidens, and the port of holy war defending the faith. Ibn Hamdis was only too well aware that all of poetic canonicity, a powerful patron, and an attentive and engaged audience were vital to completing his project. His frequent evocation of Islamic jihad, especially in his later panegyrics and elegies, is an integral component of what would evolve as his *poetics of jihad* that straddle the sacred and the profane, as I will continue to argue.

The trajectory of Ibn Hamdis's life and work runs parallel to, or perhaps follows in the path of, the Christian Reconquest of lands that had been conquered, subdued, 'colonized' and civilized by Islam for centuries. Both Muslim Spain (al-Andalus) and Muslim Sicily were peripheral areas that shared many common features: each extended into Christian territory – that is, in areas north of the Mediterranean that bordered with Christendom; both were considered *thaghr* (pl. *thughur*), frontiers of confrontation in which a constant state of war existed between *Dar al-Islam and Dar al-Harb*; and both included substantial non-Muslim populations. As peripheral areas within the greater Islamic Empire, both Spanish and Sicilian Muslim cultural histories abound in political and religious movements, as well as literary, artistic and intellectual achievements that strove to strike a balance between autonomy and distinctiveness, on the one hand, and the psychological and emotional need to be part of the centre, on the other, as articulated in Americo Castro's 'constant oscillation' or David Wasserstein's 'awkward balancing act between distancing and imitation'.[17] The wide popular appeal of the very traditional, orthodox Maliki school of Islamic law that survived the entire Muslim periods of both Spain and Sicily and the preservation and cultivation of the truly 'classical' *qasida* (notwithstanding the poetic innovations of the *zajal* and the *muwashshaha* in Spain) are two examples where Spanish and Muslim Sicilian culture aspired to be more 'mainstream' than the centre.

Islamic Spain and Sicily were also, to borrow a modern term, 'multicultural' societies. Large segments of the populations were non-Arab and non-Muslim. And as much as jihad – and I use the term here in the very contemporary and popular sense of the term – was a fact of daily life, so too were the practical politics and culture of protection (*dhimma*), of treaties and safe passage, where cross-cultural contacts and a sharing of a common life blurred the boundaries of *Dar al-Islam and Dar al-Harb*. If jihad had come to mean 'holy war', it had also come, by necessity, to include the secondary meaning of 'holy peace', especially on the turf of the royal compounds, as well as in the hunting lodges, pleasure palaces, bath houses, souks, taverns and public gardens where Muslim met non-Muslim in daily and nightly encounters.

So how was Ibn Hamdis, faithful son and loyal lover of Sicily, the paradise of wine, women and song, to fashion a *poetics of jihad*?

Historians of Arabic literature have thoroughly covered the impact of Islam on classical poetry that was deeply rooted in the *Jahiliyya* tradition. The debates concerning the Prophet Muhammad's views on the poets, for example, ranging from his early criticism of their 'all talk no action', to his eventual appropriation of poetry and poets to further the cause of his mission of monotheism, culminating in his relationship with the poet Hassan ibn Thabit, have and continue to be major themes in literary and religious debates. The stock phrases and images of man's supernatural abilities, the omnipotence of a fickle fate and the celebration of wine and sexual debauchery, all values anathema to the precepts of the new faith, carried over into the poetry of the Islamic period with seemingly little disruption. *Jahiliyya* poetry had already evolved by the first Islamic century into a highly developed and revered literary canon, and it was not likely to be undone in any measurable way. In Stetkevych's words, 'The *qasida* is thus able to impose form and meaning on changing human and societal relationships and, by explaining and directing change, exert control over it.'[18]

In the hunting lodges of eleventh- and twelfth-century Syracuse or Seville, in the palatine gardens of Palermo and Cordoba, or the public squares and taverns of Agrigento and Granada, far away in time and place from the *Jahili* warrior-poets of the Arabian wastelands, a poet such as Ibn Hamdis continued to compose and recite verses about the abandoned encampment of a former lover and the treacherous crossings of the desert terrain. Interestingly, one would find among his captivated audience men and women whose mother tongues were Berber, Latin, Hebrew, a French, Spanish or Italian vernacular, Persian or even Slavic. It is likely that few of these listeners would have actually seen a she-camel or a vast stretch of desert, nor would they have had any idea about the bitterness of the colocynth fruit or the size and shape of a wild oryx. But they could understand the poem, and they understood that this was nothing more than language, figurative language – traditional, repetitive, predictable, familiar, anticipated and performed – powerful enough to stir emotions, to entertain and instruct, to make one laugh or cry, to anger or appease, to reminisce and remind. It was the talent and skill of the poet and the sophistication of the audience, both honed and matured by long literary experience, to draw the lines between the figurative and the literal, between the artistic and the political, and between the sacred and the profane.

Ibn Hamdis fashioned a *poetics of jihad* gradually, carefully, at first subtly, then more forcefully later in his life. In an early *qasida*, untitled in his *diwan*, he injects a jihad motif within what could be described as a uni-thematic boast poem (*fakhr*). There are no specific references or indications of time, place, persons or occasions. The pure and simple style and the absence of the existential brooding and 'nationalist' angst that red-pepper his later works suggest that it was composed at an early stage of his writing, at a time preceding his departure from Sicily but one that was clearly marked with the omens of doom. Lines 1–12 constitute the boast of the individual/poet-lover, lines 13–26 shift the boast from the poet to his homeland (unspecified), and lines 27–30 form the closing supplication.

(On Bravery and the *Poetics of Jihad*)
–untitled–
Diwan #75: 114–6

1- The heart flutters in anticipation of coupling with slender maidens,
    and the branch sprouts fresh leaves with the sap of youth.

2- I was breast-fed on a passion for noble rank,
    and I race with the wind to reach its distant heights.

3- I am still grounded below, just a bit above Pisces,
    and in my ascent I look up toward the Pole-star.

4- The venerated old man is only such
    when his noble qualities are reflected in the new-born son.

5- I remember all the beauties on account of the first one,
    just as the poem is remembered by its opening line.

6- But I have witnessed that nobility is like a second wife,
    incompatible with bashful maidens.

7- I am aroused, and with me determination is aroused,
    and my rising to follow it gives me no repose.

8- There is no land that has laid my resolve to rest,
    awakening in one with no experience the inertia of a sluggish man.

9- Nor is there a soft and supple maiden living a life of idleness,
    or of the sweet fragrances of musk and aloe,

10- who bids [me] farewell in separation, hand in hand,
    chest to chest, cheek to cheek [Arabic: neck to neck].

11- Whosoever seeks glory mounts the back of a mighty horse,
    [pulling himself] away from the ample bosom of a supple maiden,

12- and hurdles into battle, with one resolution after another,
    on one night after another, and from one hostile terrain to another.

13- My homeland belongs to God, long may it live,
    as a covert for gazelles and a thicket for lions.

14- How many a gazelle fawn, with flickering eyelashes,
    reluctant to be touched, comforted by aloofness,

15- has aroused such passions with a languid blink,
    and blunted the glibness of my piercing wink.

16- And how many a lion with sharp cutting claws,
    whose mane inlaid with steel,

17- sprints forth like the tongue of a colossal conflagration
    and laps up the blood from the jugular vein.

18- Angels of Divine Justice, created for the sake of war,
    rekindle the fires of battle with their fuel.

19- Their pokers are sharp, pointy swords,
    crafted to crack skulls, in the tradition of the era of Hud.

20- They discharge forcibly what is concealed in bodies,
    whenever they smite with what is concealed in sheathes.

21- They pounce on their contemptible enemies,
    and with a vengeance they tear apart with the tips of their swords.

22- [You see them as] stars whose ascendancy sparkles in their lances,
    but whose setting is in the [enemy's] entrails.

25- Lightning, whose flash flickers
    like the fluttering of the wings of a love-struck heart.

26- You see them as the bending of the bows of the bowmen
    when they are drawn with a vigorous draw.

23- The hooves of their horses, exhausted, leave their traces
    on places of prominence (*maharib*) throughout the dusty terrain.

24- The heads of the enemy sink to the ground in battle,
    as if prostrating themselves in prayer, and oh, what a prostration! (*sujud*)

27- May God water the land of His sanctuary with a rain cloud,
    bellowing with laughter that roars like the thunder.

28- A battleground of conflict, a port for holy war (*Jihad*),
    a watering hole for stallions, and a refuge for the banished.

29- A place that brings together face to face war hero to war hero, nobleman to nobleman, and lion to lion.

30- And may the bodies of those among their living live in luxury, and the souls of their dearly departed rest in eternity.

This *qasida* is exemplary of the poet's craft in weaving the theme of jihad into the overall fabric of the traditional (read: *Jahili*) *qasida*. In the first section, the individual boast draws on familiar conceits of noble origins and successful love conquests that are common to both the amatory preface (*nasib*) and its later mutation, the love poem (*ghazal*). Lines 1–6 construct a chronology that begins with the proverbial 'twinkle in the eye', ejaculation, and conception, and passes through stages of breast-feeding, childhood, young love, to full male maturity and marriage. Lines 8–12 collapse images of both the abandoned encampment of the lover (*atlal*) and its subsequent desert crossing (*rahil*). The playfulness of this section lies in the poet's rejection of these amorous images after beautifully constructing them, and then boldly opting for what makes a man truly noble – the life of a warrior. Line 13 begins the second section with the evocation of the homeland. The boast shifts its focus from the (individual) poet to the (collective) land, while the language shifts from the feminine images of love (the soft maiden, the life of ease, the fragrance of musk, the ample bosom) to the masculine images of battle (mounting the horse, flashing swords). The homeland, we are reminded, is situated between the two: a covert for gazelles and a thicket for lions. The descriptions of the battle scenes (lines 13–26) read closely to those of the *Jahiliyya* poets, replete with stock images of shimmering points of swords, glistening like stars and thrashing of enemy skulls by the claws of lions.

The shift from the first to the second section of the poem – from the poet's boast of the feminine world of nursing and weaning to the collective boast (in the form of the land) of the masculine world of war – may be read as the universal experience of growing up, thematically built up in the first six lines of the poem, where a young boy is born and raised in a women's world under the protection of first the mother and then the young lover, only to be banished as a man to the world of mounting steeds and encounters with the enemy. To an audience of eleventh-century *qasida* aficionados, whether in Palermo or Baghdad, this meaning would be obvious. But Ibn Hamdis may have had another layer of meaning tucked between the lines: that the Sicily of his youth – a land long nestled in between war and peace, between the comfort of a privileged life and the vulnerability of being out on the edge, a land straddling two worlds, two faiths, and constantly negotiating between the religious and the worldly, between the figurative and the literal – was about to unfold.

The third section, the supplication, begins with a prayer that is haunting. Line 27 asks that his land be watered with a rain cloud, a plea commonly used for the grave of a recently departed loved one. Line 28 specifically refers to his homeland as a port of holy war (*thagr al-jihad*), an honorific in Islam for those border areas of *Dar al-Islam* that were called upon to defend the faith. The evocation of jihad in this poem has two foreshadows in the words '*maharib*' in line 23 and '*sujud*' in line 24. Both words fit literally into the immediate contexts: among the original meanings of '*mihrab*' (pl. maharib) – whose root, h-r-b, also implies war or fighting – are a 'seat or place of prominence', or a 'palace'; '*sujud*' denotes a 'prostration', an 'act of submission or bowing the head'. In the battle description, then, 'the hooves of their horses, exhausted, leave their traces on the places of prominence (*maharib*) spread out throughout the dusty terrain'; and 'the heads of the enemy sink to the ground in battle, as if prostrating themselves in submission (*sujud*)'. Both terms in their lexical semantics accurately convey the warrior-poet's victory and the enemy's submission and humiliation. However, since both '*maharib*' and '*sujud*' have evolved as Islamic liturgical terms (as 'a niche in a mosque' and 'a prostration in prayer'), they allow the poet to make a smooth and effective transition from the idiom of the profane *Jahiliyya* poetics to a religious Islamic motif. The 'prominent places' are transformed into the mosques where the word of God is spread, and 'submission to the military victor' is transformed into 'prostration in prayer' before God. The supplication asks God to protect his homeland, but the last three lines are a clear reminder of the duality that is Sicily: a place that brings different people together, and a place where they live a life of luxury and ease.

The tension between the Sicily of gazelles and the Sicily of lions – that is, of the easy life of wine, women and song versus the life of political rivalries, civil strife and war – defines the contours of Ibn Hamdis's *poetics of jihad*. By the time he became a fully professional poet, Muslim Sicily had already started to come undone at the seams. The blurring of the lines that clearly divided

Dar al-Islam from *Dar al-Harb* was growing more and more evident after two centuries of a fragile coexistence between Muslims and Christians, it should be recalled, through conversion, intermarriage, concubinage, slavery, or the laws and treaties of protection (*dhimma*). The business of daily life, agriculture, industry, commerce and the arts necessitated mutual interdependence and a degree of cohabitation that were played out in the many public spheres. All of this gave way to elastic interpretations of Islamic jihad, as I have been arguing throughout, that differed sharply or bended in different directions from those of the early generations of *mujahidin* who came from Ifriqiya to conquer, plunder and subdue, all for the sake of God (*fi sabil allah*). In addition, the many years of political corrosion, petty rivalries, local insurgencies and sectarian strife within the Muslim community – at times culminating in defections to the enemy side, as we have seen – not to mention the sporadic flare-ups of tensions between the urban and rural populations, between Arab Sicilians and Berber Sicilians, and most heatedly, between 'native' Sicilians and newly arrived North African warrior-immigrants, all had a devastating impact on the 'physical' jihad of Ibn Hamdis's times, thus, giving its 'political' evocation a hollow ring when compared to earlier times of conquest and building amid unity and purpose.

Ibn Hamdis's *poetics of jihad* is one of constant negotiation between the memory of a happy youth in Sicily and the reality of perpetual exile from it. It also entails the delicate compromise between the worldly or profane ethos of classical Arabic poetry and the potentially powerful appeal of jihad as a religio-political discourse. In other words, Ibn Hamdis as 'poet' and Ibn Hamdis as 'political exile' appealing to his patrons and co-religionists to save his homeland needed to find and poeticize a balance – between the figurative and the literal; between the artistic demands to satisfy, on the one hand, his literary critics and public audience, and, on the other, his religiously or politically fervent saviours.

Francesco Gabrieli, in assessing both Ibn Hamdis's poetry and Amari's reading of it, makes an acute observation that touches on what may be called a *poetics of jihad*:

> There is another aspect of Sicilian poetry, artistically less refined but more interesting from a human or psychological perspective, and one that appealed to the vigorous imagination of Amari and was thus brought to light with great sympathy. This was the affection and nostalgia for the homeland, an interest in its fate, and the religious and military fervor

that permeated sections of Ibn Hamdis's poems that read close to and evoked those momentous historical events that shaped the contours of his life.[19]

It is generally accepted among literary critics and fans of Ibn Hamdis, medieval and modern, that much of his best work, in terms of originality, lyrical purity and emotional effect, are his 'Sicilian' verses in which the pain of exile and the nostalgia for a lost homeland become his personal mantra and his poetic obsession. These verses may come at any time or in any juncture within any given *qasida*, and their psychological and literary effects colour or alter the mood and tone of the entire poem. The appeal to the Muslim community in the form, idiom or imagery of jihad is a strategy that is not, I argue, based upon what Gabrieli refers to as 'religious fervor', at least in the traditional – and most recently resurgent – sense of the term.

First, Ibn Hamdis's *poetics of jihad* is deeply imbedded in the long and revered tradition of classical Arabic poetry that traces its roots to the *Jahiliyya qasida*. It is a poetics that is built upon the language, stock phrases, images and themes of the aristocrat-poet-warrior of the pre-Islamic Arabian landscape. It accepts and preserves the values of a real or imagined pure ethnicity and noble lineage of 'Arabness', and it celebrates the superhuman qualities of the warrior-poet who can behead his enemy without unsheathing his sword, the might and magnanimity of the just ruler (real or imagined), and the lusty celebrations of wine, women, and song that are the privileges and rights of the poet-warrior after a hard day of battle. The fact that Ibn Hamdis could still breathe life, meaning and emotional effect into what may or might have become in other instances a hackneyed and tired poetry is testament to both his poetic skills and the survival of the *qasida* throughout the ages.

Secondly, Ibn Hamdis's *poetics of jihad* is personal, grounded in the specificities of his place(s) and time(s). His jihad is not one that supports the notion that Islam was in a constant state of war with non-Islam. His *poetics of jihad* embraces a society that revels in living life to the fullest. It is one that seeks to remember and remind of the glory days, when Islam was in the ascendancy for all its human and civilizational accomplishments. It is a *poetics of jihad* that rejects a sanctimonious theological posturing, but one that can nonetheless have a sharp political edge. For Ibn Hamdis did understand all too well its universal appeal, and he did on occasion call upon its potential power to rally the faithful to his cause. I maintain that this was a last resort, a moment of desperation, not a religious or political calling. Ibn Hamdis's 'jihad' was not universal, eternal, absolute or theological; it was a custom-made poetics to fit the particular history and geography of Sicily as extended metaphor for all that was transcendent to Islamic history and Arabic literature.

Poetic apprenticeship: The warrior-poet at the 'Abbadid court in Seville 1078–9

On a dark winter's night sometime in the year 1078, Ibn Hamdis sat despondent in his room at an inn situated on the outskirts of Seville. After what must have been a long and arduous journey across the North African desert, he crossed the Straits and arrived on Iberian soil in hopes of finding employment as a poet at one of the courts of the petty kingdoms of al-Andalus. His choice of Seville was a wise one in that its prince, al-Mu'tamid ibn 'Abbad, was renowned as a patron of culture and was, himself, a poet of considerable skill and accomplishment, as mentioned previously.

Ibn Hamdis had requested an audience with the prince-poet. Having waited a long time, he made the painful decision to pack his bags and return to his family in Safaqus. All of a sudden, the story goes, a young page appeared in the dark of night, with a horse and its rein in one hand and a lantern in the other, approached the inn, and called up to the dejected poet to announce that the prince was granting him an audience. When Ibn Hamdis arrived at the palace, al-Mu'tamid offered him a seat, and, after some time, commanded him to stand up and look out from a small window. In the distance, he saw an ironsmith's furnace, encased in glass, with two small portals that a woman was periodically opening and closing to stoke the flames. Al-Mu'tamid then suddenly hurled a line of poetry at Ibn Hamdis describing the fire and challenged him to match it or best it. After three quick rounds of poetic sparring, al-Mu'tamid was sufficiently impressed and asked Ibn Hamdis to join his royal retinue.

The anecdote, preserved for us in al-Maqarri's (d.1631) monumental history of the Arabs in Spain, *Nafh al-Tib*,[20] is a wonderful snapshot of medieval court life and one that illustrates the ups and downs of a struggling poet seeking to find fame and fortune. It draws attention to the power and importance of patronage. Above all, it reinforces what we already know to be *de rigeur* for an aspiring poet: that wherever he go, he must carry the proverbial trunk of poetic knowledge and lore – centuries of textuality and intertextuality, of millions of words and stock phrases, of rhetorical devices and images, of metres and rhymes – that he be forever ready to draw from his pouch a line or two, or a whole poem, on the spot, on any given subject, with mastery of the traditions and artistic originality; and that he rise and succeed to the challenge and respond to any new situation.

Among the many poems that Ibn Hamdis composed in Seville, a panegyric (*madih*) to al-Mu'tamid best exemplifies the classic features of the Ibn Hamdis's 'insignia madih'. Previously, we saw in poem #98 (*When she approaches at night I extend my cheek in joy*) how Ibn Hamdis superimposed a subtext of Sicily onto a poem or a segment of a poem without making any direct reference to it. In poem #75 (*The heart flutters in anticipation of coupling with slender figures*), we saw how he fashioned a *poetics of jihad* and wove it throughout a poem. With the following *qasida*, we see how the panegyric proper in his work acts as a preferred site to expand the jihad motif into wider literary and political terrain.

The panegyric is only twenty-eight lines long, and several references within it suggest that it was composed early on in his Seville period, sometime soon after his arrival in 1078. The mood is upbeat and the substance and tone of the praise proper are both high quality and sincere. Although the entire piece falls within the monotheme of panegyric, it may be divided into two major segments: lines 1–22 comprise the panegyric proper (*madih*); lines 23–28 comprise the poet's boast (*fakhr*).

Panegyric to al-Mu'tamid
Diwan #101: 170–1

1- Your countenance has removed all inflammation from our eyes,
   and in beholding you we see what God has brought forth from afar.

2- Your noble pedigree manifests itself in four images:
   the full moon; the lofty peak; the deep blue sea; and the mighty lion.

3- The human eye gleams a sparkling black (pupil) when it catches sight of you,
   and chases away all worry and grief.

4- We rejoice in a face in whose features glows with a light
   that makes a true believer all the more devout.

5- Your sword has been distinguished for its defense of the righteous faith,
   while you remain forever distinguished by your incomparable generosity.

6- [You are] a lion one imagines as having swords as its claws,
   and its coat of mail as thick skin and a mane.

7- It is as though its sheathes rush into war to drink blood
   in the tradition of the [mighty] Hindi sword.

8- Because of the sheer courage in its right hand [alone],
   its strike becomes all the fiercer when drunk on blood.

9- On the day of battle its spear is raised,
   and it chomps on the livers of lions.

10- Our religion derives its strength (*mu'tamad*) from a king who spends his waking hours
    drawing strength (*mu'tamid*) from the Most Compassionate.

11- His spears are like the shooting stars with which
    he destroys all the tyrants of infidelity who to the fore appear.

12- Whenever he raises the banner of war with full resolve,
    his hands untie every knot with his judgements.

13- Vigorous yet patient, whenever any master comes to contest him,
    you picture it to be the [great] battle of *Uhud*,

14- [whose soldiers are] pure thoroughbreds mounted by valiant knights of fury advancing,
    like female demons carrying lions on their backs.

15- Whenever the sky clouds up with billows of battle dust,
    the Samhari swords before them like pillars stand erect.

16- Every courageous soldier is covered from head to toe in steel,
    its coldness coagulates blood into foam [that rises] above them.

17- Rushing forth a sharp [sword] in hand with its tip aroused on the day of battle,
    it brings sleep to the eyes of the sleepless.

18- It does not drink the sap of the body sheathed in chain mail
   until it sees the tip of its sword devouring the flesh.

19- You make a river of blood flow from your enemies,
   you leave purposely the land where they stood soaked in blood.

20- O you who rotate the cycle of generosity
   and whose justice supports every man in need,

21- the people of hope flock to you, and by your very mention
   they inhale the aroma of musk and find a cure in you.

22- You have never disappointed one hopeful of your magnanimity,
   nor have you left a thirsty *[saadd]* man with nothing to quench his thirst.
   or: you never turned away a man in exile *[sadda]*.

23- I now have no distance in my distant wandering from my homeland,
   after it you have made *Hims [Homs]* a country for me.

24- As a substitute for my closest kin I was given its kin;
   May God not separate me from them in all eternity.

25- How many of my people in a land far away does the earth embrace,
   whom I could not see because of my distance.

26- Even the death of my father did not compel me to depart your abode,
   however much the death of a father may deeply distress the son.

27- You did not block my path to return to them;
   you made my separation *[sifaad]* from them a blessing *[safad]*.

28- This most tender loving care, whose sweetness abounds in my heart,
   cools off the scorching heat of [my] sorrow.

Lines 1–4 address the physical features of the patron subject and the aura he casts over people. Lines 5–10 shift the focus of praise to his military qualities, done masterfully through the extended metaphor of a lion. The thematic transition between the two segments comes gradually, beginning with the suggestion in line 4 that the true believer becomes more devout, and then followed by the epithet of 'defender of the faith' in line 5. This is significant in that this quality is perhaps the most evoked in the Arabic panegyric's shift from the *Jahiliyya* to Islam. Having adjusted the tone of the *qasida* thus far to resonate with his Muslim audience, Ibn Hamdis is free to explode in the next four lines the classical *Jahili* style, building on the lion metaphor with its claws as swords drunk on the excess of blood, exemplary of 'the metaphorical (and ritually symbolic) equivalence of blood and wine in the Arabic tradition whereby to drink wine is a metaphor for quenching one's thirst for blood vengeance'.[21]

Line 10 returns to the religious tenor with the poet's use of the rhetorical device of paronomasia (*jinas*). The punning of '*al-muʿtamid*', which is the official honorific (*laqab*) of the patron, combined with the active participle meaning 'relying upon', or 'deriving strength from', constructs a chain of divine command, whereby the faithful subjects, including the poet himself, rely upon al-Muʿtamid, who in turn relies upon God. This conjures the image of the legitimate Islamic ruler, one that, as argued throughout this book, is crucial to the post-scriptural sense and understanding of jihad. The interlacing of religious motifs into the overall *Jahili* weave of the panegyric continues from lines 11–14, with the linking of tyranny to disbelief (*kufr*) and the evocation of the famous Battle of Uhud. Curiously, this was an early battle between the Meccan enemies of the Prophet Muhammad and the Muslims that ended in defeat for the Muslims due to poor communication and coordination. Its evocation here may simply be that the word 'Uhud' fits neatly into the rhyme scheme of the poem. However, the battle's symbolism in Islamic history as a warning against disunity and poor planning in the face of the enemy adds another layer of meaning to the poem, in that the petty kingdoms of al-Andalus (*muluk al-tawaʾif*) were warring among themselves and allowing the Christian Reconquest to make significant advances into Muslim territories.

Lines 14–19 constitute a classic battle description (*harbiyya*) in which the poet, through the use of compacted sensual and visual images and lively animated verses in full colour, narrates and poeticizes the high points of al-Muʿtamid's victory in the idiom of the classical *qasida*. Like the extended metaphor of the lion earlier in the poem, here we see the poet deploy the extended metaphor of the anthropomorphic sword.

Lines 20–22 shift the praise from the qualities of might to that of magnanimity. Al-Muʿtamid is praised as the essence of generosity, the very source of bounty and life affirmation, and the refuge for all in need. The second hemistich of line 22 may be read in a variety of ways. Based on the punning of '*saad[d]*', that is, 'one who thirsts' or 'one who has turned away from or departed a place' and '*sadd*', as '[front of the] hand', we may read it as al-Mu'tamid being the quencher of a thirsty man, or the provider of shelter for one without a home. Both readings are close enough in meaning, and both fit comfortably in the passage; but the second would allow for a smoother transition to the next segment of the poem.

Lines 23–28 introduce the first person voice of the panegyrist, thus allowing this last segment to construct a boast without any rupture or departure from the general theme (intention, aim: *gharad*) of the poem. In these six lines, Ibn Hamdis collapses his own personal experiences of departure from his homeland, separation from his kin who are now far away, the loss of his father while in exile, and his welcome into the court of al-Mu'tamid, whose loving care cools the fires of the poet's grief, being the attribute that brings the panegyric to its culmination. Once again, we can see here Stetkevych's 'mythic concordance' between poet and patron, a ritual exchange by which al-Mu'tamid is erected onto the eternal panoply of the aristocratic poet-warriors and legitimate heirs to Arabo-Islamic political legitimacy, and Ibn Hamdis is rewarded with a sanctuary from exile and, more importantly, a forum from which he could espouse his greatest cause.

More significantly, this first person and final segment of the poem is another example that demonstrates Ibn Hamdis's *poetics of jihad*. Having expressed in earlier verses the many aspects and attributes of the physical jihad through the noble qualities of courage, strength, and defence of the faith, the poet-panegyrist gives expression to a personal, spiritual, if not existential, jihad. Living in the time of the Norman Conquest of Sicily, Ibn Hamdis was experiencing exile from his homeland, separation from loved ones and the death of family members, including his own father for whom he composed an elegy early after his arrival in Seville (*Diwan* #330, *Elegy to the Father*). These personal life experiences, as a result of a pending defeat of Muslim Sicily, would become an integral part of all his jihad verses.

* * *

In the year 1086, some eight years after that fortuitous night when Ibn Hamdis first met and locked poetic horns with al-Mu'tamid, securing for himself a position within the royal court inner circle, the 'Abbadid kingdom faced its greatest challenge in a confrontation with the Castilian Alfonse VI that lead to the battle of al-Zallaqa (a plain in the area of Badajoz in southwest Spain). The battle ended in a highly publicized victory for al-Muʿtamid. For this joyous occasion, Ibn Hamdis composed a *qasida*.

From his arrival in Seville until the Battle of Zallaqa, much had happened in Ibn Hamdis's life – personally, politically and professionally. In addition to suffering separation from family and the death of loved ones, he was witnessing a series of military successes of the Christian Reconquest around the Mediterranean Basin. Professionally, things were much better. As an employed poet much in demand, he enjoyed the company of not only of a poet-patron, but that of other court poets with whom he could spar in robust competition. He enjoyed ample opportunity to refine his skills in the arts of panegyric, elegy and especially in description poetry (*wasf*) that was flourishing among *literati* and philologists throughout Muslim Spain. But while life at the ʿAbbadid court allowed him to grow and mature as a poet, it also brought him closer to the battleground of the Christian Reconquest. As a young man living in Syracuse, we can assume that he had only heard about the Norman advances into Sicily that were taking place on the northern littoral of the island. Also, given that Noto and Syracuse, situated on the southeastern province of Sicily, were the last strongholds to Muslim Sicilian resistance to the Norman armies around 1090, again it is safe to assume that Ibn Hamdis was not directly in the line of fire and fury he so exuberantly and artistically described in his verses. Al-Andalus was thus not only the site of his poetic maturation, but also of his political awakening. What he came to experience first-hand through al-Muʿtamid's battles with Alfonse VI, as well as through skirmishes with rival (Muslim) petty princes throughout al-Andalus, transformed the villains of his poetics from the distant and abstract enemy of classical Arabic literary tradition into real, actual people with names and identities. It thus allowed him to recast the universal enemy of *Jahili* poetics into the face of the Christian Reconquest. As Carole Hillenbrand recently reminded us, 'An intensifying of the Muslim jihad spirit was to return as a result of the Crusades.'[22]

On the Friday following the battle, Ibn Hamdis, as well as the other court poets, was called upon to deliver an ode of congratulations to his victorious, albeit severely injured, patron. He composed a *qasida* of forty-six lines: lines 1–10 constitute a wine song (*khamriyya*), lines 11–16 may be read as a battle narrative (*harbiyya*), and line 17–46 form the panegyric proper (*madh*). This last segment encompasses as well an invective (lines 27–36) towards the enemy (*hija'*) and lines 45–46 also comprise the conventional supplicatory closing (*du'a'*).²³

In Praise of al-Mu'tamid ibn 'Abbad on the Occasion of His
Defeat of Alfonse VI
[at the Battle] of al-Zallaqa in 1086
Diwan #283

1- I clothed the dear little daughters of the vine
  with embellishments the remains of abodes once donned;

2- I followed the path of al-Hakami* in pursuing them;
  How could I turn away from this wise man's theme?
  * Abü Nuwas, al-Hasan ibn Hanii al-Hakım (d. 815), early Abbasid poet famed for his wine songs.

3- How can abandoned ruins surpass the quality of fresh wine
  when it exudes musk into the breath of fresh air?

4- The love of wine is renewed in every heart,
  since wine polishes away the rust of anxieties.

5- In the days of old, I longed for the pleasures
  [that awaited me] in the ancient castle.

6- If I thirsted, then my cup was returned to me,
  just as the full breast is returned to the weaned child.

7- I would not ask a muted ruin to converse,
  as though it possessed the signs of one who could speak.

8- But rather I would seek out melodies from a lute,
  which arouse pleasures in the bosom of a gazelle.

9- And many a wine would put to sleep my drinking companions from drunkenness,
  but with it I could chase away their slumber.

10- The drinking companion would awake, as the eye of early morning
  has the [shimmering] residue of the dark night;

11- as though the early morning, face to face with its darkness,
   was a combatant who stares down his opponent in disdain;

12- as though the East, between the one and the other,
   was a battle line, across which Zanj and Rum come face to face.

13- The night [was] like a black stallion, but when the light of day
   burst forth, it was like a young [weaned] camel on the attack.

14- Throughout night's darkness we crossed a vast terrain,
   on a camel with flesh stripped from the bone.

15- With its hooves bleeding profusely, we crossed the open desert with her,
   leaving our traces [firmly implanted on the sand].

16- And we wandered from town to town,
   like people whose souls have been comforted by the body's fatigue.

17- And in the abode of Ibn 'Abbad, we alighted,
   and we were regaled with munificence from one so resolute.

18- Such that kings would lower their eyes
   to pay homage to the aura of the mightiest king.

19- Noble qualities are neatly arranged within his ranks,
   and you would think that they were the [brightest] stars.

20- Acts of generosity flow from his fingertips,
   and you would think that they were the [fullest] rain clouds.

21- If hopes come to him thirsting with passion,
   then they leave quenched by the copious dew of his hand.

22- Where generous men are relegated to oblivion,
   he brings forth a memory that travels in the mouth of time to come.

23- The sharpness of his vision whispers privately to him
   secrets which are hidden deep within the heart.

24- O scion of [the royal tribe of] Lakhm,
   whose members are moons that shine brightest among the noblest tribes.

25- When they are generous, they bring downpours of generosity,
   and when they are gentle, they erect mountains of gentility.

26- In your right hand is a sword which is inviolable,
   and by using it you safeguard that which is sacred.

27- And a battle in which Alfonse encountered an opponent,
   one who causes havoc on the soul of [his] adversary.

28- He took cover in the dark of night, and then fled in fear,
   with a terror that could shatter the ears of an ostrich.

29- And because of Yusuf, endowed with bravery, he [Alfonse] was made to taste misery,
   and the sweetness of a graced life was rendered bitter.

30- The serpentine blades tore him apart with their sharp teeth,
   so, ask the sound (*salim*) night about the one bitten (*salim*) by the snake.

31- Your monotheism dissuaded him of his [trinitarian] polytheism,
   snipping at the hands of [his] fear, raging with anger.

32- Insulted, he watches you as you grin like like a hunting hound
   who even when he yawns he bares his fangs.

33- In early morning he comes with crosses that lead infidels astray,
   having concocted the schemes of a mongrel army.

34- It was though they [appeared] like devils,
   but [it was] you hurled at them the fire of stars.

35- Infidels, their battle coats are concealed with armor,
   but the whiff of their odor gives them away.

36- A tyrant [even] to them leads them to their demise,
   and woe unto the tyrant!

37- He brought them to graze on a pasture of *washij*** trees, and they tottered about,
   and such are the consequences of evil grazing.

   ** *Washij* is a kind of tree from the wood of which swords were made

38- He lead them to watering holes amidst the sharp lances,
   and like a water boy he served the waters of death from the well.

39- And then when he came to you with a people from 'Aad,***
   along you came with the howling destructive wind.
   *** 'Aad and Thamud, evoked by Arabs as being ancient Arabian tribes in the *Jahiliyya*, meaning *kuffar*): Qur'an reference that God punished with the people of 'Aad: **Surat al-Haqqa 69: 6; and Surat 'Aad 89: 6–9.**

40- You rekindled the fires of battle,
   and its moans related that they were the sparks from hell.

41- With the gallop of sturdy horses there arose a dark gloom,
   by which they clothed the dawn (*sarim*) with the night. (*sarim*)

42- The robe of the air was frayed at the edges,
   and the face of the earth was scorched at the surface.

43- And the ascending Khatt spears were inebriated,
   until every pliant straight arrow was arched.

44- They drank only from the wine of collarbones,
   and they inhaled only the scent of head wounds.

45- So, Pray to your God who is worshipped, and make a sacrifice
   to Him of their leaders, one after the other.

46- And celebrate with divine guidance, and prepare for the enemy
   the punishment of war, with the most painful of pain.

The opening of the poem with the wine song sets a celebratory mood and it conjures images of male bonding that extend into the battle descriptions. These may be read as nothing more than the poet's attempts at paying homage to poetic conventions and/or as a strategy to remain within the horizon of expectation of an audience well versed in those conventions. As in many of his poems, Ibn Hamdis employs the image of 'the morning after' when the daylight of sobriety extinguishes the glow of nocturnal pleasures of music, feasting and inebriation. Key to understanding his manipulation of that imagery here is reading lines 10 and 11, in which he shifts nimbly from the universal combatant and his adversary to the very real and now *Zanj* (read:

Arab, East) and *Rum* (read: Christian, West) in line 12. This shift in these lines will continue throughout the poem, especially in the 'al-Muʿtamid versus Alfonse' binary that forms the core of the panegyric/invective. In line 31, the poet casts the praise and invective within the frame of the Christian-Muslim theological binary opposition between 'monotheism' (*tawhid*) and 'polytheism/trinitarianism' (*tathlith*).

Secondly, he names Alfonse and Yusuf, and he documents and describes the battle with factual historical events: the scheming of Alfonse, his abandoning his own forces and escape at night, and the intervention and support of the Almoravid chieftain, Yusuf ibn Tashufin, whose aid al-Muʿtamid sought against the advice of the other Andalusian princes.[24] Ibn Hamdis's evocation in line 13 of the *Battle of Uhud* (625 AD), in which the Prophet Muhammad led his Medina forces against their Meccan enemies, as was mentioned, allowed him this time to memorialize the *Battle of Zallaqa*, and by extension its leader, al-Muʿtamid, onto sacred Islamic history.

Ironically, a mere five years later Yusuf would return to Seville, this time as conqueror, and put a violent end to the ʿAbbadid Emirate, sentencing al-Muʿtamid and his family to a prison in the Maghribi city of Aghmat. Evocative of that first encounter thirteen years earlier in which patron and poet engaged in poetic competition, Ibn Hamdis and al-Mutamid were fated to exchange verses one last time. The occasion was not the same and the relationship between patron and poet had been totally altered. In his prison cell, al-Muʿtamid composed a poem and addressed it to his former court panegyrist and loyal subject. In it he ponders his fate, expresses his painful longing for his paradise lost, and wonders if there will ever be a return to his homeland, questions, feelings and poetic themes all too familiar to the Sicilian exile. Ibn Hamdis's response *qasida* expresses the shared pain and humiliation of defeat, the fear of a future unknown and anticipation of hostile terrains yet to be crossed. Both men, I have argued, found their means of expression in the language and diction of the classical *qasida*, through the *Jahili* notion of the unpredictable and arbitrary hand of fate, of the separation from loved ones, and the abandonment of the abode, but at the same time through an Islamic *poetics of jihad* that embraces at once a stubborn loyalty to the sanctity of faith and the worldliness of art.

Return to the old world: Politics and the panegyric at the Zirid court 1091–133

One can imagine, and with a good deal of certainty, that Ibn Hamdis's departure from Seville and his arrival at the Zirid court in al-Mahdiyya was a reverse trajectory across the North African littoral he had made thirteen years prior. Times were changing, rapidly and radically. The Seljuk Turks had taken control of Baghdad, and, with the force of their military might and patronage of conservative, Orthodox Muslim institutions, they reduced the classical Islamic caliphate to a symbolic figurehead. At this time, the Almoravids were following suit in the lands of the west, and Seville as 'abode' of the idyllic life of religious tolerance and cultural eclecticism was to become, at least in the mind of Ibn Hamdis, like Sicily, the locus of the abandoned encampment, the memory palace of lost love and the symbolic landscape of youthful pleasures.

The Ifriqiya of 1091 must have been an abrupt jolt of reality, an experience much conveyed in the image of the crude awakening Ibn Hamdis was so fond of conjuring in his wine songs, when after a night of blissful intoxication, melodious strummings of the lute, and ample-bosomed, slender-waisted maidens, the imbiber faces the early morning of a day of battle. The Fatimid caliphate was completing its first century in Cairo, having bequeathed its North African domain to the rulers of rival Berber tribes. Their most loyal supporters, the Bani Ziri (Zirids), had won the lion's share with the reign of Ifriqiya, at whose court in al-Mahdiyya Ibn Hamdis set his sights and was to spend much of the remainder of his long life.

The political upheavals and rivalries following the gradual Fatimid disengagement from North Africa marred the entire history of the Zirid dynasty (1016–1167). The resulting rise of local Berber 'princedoms' were often drawn along the fault lines of tribal divisions, especially the Zanata on the one side and the Sanhaja and Kutama on the other. This mini 'petty kingdoms' (*muluk al-tawa'if*) partition of the once vast Fatimid North African domain created porous boundaries for *Dar al-Islam*, replicating what Ibn Hamdis witnessed in Seville, that would eventually be exploited and penetrated by the Christian Reconquest of Muslim lands north of the Mediterranean, in both Spain and Sicily. More significantly, the decision taken by the Zirid prince al-Mu'izz ibn Badis (r.1016–62) in 1047 to renounce allegiance to the (Shi'ite) Fatimids of

Cairo and pledge his fealty to the (Sunni) 'Abbasid caliphate in Baghdad added greater stress to these precarious times in North African history. Not only did it deal a severe blow to any residual Shi'ite influence on Islamic religious and intellectual life, reaffirming in essence, the restoration of a Maliki orthodox Islam as premier sect, but it prompted the Fatimids of Egypt to take their revenge by unleashing the hordes of Arabian Bedouin tribes, the Bani Hilal and the Bani Sulaym, to invade North Africa. This contributed, in the estimation of many later medieval and some modern historians – Ibn Khaldun standing among the most vocal – to the massive destruction of cities and rural areas, causing the catastrophic and long-term destruction of the Ifriqiyan economy.

Most ironically, the year 1091 also saw the Norman capture of the Sicilian cities of Syracuse and Noto, completing, in effect, their conquest of the island that began in 1061. Upon his arrival at the Zirid court, which by all indications was soon thereafter, Ibn Hamdis used the occasion to compose and perform a panegyric to his new patron, the Zirid prince Tamim ibn al-Mu'izz (r.1062–1108). This is the only panegyric to Tamim in the diwan.[25] The importance of this poem, one of the most unusual in terms of shifting themes and discordant tones, is the radically different locale and historical moment in which it was composed. The 'Tamim panegyric' reflects the angst and indignation of a second exile. Now back in Ifriqiya, Ibn Hamdis was being drawn closer to the maelstrom of Muslim Sicilian defeat. Much as he followed events as best he could from Seville, Sicily had been far away, comfortably ensconced in the poetic recollections of his verses of nostalgia and in his supplications for its survival and his return to it. But now the dwindling hopes of reconnecting to his youthful paradise were brought home at disturbing proximity as tens of thousands of Muslim Sicilians seeking refuge in their ancestors' towns in Ifriqiya brought back stories of political divisions among Muslims and the Norman advances. The 'Tamim panegyric' also marks a turning point in the poetics of Ibn Hamdis. His post-Andalus work becomes more political, as reflected in the growing proportion of the panegyric in relation to other themes, with frequent injections of biting invective; and it conveys a bitter scepticism through verses of existential brooding and angst dominating the repetitive – if somewhat hackneyed – reworkings of the classical motifs. Above all, we can safely surmise that the poem carries with it a bitter personal indictment toward Tamim under whose reign Sicily had suffered its ultimate demise. This may well be the reason why Ibn Hamdis refrained from writing further praise poems to him.

The Tamim panegyric comprises sixty-two lines: lines 1–15 form a gnomic introduction (*muqaddima hikamiyya*) that taps heavily into traditional 'crying over abandoned ruins' (*al-buka' 'ala al-atlal*) and boast (*fakhr*) imagery, lines 16–25 may be read as a desert crossing (*rahil*) of sorts, lines 26–35 constitute the panegyric (*madih*) part I, lines 36–42 are what I call a 'Sicilian interlude' lines 43–58 are the panegyric part II and lines 59–62 complete the poem as a 'Sicilian finale'.

Panegyric to Tamim and Lament on Norman Invasion of Sicily

Diwan #27: 28–33

1- I have donned the armor of patience against calamities.
   If you do not make peace, O Time, then make war.

2- You have ground your teeth on stones that crush [the hooves] of camels,
   and broken in a wild horse that allows no rider.

3- You weren't even satisfied that my soul suffered banishment,
   since I never dug my heels in the lands of the west.

4- A country whose water flows above the rocks,
   from which every imbiber drinks and wants more.

5- I was prevented (weaned) from enjoying every cup and pleasure,
   and I squandered the treasure of life on frivolity.

6- The hilt of the sword rests in the fold of my forearm,
   compensating a coy, ample-bosomed maiden for a horse.

7- The Indian sword only beds down a blunted blade;
   its strike on the day of battle falls on the readily stricken.

8- If I had good company in a sword, I would cling to it;
   for, I have but loneliness for losing loved ones.

9- In youth, my height was the height of the sword,
   and I entrusted it to be my shield.

10- If I had any ambitions with this sword,
    just think how many Moses had with his staff.

11- You think that I am forgetting, but I still remember
the treason of my time and the treason of my companion.

12- [My sword] was nurtured by my character as a young man,
and it struck only against the blows against me.

13- Many a plant has been overwhelmed by bitterness
that had once been sweetened by the water of rain clouds.

14- I learned through experience things of which I had been ignorant;
things are indeed unknown before they are tried.

15- Whoever thinks that the abundant fresh waters of Hadramaut were sweet,
passes by the watering holes with a distorted view.

16- I rode the vast no-man's land on the saddle of many a mount
clutching the reins as we tore through the desert.

17- Young she-camels, backs arched by emaciation,
scant of milk like the bows of a tree,

18- When they came upon wells with clear, blue water,
they surrounded it like eyebrows surrounding an eye.

19- Firmly resolved in my hopes, I was made to alight
on the false hope of removing anxiety from my mind.

20- There is no safe place save in private thoughts,
where I seem to summon everything absent.

21- When I encountered people whose evil was feared,
I avoided them and chose the ascetic's life.

22- I was even fortunate to be visited by a phantom
who repelled every reproacher from my bed as I slept.

23- Have the leanness of my body and the hoariness of my forelocks
now altered my appearance so that it no longer visits?

24- If whosoever is absent counts the months of his exile,
then I have counted eons upon eons for mine.

25- How many a sincere resolution like drawn swords
   has been peeled away by the grip of false hope.

26- I have in the skies of the East a constellation that shines
   whenever I reach for its highest stars.

27- I have become so accustomed to my exile from it,
   that the string of days have piled up as if in the palm of an accountant.

28- Whenever Gemini in the heavens hears my poetry,
   it listens to me because of my improvising marvelous verse.

29- How many a soulmate have I in the sky who protects
   without blame even the shameful from his enemies.

30- My brother, confidant, I often drank wine with him,
   whose youth from the hand of time has not been snatched.

31- A fine vintage, [count] how often its long age is mentioned,
   from it the paws of the accountants have been filled.

32- When the water wades into the wine's hidden entrails,
   pearls appear from it, some floating, some suspended.

33- My evenings in the two Mahdiyya(s) were like pearls,
   in your world, set upon the neckline.

34- These evenings will not be changed, but will remain as pearls,
   strung like necklaces for years on end.

35- If I wanted to glance at the crescent moon,
   I would notice Tamim in the firmament of noble qualities.

36- If my country were free I would go to it with a resolve
   that considers separation a constant affliction.

37- But how can my country be ransomed for me from captivity,
   while it sits in the clutches of the usurping infidels?

38- These dogs have prevailed by devouring my lands,
   and after a lull they lunged for the veins.

39- Before my eyes my compatriots perished by submitting to civil strife,
   in which every woodsman lit a bonfire.

40- And their desires for it became such that they conducted themselves
   in ways contrary to our faith.

41- Kinfolk showed no mercy to their own people,
   as swords were dripping with the blood of kin.

42- Like the joints of the fingers that have been ripped apart,
   that were once held together by the flesh of the hand.

43- Protectors, if you saw them in battle,
   you would be gratified by the vision of their most ferocious lion.

44- If they go to fight in the fiercest of battles,
   they unleash from their hands thunderbolts in the clouds.

45- On the days of piercing lances, they have strong hands
   that deliver the lion's liver to the fox in their attack.

46- They have camel stallions that gallop through enemy territory,
   whose neighing prolongs the wailing of mourning women,

47- with the camels' ears pointed beneath their swords,
   just like the pens of writers made pointed by sharpening.

48- If the ears go around in circles, you would imagine them
   striving to hear what is beyond the clouds.

49- If they be silenced in the throes of death, they articulate
   with the clash of their swords the flash of their slender sharp edges.

50- You see the flames of fires on the tips of their swords,
   from the hands of swordsmen people are made to taste death.

51- Fear not that these people will turn away from death,
   [fiercer are they] than lions who retreat in fear to their dens.

52- While some people stray from the path of guidance,
   they are guided away from straying and toward the most luminous stars.

53- How many brave, thoughtful ones are among them,
   who attacks from the front and not from behind.

54- When he attacks he splits the enemy army in half,
   as one would butcher a sheep in a playground.

55- If they did not attack the Normans, their entering would be
on the inside of ships, on the backs of sturdy horses.

56- They would die the death of glory in the thick of battle,
while cowards die in the arms of beautiful women.

57- They stuffed pillows with the dust of holy war,
which they will recline upon in their graves.

58- They have fallen like falling stars into the cavity of decline,
and perpetuated the blackness of night on earth.

59- Is there not in God's protection an abode in Noto
upon which the clouds pour forth their abundant rains?

60- I fashion its memory in my mind at every waking moment,
and I draw forth for it the drops of gushing tears.

61- I yearn like the old she-camels for a homeland,
to which the abodes of beautiful maidens are drawing me.

62- Whoever leaves a homeland but whose heart remains therein,
hopes the return of the repentant heart to its body.

The first segment of the poem, the gnomic introduction, is a feature that appears prominently in the Ibn Hamdis panegyric to the Zirid princes. As stated above, it manipulates the emotional effects of the classical 'crying over abandoned ruins' and boast tropes to articulate both the personal (past) and the present voice of the poet. In this segment, Ibn Hamdis brings together his past experiences, present predicaments and future aspirations within the poetic idiom and generic boundaries expected by his audience. The familiar Hamdisian-favoured themes – fate's power of man, his banishment and exile from his homeland, lost youth and separation of his loved ones – along with calling attention to his own poetic prowess in the form of the boast all coalesce in a sequence of back-and-forth shifts from the general to the particular; from the collective to the individual. If lines 1–2, for example, are typical of any classical Arabic *diwan*, lines 3–4 point specifically to the relatively short period Ibn Hamdis spent in Spain. Line 11 points to his own painful realization that 'treasonous' Muslims, as was the case in both al-Andalus and Sicily, bear some of the responsibility for Sicily's defeat, and thus, for his continuous exile, as the following verses shift back to the classical *qasidas* images of the life-death cycle.

The second segment (lines 16–25) mimics the classical desert-journey segment (*rahil*). He reworks familiar images of crossing hostile terrain, she-camels with bloody hooves and alighting at desert oases, which at first hold his audience's attention and raises their expectations, and then jolts them by injecting his feelings of false hopes. He finishes this segment with the *Jahili* motif of the 'phantom of separation' (*al-bayn*), where the poet cuts off the account of his own journey, withdraws into his privacy and bemoans the illusory nature of his existence with a sharp pessimism.

Line 26 introduces the panegyric proper. The transition suggests that there is light at the end of his tunnel in the personage of Tamim. The panegyric, in the main, draws upon a cluster of celestial images to describe both the character of his rule and the power of his kingdom. The poet uses the conceit of the 'boon companion', and, through the wine song images (lines 30–32), establishes a personal and long-standing connectedness between patron and poet (which, if read literally, was highly unlikely).

The Sicilian interlude of lines 36–42, some of the most oft-cited verses by modern critics, articulates unequivocally, as I argued earlier, the personal anguish of the Sicilian poet-in-exile. Its seemingly abrupt interjection into the panegyric, with its uncharacteristic evocation of Muslim backbiting and political divisiveness, carries an important function not only in its stark and honest realism, but also in its exact – and, once again, highly strategic – location within the poem. As an expression of loss and separation, its proffers for Tamim the noble qualities of hospitality (*diyafa*) and protection (*ijara*) to the wayfarer or downtrodden that are prerequisite to the image of the legitimate ruler in both the *Jahili* and Islamic Arab traditions. Also, and equally important, this interlude's stark and bleak assessment, shared undoubtedly by the masses of the Ifriqiyan populace and the throngs of new emigres from Sicily, pose a direct and audacious challenge to Tamim to earn the title of 'defender of the faith', the most crucial attribute to Arabo-Islamic political legitimacy, by actually doing his political – and religious – duty.

The return to the panegyric in line 42 is most remarkable in its shift in address from the singular (*Tamim*) to the plural (*Hummat*: Protectors). To whom the collective address refers is a tantalizing ambiguity in the poem. On the surface, and within the logic and the occasion of the panegyric proper, it would read as Tamim and all the members of the Zirid dynasty, past and future included, who engage in struggle against the Normans to liberate Sicily. It may also refer to those Muslim Sicilians, especially those of the towns of Syracuse, Enna, and Noto, who valiantly resisted the Normans until the end.

In either case, it is clearly an appeal, or perhaps even a kind of baiting, the poet directs to both Tamim and his fellow Muslims. True nobility, hospitality and protection of the downtrodden can only be completed with bravery in battle. Ibn Hamdis conveys this message skilfully and poetically, through his mastery of the idiom, stock phrases and imagery of the classical Arabic battle description (*harbiyya*) that explode throughout lines 43–58. Also, given the current military and political defeats of Muslim Sicily and the political and economic turmoil of Ifrıqiya, the highly accomplished and battle-tested Ibn Hamdis is drawing from his arrow pouch a well-honed weapon of classical Arabic rhetoric, 'rendering what is false in the form of what is true' (*taswir al-batil fi surat al-haqq*). By rendering the 'ugliness' (*qubh*) of defeat and weakness into the 'beauty' (*husn*) of victory (and ultimately, political and religious legitimacy), Ibn Hamdis completes his panegyric to Tamim in the form of a 'fictional' hypothesis in which the Zirid prince receives his position among the great warrior-heroes of the classical *qasida* by actually earning it. The poem ends with the familiar 'Sicilian' insignia of Ibn Hamdis, a finale in the form of a supplication asking God's protection (line 59) for what is and will continue to be his poetic appeal to all those who were or will ever be exiled from the homeland.

Ibn Hamdis would live out the second forty years of his life in the service of the Zirid princes, Tamim, Yahya, 'Ali, and al-Hasan, on whom he, as well as other Sicilian Muslims in situ or in exile, depended to liberate the homeland from the Normans. Among the many panegyrics he composed to them, the lion's share belongs to 'Ali ibn Yahya whose relatively brief reign (r.1115–21) witnessed what the chronicles report of the most serious military attempts against the Norman advances around the central Mediterranean Basin. While the sole Tamim panegyric brings the Hamdisian *poetics of jihad* into a second and final phase of development, politically and artistically, it was especially in the poems to 'Ali where we hear the voice of the poet repeating that pleading, desperate angst he so articulately directed to Tamim soon after his return from his Andalusian exile in 1091.

At the beginning of the last decade of his life, Ibn Hamdis would have the brief but fleeting fortune to witness an Arab military victory over the Normans in a small island off the coast of Ifriqiya. The Battle of al-Dimas (c.1123) would be the occasion on which Ibn Hamdis composed and delivered one of his last panegyrics to the Bani Ziri. The Zirid prince al-Hasan, the young pre-pubescent son of 'Ali, inherited the throne upon the sudden and unexpected death of his father, and by all indications had no connection at all to the victory. Yet Ibn Hamdis chose the form of the panegyric to make what could very well be read as his last public appeal to the ruling dynasty. As argued elsewhere, this poem is less a tribute to a righteous monarch and *defender of the faith* as it was a literary memorial to a falling homeland.[26]

Ibn Hamdis's *poetics of jihad* had evolved over the many years of his life, built on and encompassing the many lived experiences of living on the frontiers of Islam that included constant interaction with the Christian world, including its monarchs, soldiers and its ordinary citizens. It begins from a distance, with the rumblings of the Norman Conquest to the battlefield accounts that punctuated the nonetheless idyllic life at the 'Abbadid court in Seville. It changes course with his return to Ifriqiya where the battle for Sicily between the Muslims and Christians is brought home by physical proximity and contacts with fellow exiles. From the many manifestations of the abstract enemy of poetry to the real names, faces and events that have come to confront him head on, Ibn Hamdis's poetic jihad grows sharp, biting, penetrating and relentless, much like the armoury of weapons he so skilfully personifies in his verses. While he is fated to watch in despair his homeland falling into the hands of the rapacious infidels, his voice increases in volume with the appeal to all Muslims, rulers and ruled, for jihad, in all its spiritual and physical significations. And, however sharp the religious and political tones of these verses grow, there is always a glimmer of hope.

Secondly, Ibn Hamdis's *poetics of jihad* remains deeply grounded in the bedrock of Arabic poetic tradition, as has been demonstrated repeatedly throughout this chapter. He appeals to his fellow Arabs' common faith as much as he does to their artistic sensibilities and their love and devotion to the Arabic tradition. The fact that he often shifted, with impressive craft, from the image of celebrating a fine wine to defending the true faith of Islam that unequivocally prohibits it is testament to a poet devoted in equal measure to his profession.

Finally, Ibn Hamdis's *poetics of jihad* was crafted from the lived experiences in the times and places of his own life. It was local, targeted and meaningful. We hear his outburst in the Tamim panegyric, but in a monothematic *qasida* he composed not long after we hear Ibn Hamdis at his most lyrical. The poem was delivered as a sermon to his fellow Muslim Sicilian compatriots in which he expressed the thoughts and emotions of a true *mujadid,* kin to the modern nationalist crying out to save his nation:

Sermon to His Compatriots on Fighting a Jihad
Diwan # 270

1- O people of the frontier [of Syracuse] you are not my kinfolk
   if you do not do as good Arabs do and attack the Barbarians.

2- Do not sleep, for I fear that disasters will crush you
   while you dream [false] hopes.

3- How many a cup full to the brim with venom
   did the cupbearer serve to the imbiber as the daughter of the vine [wine]!

4- So, direct the faces of your horses towards a battle
   that bestows to the Normans fatherless children and bereaved mothers,

5- [horses] that kick up the dust that dims the light of the sun,
   just as they do with the stars in the dark of night.

6- In the thick of the murky battle clouds, attack with your swords
   as if they were flashes of lightning stained red by chopping heads.

7- Let not the swords cease to be drawn from their sheathes,
   like rivulets that lie shielded beneath piles of rock.

8- The sword's severing of the head of every infidel
   is music to my ears sweeter than the strumming of the lute.

9- I swear by God! Every one of you is as sharp and penetrating as your swords,
   rushing to battle, shimmering with determination,

10- [Each a hero] invigorated by plunging himself into the foray,
    as though he were yearning for battle, not for peace.

11- [A hero] whose steadfastness sets him on fire,
    as the rings in his armor shield him from every thrust and blow,

12- and who attacks with his weapons concealed,
    and when he appears, he breaks out like the dawn after the dark of night.

13- He [makes] a thrust into the body which extracts the soul,
    even before the tip exits the flesh.

14- Nothing can be ransomed of flesh or blood
    except what is left on the bones after they have been stripped.

15- Steadfast, whenever death approaches with jaws wide open,
    the rumbling sound of horses throbs repeatedly like music to his ears.

16- He has the eyes of the killer lion,
    and his heart has the knowledge to turn passivity into action.
    (a grammatical reference: The heart knows how to make active the massive mood.)

17- This is God's country! If you lose its wide open space (*hawa'*)
    then your aspirations (*ahwa'*) on earth will be scattered.

18- Your glory will end up in humiliation and exile,
    and the unity among you will be obliterated by separation.

19- The land of others is not your land,
    nor are its friends and neighbors your friends and neighbors.

20- Can the land of someone else take the place of your land?
    Can a milk-less aunt take the place of a mother?

21- O friend, who has connected your love to my love,
    just as the second rains connect to the first rains,

22- chain yourself to the country which is your beloved homeland,
    and die in your own abode.

23- Never try for even a day to experience exile,
    since the mind will never savor the experience of poison.

5

In Praise of Norman Kings: Arabic Panegyrics beyond Its Boundaries

jabara allah[u] kull[a] ghariib[in] ila watanih[i]:
May God return every foreigner to his homeland!

The venerated monarch Roger, empowered by God (*al-Mu'tazz billah*), ruler of Sicily, Italy, Lombardy and Calabria, leader of the Roman Empire, victor of the Christians, the best of those who reign over them in withholding and granting abundance (bastan wa qabdan); who administers the affairs of state as he wills, solidly and thoroughly; who rules with justice over all his subjects, providing equal protection and welfare, and dispensing favors fairly; who conducts himself with dignity, enacting laws in the most efficient and orderly manner; who, in conquering the territories east and west, humiliates all those among his co-religionists, near and far, who act arrogantly, and does so with what he assembles in vast and well-equipped armies and navies; who is well informed and experienced, whose fame and efficiency is confirmed, in sight and in sound; whose ambitious goals he never fails to reach, nor any lofty thought passes him by, nor any difficult desire he holds he does not achieve; to whom Fate runs its course according to his goals and desires; to whom prosperity is dispensed in whatever manner he chooses; whose intimate friends enjoy perpetual glory and esteem while his nemeses remain despondent and defeated; who crafts so many positions of power and erects summits of high-mindedness that reach the stars; and who brightens the lands and turns their fields into lush and fertile gardens!

[A king] who combines noble origins to a noble character, kind deeds to a kind disposition, a valiant spirit to clarity of mind, a profound intellect to a dignified forbearance, sound judgment, and wise stewardship; who possesses knowledge in attending to matters with deep and complete understanding;

whose aims are like arrows that hit their mark; and to whom the locked [secrets] of events are pried open.

– Muhammad b. Muhammad b. ʿAbdallah al-Idrisi (c.1099–1160)[1]

By the beginning of the twelfth century, Sicilian exile poet Ibn Hamdis had already made his way back to North Africa where his ancestors first settled as soldiers in the Muslim wars of Conquest and from where his great- (great) grandfather eventually departed to participate in the jihad of Sicily. Since his own departure from Syracuse in 1078 (about the time when Palermo fell to the forces under the command of Roger of Hauteville) and the first of his traumatic exiles, Ibn Hamdis was fated to live through the political divisions among Muslims and the dramatic successes of the Christian Reconquest. After thirteen years of fame and fortune under the royal patronage of the ʿAbbadid court in Seville, and having survived the decisive Battle of Zallaqa in 1086 in which the emir al-Muʿtamid ibn ʿAbbad defeated Alfonse VI, king of Leon-Castille, and only with the assistance of Berber warlord Yusuf ibn Tashufin, Ibn Hamdis experienced his second exile in 1091 when Yusuf returned to Seville as conqueror and dethroned, banished and ultimately imprisoned his beloved patron. As Ibn Hamdis made the treacherous journey back to Ifriqiya in 1091, the abode of his ancestry, he was forced to follow the news of the fall of the last Muslim bastions on the island, including Syracuse and Noto, the lands of his cherished youth. He spent the last decades of his long life as court poet to the petty princes of the Zirid courts of Ifriqiya, taking every advantage that came his way to vilify the infidel usurpers of his beloved homeland.

Ibn Hamdis's caustic verses towards the invading Norman armies, as we have seen, were more often than not accompanied by sarcastic quips and painful asides concerning the breaking of ranks and downright treasonous acts perpetrated by Muslims themselves. If the realization of Muslim betrayal as a cause for (Muslim) Sicily's downfall was not painful enough, how could Ibn Hamdis comprehend, rationalize or process the fact that Muslims, Islam and Arabic culture all seemed to survive and flourish throughout these early decades of the same twelfth century, under the rule of the very enemies he cursed and ridiculed throughout much of his poetry? It would be no comfort to Ibn Hamdis to read contemporaneous and later historical accounts, penned by righteous believing Arab Muslims, poets and historians alike, on the benevolence and tolerance of the Norman kings. Ironically, while Ibn Hamdis was composing his invectives towards Roger II from al-Mahdiyya (who in the meantime not only married Elvira, the daughter of Alfonse VI, but was making alliances with tribal warlords in competition with the Zirid government of al-Mahdiyya), somewhere north of the Mediterranean divide in the suburbs of Palermo, fellow Arabic poets were composing verses of praise.

If Muslim Sicily's 'national poet' has survived in history as the voice of Muslim resistance to the Norman Conquest, then famed geographer al-Idrisi (1099–1160) undoubtedly represents the articulate voice of assimilation and cross-cultural coexistence that grace the historical archive of Norman Sicily. Muhammad ibn Muhammad ibn 'Abdallah al-Idrisi was invited to the court of Roger II most likely within a few years after the death of Ibn Hamdis in 1133. A scion of an Arab family with deep roots in Muslim Spain (al-Andalus), al-Idrisi traces his ancestry to the Hammudid family of Malaga, a family which also encountered its own experiences of exile during periods of Muslim political upheavals of the eleventh century. When al-Idrisi's father, Muhammad ibn 'Abdallah, took refuge in Sicily, word of his lineage to the Prophet's family via the Idrisids of Morocco reached Count Roger I, who in turn welcomed him with safe passage and patronage. Given that there is no conclusive evidence of where al-Idrisi himself was actually born, the general assumption being in al-Andalus, it is well within the realm of possibility that he was born a Sicilian, or at least raised as one, and that his year of birth is a clear indication that he was born in the post-Norman Conquest. As much as he was an Arab Muslim fully formed and educated within the Arabo-Islamic traditional, as is clearly reflected in his scholarly output, his 'citizenship' (i.e. his political loyalty) was unlike that of Ibn Hamdis, open to question, and thus one possible explanation for their different world views. In any event, his *Book of Roger* represents a high point in Arabic geographical writing, and its very existence has always been viewed as a stellar example of royal Norman patronage of Arabic culture.

The quotation that opens this chapter is taken from al-Idrisi's introduction to his magnum opus on world geography, *Kitab Nuzhat al-Mushtaq fi ikhtiraq al-Afaq* (*The Excursion of One Longing to Cross the Horizons*), commissioned by King Roger II and presented to him in 1154, only several months before the king's death. Al-Idrisi's *Introduction* stands as the most articulate testimony of Arabic panegyrics to a Norman, and when read against the invectives culled from the many poems of Ibn Hamdis, one encounters a zone of contradiction of enormous proportions. This contradiction will be explored in this chapter.

Al-Idrisi's *Introduction* falls well within the language and idiom of medieval literary works that sing the praises of patrons and benefactors. It is therefore logical and well within the 'horizons of expectation', to use a modern term, that al-Idrisi acknowledge the generosity and a host of other qualities of the man who lavished monetary and professional abundance upon him. Also, in the – even remote – event that al-Idrisi was born and raised in Sicily around 1099, he may never have known nor experienced anything other than Norman rule, as alluded to above, and thus felt himself as an ordinary, loyal subject of the Norman court in Palermo. Ibn Hamdis, by contrast, chose to depart from Sicily as a young man while Muslim sovereignty, however brittle at the time, remained intact. With the likely possibility that he himself chose not to return, and with the pangs of guilt that haunt his *Diwan*, Ibn Hamdis's fate defined his eternal enmity towards those who stood in his way from ever returning to Sicily.

The litany of qualities al-Idrisi attributes to Roger II, from the physical to the metaphysical, are all well within the Arabo-Muslim lexicon on good governance and shared by and large with both western Latin and Byzantine Greek traditions: a strong leader who derives his authority from God, a wise and capable administrator, a just ruler, a provider of security and welfare, a ruler of honourable conduct, an able legislator, a strong soldier and defender of the realm, a staunch foe against the enemy, and high-minded and lofty in thought and spirit etc.

The combination of these attributes, long the essential ingredients of Arabic panegyrics, biographical dictionaries and historical accounts of the reigns of men in political and intellectual power, would not necessarily disturb a twelfth-century educated Muslim, wise to the ways of the world, except of course those with staunchly conservative religious views or with a political axe to grind. Perhaps one phrase – '*huwa khayru man malaka al-rum bastan wa qabdan*' (He is the best of those who ruled the Christians in granting abundance or withholding it) – might have raised a disapproving eyebrow, because the phrase *bastan wa qabdan* resonates clearly with the Qur'anic verse '*wa-allahu **yaqbidu wa yabsutu** wa ilayhi turja'un*' (It is God who withholds abundance or grants it, and to Him you are returned: Qur'an II: 245), possibly suggesting, or being misread as such, that Roger II was on par with God. But al-Idrisi was careful to contextualize the phrase by reminding the reader (and we must make the assumption that the book was targeted to an Arabic-reading audience) that the attribute is given to a Christian king in the way he governs a Christian realm.

Thus remains the perplexing question of why Sicilian Arab poets – as well as other Muslim scholars and writers – sang the praises of Roger II, while the ruler of the Norman Kingdom of Sicily was spearheading the defeat of Islam as the once military, commercial and cultural power in the central Mediterranean. Much of the intrigue around this question stems from an equal, if not greater, amount of invective written against the Normans, as illustrated by the examples throughout previous chapters, by Sicilians who remained on the island after Islam's defeat, by exiled Muslim Sicilians who followed from afar reports of Norman ascendancy on their homeland, and by Arab chroniclers and historians writing outside Sicily or throughout the many years that followed. The standard narrative bequeathed to us embraces the thesis of a great Norman synthesis that fused Christian Latin, Byzantine Greek and Muslim Arabic cultural production and practices to forge a Norman kingdom that many of us have read as multicultural and multi-ethnic, uncannily resembling a modern state. Historical – that is, literary, linguistic and architectural – sources support this thesis, but there still remains significant textual evidence of widespread oppression and resistance to Norman rule that disturbs a picture-perfect world of medieval Sicilian *convivencia*.

This final chapter looks more closely at the intrinsic – dare I say philological – aspects of Arabic panegyrics penned by Arab travellers and court poets of the Norman court, especially during the reigns of Roger II (d.1154) and William II (d.1189), which may open up to a wider range of ambiguity that invites alternate readings of these praises. Leaving the obvious and unambiguous bulk of Norman invective aside, including Sicilian Arabic poetry that was composed (i) during the period of Muslim Sicilian political decline in the mid-eleventh century, (ii) in the decades of the Norman campaign culminating in the fall of Syracuse and Noto in 1091 and (iii) throughout much of the twelfth century under Norman rule itself, I will focus on an extant selection of Arabic prose and poetry in praise of the Norman kings to offer variant interpretations within the context of what poets and historians refer to as *fitna*.

The fall of Muslim Sicily to the Norman invasion resulted in waves of emigration, particularly among the island's political, cultural and professional elite, to Ifriqiya (Tunisia), al-Andalus (Spain) and Egypt, while massive numbers of Christians from the Italian mainland, especially 'Lombards', poured into the island and eventually became the nemeses of the Muslim community. Those Muslims who either chose or were forced to remain eventually came to live their lives as a disempowered minority but with varying degrees of status and security. Many continued to participate in public life as farmers, craftsmen and merchants; others enjoyed the security of military or civilian employment under the new government with court protection. The 'palace Saracens', eunuchs who may or may not have been forced to convert to Christianity,[2] as well as scribes, accountants, translators and other skilled labourers, not to mention the many slaves of various categories and ranks, were all brought into the system in ways that replicated previous Muslim practices. The new circumstances in which most Muslims found themselves as a minority constituted, in effect, a kind of *dhimmi* status, all too familiar to Muslims. In a situation of the tables being turned, these Arabs must clearly have known the rules of the game and the codes of how to accept, survive, assimilate or dissimilate to the new world order. At the same time, the collective experience of losing a homeland, suffering a diminished status and witnessing Muslims defeats across the Mediterranean basin contributed to Muslim solidarity, as Alex Metcalfe has argued.[3] It is in this vast blurry grey area between Norman tolerance and Norman conquest that I seek to reread Arabic panegyrics.

The *Fitna* of Ibn Jubayr: *Seduction and chaos*

In his quest to build a kingdom incorporating the best of three local cultures, a project now referred to as the *Norman Synthesis*, it was only natural that Roger II, in imitation of the Arab princes he replaced, would invite scholars, scientists and poets to grace his court and cultivate his realm. Historical accounts, in both Arabic and Latin, amply attest to Roger's predilection and patronage of Arab-Islamic scholarship and institutions, and there is no reason

...ity of Arabic poets' verses on him. However, the wide ...e of contradiction – between the court poets' favourable ...and the prolific invectives hurled against the Norman Conquest ...n prose and poetry could be clarified in Ibn Jubayr's by now oft-cited account of his sojourn in Sicily during the reign of King William II in 1183, whose own stances towards Muslims and Muslim culture replicated those of his grandfather. A brief excursion back to this account will reveal useful clues to understanding the range and nuances of this contradiction.[4]

Shipwrecked off the coast of Messina with a group of pilgrims returning from Mecca en route to Spain, Ibn Jubayr relates that the king (William II), while on an inspection tour of his fleet, came personally to the port, paid the passengers' disembarkation fees, provided them with money and granted them safe passage during their visit. These comments immediately and unequivocally conjure the diptych image of *diyafa* (hospitality) and *ijara* (protection), two key traits in the poetics of panegyric essential to legitimate rulership in the Arabic-Islamic tradition. In his three-month visit, Ibn Jubayr travels across the northern coast of Sicily, from Messina in the east to Trapani in the west, and bears witness to a Muslim presence of merchants, bureaucrats, craftsmen, farmers, scholars and mystics, living their lives, at times secure, at times insecure, enjoying in places both the protection of the royal court and the tolerance and good will of Sicilian Christian citizens.

Ibn Jubayr's trajectory along the northern littoral of the island from east to west maps out for the reader the story of cross-culture at the end of the twelfth century. It recounts in reverse the history of the Muslim conquest and settlement of the island that had taken place, from rise to fall, in the previous centuries. If we recall Amari's observation from reading the Arabic chronicles that the jihad project started in the west of the island, with the landing at Mazara in 827 and the capture and installation of Palermo as 'capital' city in 831, moving east with the conquests of the Byzantine strongholds of Castrogiovanni (Enna) and Syracuse in the middle of the island, culminating in the fall of cities in the east of the island (i.e. Taormina and Messina c.909), we can easily imagine the island scantily populated with Muslims and Islam in the (north)eastern parts but increasing in size as Ibn Jubayr was making his way to the west. He describes Messina as a dirty and hostile city, with very few Muslims. He recounts a meeting with an Arab named 'Abd al-Masih (Servant of the Messiah), possibly a convert to Christianity, who pleads with shipwrecked Muslim pilgrims for news and souvenirs from Mecca (*Rihla*, p. 299). Ibn Jubayr describes Cefalu, situated at the centre of the northern Sicilian coast, as having a mixed population with shared Muslim/Christian spaces in the city but with Muslims inhabiting their own suburbs and adjacent farms and villages. The stretch of road from Cefalu to Palermo is perhaps the most interesting: Ibn Jubayr paints a picture of intense human traffic, Christians and Muslims alike, with roads teaming with markets, merchants and pedestrians. Especially noteworthy is his mention of Qasr Sa'd, situated on the coast a few miles from the gates of Palermo. This was a Muslim palatine village built in the heyday of the Islamic era and one populated with (Muslim) worshippers next to which lay the many gravesites of Muslim ascetics and saints (*Rihla*, p. 303). Given the emergence of Sufism in the curricula vitae of late eleventh- and twelfth-century Sicilian and North African Muslim scholars, and in light of the flourishing of mystical movements across the three monotheistic faiths there and then, one can safely speculate that this small patch of land survived as a site of cross-religious intersections and one where economic exchanges, religious visitations and other aspects of human activity we might brand today as tourism took place away from the scrutinizing eye of unlike-minded government and religious officials.

Palermo, as to be expected, is described by Ibn Jubayr in terms not totally unrecognizable to the Palermo of Ibn Hawqal in 973. Apart from the passage of two centuries, and the change from Muslim to Christian rule with all that entails, Palermo maintained its multi-ethnic, relatively cosmopolitan flavour, with Muslims interacting with Christians in many public places, enjoying aspects of court patronage and government employment and living their daily lives in the security of their own suburbs and adjacent farms and hamlets. Further west, in Trapani, Ibn Jubayr paints a picture of a totally mixed population in terms of public spaces, again reflecting the long history of Muslim settlement patterns in Sicily.

As the narrative moves westward, however, the voices of individual Muslims emerge and disturb the image of just rule and tolerance, with instances of unfair treatment, fiscal and religious oppression, and harassment. The projection of William II as a just ruler back on the docks of Messina blurs with these complaints, and the attributing of hospitality and protection to him is gradually rendered null and void. Modern scholarship suggests that the good intentions of the Norman Court, as espoused and put into practice by both Roger II and William II, had to give way to the changing demographics on the island: the influx of hostile Lombards from the mainland, pressures from the Vatican especially in light of the wider Crusader movement and the rising power of the Sicilian baron classes. Somewhere between the benign royal policies and the shifting politics outside the inner circle of the Norman royal court I read the zone of contradiction bearing in mind Ibn Jubayr's repetition on *fitna*.

The term *fitna* has been mentioned in previous chapters on numerous occasions in accounts from Arab chroniclers, travellers and poets to give meaning to political and social events that I have been arguing contest, challenge and violate the grand project of Muslim jihad in Sicily. According to Edward William Lane, the term has a wide lexical range:

> A burning with fire; melting of gold or silver to separate the bad from the good; trial, probation; affliction, distress of hardship; an affliction whereby one is tried, proved or tested; punishment, castigation or chastisement; civil war or conflict among people; slaughter, war, faction, or sedition among the parties of the Muslims when they form themselves into parties; discord, dissent, or difference of opinions among the peoples; a misleading or causing to err or go astray; seduction or temptation; the showing of desires and lusts of the present life or world whereby one is tried; the cause of one's being pleased with a thing; madness, insanity, (diabolical insanity); error, deviation from the right path; infidelity or unbelief; and the devil's prompting or suggesting some evil idea.[5]

Heretofore, the term *fitna* has been generally understood to mean the state of chaos emanating from political division or civil strife. However, it is precisely in the more commonly understood lexical dichotomy of 'civil strife' and 'seduction/temptation' that I read as the intended meaning Ibn Jubayr wishes to convey in his reading of Muslim-Christian relations in late twelfth-century Sicily. The two meanings, and the ambiguities that lie therein, flesh out the nuances of the zone of contradiction that define the poetics of Arabic praise (or invective) for the Norman kings. In the case of William II, we are treated to Ibn Jubayr's (initial) litany of praises for his generosity, protection, wise governance, skill in building magnificent buildings and gardens, judicious and generous treatment of Muslims doctors, lawyers, bureaucrats, teachers, pages, slaves, and concubines, patronage of Muslim sciences, and his own literacy in Arabic language and culture. But along the road from Messina to Trapani, the various voices of Muslim Sicilians rise in cacophony, and the praises of a benevolent enemy king devolve into invectives of abuse, injustice and tyranny. And with each report of these accounts Ibn Jubayr ends with a supplication to God (*du'a'*), much the way poets sign off their *qasidas* to ask God for a favour – in this case, to dissolve William's rule and restore Sicily to Islam.

While the historians and poets I cited in previous chapters evoked the term *fitna* to convey basically the internal divisions or the breaking of ranks among Muslims, individually or collectively, especially in facing enemy aggression, Ibn Jubayr more often than not comes much closer to the meaning of *fitna* as temptation or seduction, and his numerous uses of the term cluster around four areas of temptation that he warns his fellow Arabs to avoid: (i) Norman royal patronage, (ii) the (overt) friendliness and gentility of Christians towards Muslims, (iii) the beauty and splendour of Norman Christian material culture and civilization and (iv) (the benefits of) conversion to Christianity.

In his lavish praise of the Norman Kingdom, resplendent with all the attributes and accomplishments that were the hallmark of Muslim praise of good governance, Ibn Jubayr reports that William lavished considerable attention to his Muslim physicians and astrologers and that he seized every opportunity to lure such people passing through the island to remain and take advantage of his generous patronage. Ibn Jubayr asks God to preserve the Muslims from the seduction (*allah yu'idh al-muslimin min al-fitna bihi bimannihi* (*Rihla*, p. 298)), and he takes the supplication further by asking God's protection from the king's hostility and extension of powers.

On the road from Cefalu to Palermo, Ibn Jubayr's party of Muslim travellers encounters a group of Christians who greet them warmly and courteously (*Rihla*: 302). In a later passage, he recounts the story of a Christian Sicilian who offers him advice about how to conceal taxable commodities he may be carrying from greedy customs officials and of a second Christian who wishes him prosperity while in Sicily. In all cases, Ibn Jubayr cautions his reader not to be seduced by these seductive kindnesses (*min al-umur al-fattana*) (*Rihla*, p. 304).

In his citing of the many Norman palaces and gardens built by William II, as well as the vivid details of the luxurious cathedral built by George of

Antioch, minister to Roger II, known today as Santa Maria dell'Ammiraglio, or La Martorana, Ibn Jubayr acknowledges the magnificence of Norman civilization that rivals his own Muslim civilization and once again lectures his readers about the dangers of being seduced by Norman culture (*tuhdith fi al-nufus fitna na'udhu bi-allah minha*) (*Rihla*, p. 306).

Fourthly, and most curiously, Ibn Jubayr, echoing the sharp tones of Muslim writers from the other side of the Mediterranean, warns Muslims of the pitfalls of being seduced into converting to Christianity. Here, we must read between and under the lines to comprehend what Ibn Jubayr was facing in the last chapters of his *Rihla*: the reality that there were Muslims in the late twelfth-century Sicily, very much like Christians of the ninth and tenth centuries, who survived the passage of time and the extraordinary changes wrought by the shifts from Christianity to Islam and back to Christianity, by way of conversion, either through compulsion, persuasion, conviction or opportunism. (Refer to Chapter 2 where shifting loyalties are discussed.) He cites three examples and attributes all of them to a combination of coercion on the part of Norman tyranny and the devious temptations of a seductive culture to which weak Muslims succumb: first is the case of Ibn Zur'a, respected Muslim jurist, who converts to Christianity upon the arm-twisting of Norman government officials and who adjudicates on cases involving Christians and Muslims, based on his knowledge of both religions and legal systems; the second is a practice, we are led to believe, prevailing at the time, whereby an aggrieved family member who was facing anger or disagreement from another family member could take refuge in a church and, upon agreement to convert to Christianity, escape the family's wrath and authority; third is a case where a local Muslim offered to marry his young virgin daughter to any member among the visiting Muslim pilgrims in order that she escape the temptation to convert and marry a Christian. The incident comes to a narrative climax with the praise of this young saintly girl who was willing to bear eternal separation from her family in order to maintain her faith (*Rihla*, pp. 315–6), an all-too-familiar trope in the long history of Christian-Muslim cross-cultural conflict.

Ibn Jubayr's repeated use of the term *fitna* to denote what he sees as dangerous consequences for cross-cultural/cross-religious contact taps into the wide lexical breadth of the term itself, allowing for the subtle nuances and ambivalence in his understanding and judgement of what he sees unfolding before him. How ordinary Sicilians whom he encountered, Christians and Muslims alike, lived their lives defies any clear-cut delineations that ordinarily mapped out the worlds of Islam and Christendom in the medieval Mediterranean. The attraction to the 'other' and the crossing of religious, social, legal and linguistic boundaries were indeed two-way streets that were well travelled in both directions. Muslim physicians and astrologers, not to mention court poets, as we shall soon see, were persuaded to accept the financial and professional benefits of Norman patronage, in the same ways that Christians and Jews embraced Islamic patronage well into the heyday of Muslim sovereignty. And, if Ibn Jubayr is to be believed, these practices continued during William II's reign in the later decades of the twelfth century. He writes that an Arab palace tailor (Yahya ibn Fityan al-Tarraz) reported to him that Christian women came to his palace and were converted by the Muslim harem servants (*Rihla*, p. 299). All this points to a continuum in the practices of cross-culture that could earn the approval or disapproval at any time or place. If one recalls Ibn Hawqal's acerbic remarks about Muslim Sicilians who dwelt on the outskirts of Palermo and married Christian women living their lives with one foot in *Dar al-Islam* and the other in *Dar al-Harb*, we see something very similar still happening two centuries later.

Poets and the Norman court patronage

The zone of contradiction between Arabic praise and invective towards the Norman kings of Sicily extends well into the extant handful of panegyric poems that celebrated the court of King Roger II, but such poems are conspicuously absent, at least by indigenous Sicilians, in the court of his grandson, William II, some thirty years later. Had those thirty years wrought significant political or cultural changes that no longer allowed for such longstanding cultural practices? Had Christendom's political and cultural dominance in Sicily rendered unnecessary and obsolete the propagandistic appeal of Arabic courtly panegyric poetry, especially at a time of dwindling Arabic political and cultural influence?

Karla Mallette's groundbreaking study of Norman literary history that situates these praise texts against the currents of literary production in the

Norman period is a useful way to proceed. Mallette offers a broad and reliable framework for drawing the artistic and intellectual contours of Norman Sicily with the following observations: literary works penned in the 'mainland' languages of Arabic, Latin and Greek during the Norman period were conservative in their adherence to their own literary traditions. Latin was the language of chronicles and 'books of the deeds of rulers' that richly document political history; Greek was the language of liturgical writings; Arabic was the language of philosophy and poetry.[6] But a lingering question yet to be satisfactorily answered is: Were the Norman princes and courtiers reading and understanding these Arabic panegyrics in ways similar to how Sicilian Arabs, well versed in the traditions (conventions and subversions) of the classical Arabic poetic canon, read them or intended them to be understood?

To recapitulate, the panegyric (*madih*), that is, praise of a patron or esteemed family or tribal member, is a variation on the broader 'boast' segment that constituted the third part of the classical Arabic tripartite *qasida*. Its opposite, the invective (*hija'*), was hurled against an enemy or rival. Implied in both praise and invective is the ideal of '*hasab and nasab*': *Hasab* is the sum total of the qualities and generous deeds of one's ancestors; *nasab* is the tribal lineage that the proud Arabs were careful to preserve unsullied by marriage with inferiors. The aesthetics of praise, of course, was not restricted to the *qasida* or poetry proper but also extended into other genres of Arabic writing, as we have seen, for example, in the cases of al-Idrisi and Ibn Jubayr. Those noble traits of bravery, generosity, forbearance, hospitality and military prowess – or the lack thereof – continued to dominate the language with which Muslims cast their praise or blame on self and other in equal measure across the wide range of Arabic literary expression and genres throughout the twelfth century.

To understand in more nuanced ways the meanings and implications of Arabic praises of the Norman kings at a time of political instability and submission, it is useful to look to the conventions of the classical Arabic *qasida* in which the language, idiom and imagery of panegyric developed. Three aspects of the *qasida* form a template for my reading of the twelfth-century Sicilian Arabic panegyric: mobility, dichotomy and advocacy.

By mobility, I mean the ability to move, shift or relocate, geographically and generically. As a product of a desert environment that expressed the world view of a nomadic, tribal way of life, the Arabic *qasida* followed the Islamic wars of conquest emigrating from the Arabian Peninsula and comfortably settling first in the garrison towns of Mesopotamia, then in the urban centres of the Eastern Mediterranean and Egypt. As Islam moved West, the Arabic *qasida* moved with it, finding its place in urban and rural areas of Berber North Africa until it crossed the Mediterranean and found a new habitat in Spain (al-Andalus) and Sicily. The old Arabian tropes of crying over abandoned ruins, the treacherous journey through hostile lands, and the extolling of noble Bedouin virtues of manliness (*muruwwa*) and tribal pride and loyalty not only survived but found new meanings in these faraway places. One need to only recall the verses of Ibn Hamdis whose influence on his compatriots on the island must have been considerable.

Generically, the *qasida* was able to wrestle itself away from the conventions of the classical tripartite structure. In time, it gave way to a bipartite poem and even the monothematic occasional poem, allowing the poet more creative freedom and flexibility, especially by a mixing and weaving of thematic clusters in unpredictable order. It goes without saying that the Arabic *qasida* also made a successful transition during radical shifts in Arab history. Both the advent of Islam in the middle of the seventh century and the Muslim discovery of the Greek sciences and logic two centuries later each had a distinct, massive impact on Arabic poetry and poetics, with the Arabic *qasida* and its constituent parts adjusting easily and artistically to the changes.

Secondly, dichotomy as a feature of the classical Arabic *qasida* is vital in understanding the various and possibly contradictory meanings in a single poem. James Montgomery has argued convincingly that dichotomy is rooted in the 'ritualistic function of the poet' that may cause 'personal or inward aspects of the poem to be neglected' and that a certain 'equivocalness of the movements' leads to a double edge in the poem, 'being both subordinate to the overall *qasida* and valid expressions of the bedouin world view in their own right'.[7] Thus, when the *madih* broke away from its supporting role in the classical *qasida* to become a major literary force in its own right, and while the poet evolved from the voice of the tribe in a desert setting to the highly visible public figure charged with extolling the virtues, real or imagined, of caliphs, sultans and even petty warlords in search of legitimation, the panegyric came to express the public and private – at times harmoniously, at times in discord. When the repeatedly exiled Ibn Hamdis delivered a bipartite poem he composed to Zirid prince Tamim ibn al-Muʻizz (d.1108), he interrupted the long panegyric segment, as we have seen, with a ten-line diatribe against the Normans who had recently completed their conquest of his homeland. By the time he returned to the panegyric, the damage was done: the (explicit) panegyric turned to (implicit) invective as the Muslim prince was poetically implicated, and possibly publicly shamed, in failing to defend Sicily and, by extension, the Islamic faith.

Thirdly, the power of advocacy – that is, the ability of the *qasida* to carry social and political messages – has been a hallmark of the classical Arabic *qasida* and perhaps the secret to its popularity and longevity. From archiving tribal rivalries in sixth- and seventh-century Arabia to articulating Arab nationalist demands for independence and resistance to European imperialism as late as the mid-twentieth century, the spirit and form of the Arabian ode – in all its themes of crying over abandoned abodes, lamenting lost love, embarking on dangerous journeys in hostile territory, and self-boasting, praise and invective – have survived and flourished in worldly relevance in distant places and times. There is no more compelling example of advocacy than the poetry of Ibn Hamdis whose own life experiences of exile, loss of loved ones and homeland, and the struggle to survive in the twelfth-century Mediterranean were articulated with such emotional force in the reworkings of the sixth-century Arabian ode.

As much as the Arabian ode, Bedouin and pagan in world view, survived the transition to Islam, capable of reconciling itself to a new historical consciousness and a radically different system of beliefs and practices, it was the incessant political twists and turns in the new Islamic Empire that posed the greatest challenges and opportunities to a court poet. As the Empire simultaneously grew and fragmented politically, the demands for talented poets to sing the praises of a ruler in competition for political legitimacy rendered panegyric poetry a potentially lucrative and powerful profession. However, over the centuries, many a poet found himself, by choice or necessity, extolling the virtues of a patron being compelled to adhere to classical Arabic literary conventions on the one hand, while maintaining credibility with his audience, on the other. In the best of times, poets could enjoy the patronage of a caliph, sultan, war hero or eminent scholar. More often, they found themselves standing before throngs of people reciting their verses in praise of eunuch slaves, Turkic sultans and Berber warlords who shoved their way into power and employed these poets as propagandists. Arabic panegyrics was pushed and pulled in many directions throughout its long history – had seen and done it all, so to speak – but never seemed to be at a loss for words.

***

The following verses, penned by four different poets, are the surviving extracts of Sicilian Arabic panegyrics to Roger II, recently re-edited and collated into a volume by Ihsan Abbas.[8] From the outset, I readily acknowledge the problem triggered by contemporaneous and later anthologists who chose to exclude verses from these poems they deemed unfit to print, that is, poems in praise of infidels (*kuffar*). We can only imagine what exactly offended these compilers: possibly portraying Norman rulers in an Islamic religious idiom and imagery or voicing support for the Normans while breaking ranks with Sicilian Muslims engaged in holy war to liberate the homeland. One could also ask to what extent these censoring anthologists actually read or misread the sequence of tropes or highly referential use of language the Sicilians poets used to express the ambivalences and complexities of their situation. Conscious of these challenges in my readings and conclusions, I nonetheless persist in working with these extant verses, being our only options, if only to glean historically meaningful insights from them.

'Abd al-Rahman ibn Muhammad ibn 'Umar al-Buthayri (*Mu'jam* #60: 58–9) was a scholar from the city of Buthayra (modern Butera), located on the southern central coast of the island. According to *al-Mu'jam*, his biographers describe him as having memorized the Qur'an and as being a highly competitive scholar, skilled in the epistolary arts, i.e. official correspondence, diplomatics, essays (*tarassul*), and a master of expository prose (*nathr*).

We have twelve lines of a poem he composed in praise of Roger II, the bulk of which is dedicated to extolling the king's architectural accomplishments. Immediately following these verses quoted in the collection are ten lines of another poem composed by the anthologist Ibn Bashrun who was challenged by al-Buthayri himself to best his poem, highly likely included in this biographical entry as an illustration of al-Buthayri's description of being competitive. Since the intention of Ibn Bashrun was not to praise Roger II but to engage in poetic sparring (reminiscent perhaps of Ibn Hamdis's first encounter with al-Mu'tamid ibn 'Abbad in Seville in 1071, cited in Chapter 4), I cite here and focus only on al-Buthayri's verses.

The four lines before the poem's break (as shown below) comprise a wine song replete with the familiar tropes of passing the goblet from imbiber to imbiber, keeping beat to accompanying music and, most conducive to my thesis, staking claim to Sicily as (paradisiacal) abode. The fourth line, seemingly innocuous, is nonetheless a reminder to the would-be revellers (i.e. to the poem's audience) that we are outside of *Dar al-Islam* – that is, in the land of the Caesars.

Following the break, the remaining eight lines of the same poem are devoted to descriptions of Roger's palaces, including gardens, loggias and fountains. The adjective *mansuriyya* to describe the plural palaces (*qusur*) in the first of these eight lines carries possible opposite or ambiguous meanings. As an adjective derived from the passive participle of the verb *nasara*, meaning to be awarded 'victory', the implication exists that where there are 'victors', there are the 'vanquished'. Also, the fact that the root '*nsr*' carries the meaning of both *al-Nasira* (i.e. the city of Nazareth) and the by-then highly used epithet for Christians (*al-Nasara*) may have conveyed to a Christian a positive connotation of palaces (belonging to) victorious Christians. To a Muslim, however, the noun-adjective phrase, *qusur mansuriyya*, would carry, for obvious historical reasons, the opposite meaning. The following line explicitly states that the beauty of these buildings has been completed by God, the Islamic 'al-Rahman'. To a devout Muslim, this would be understood as a stark reminder, 'We are no longer in *Dar al-Islam*.'

1- Pass around the golden carnelian-red [wine]
   and join the morning to the evening [in your revelry]

2- Drink at the tempo of the lute chords
   and the songs of Ma'bad

3- No living is serene, save
   in the sweet heights of Sicily

4- In a dynasty that rivals
   the empires of the Caesars.
   ...

5- And in the palaces of the victorious state
   joy breaks its journey and settles

6- How admirable its site:
   the Compassionate [Lord] has perfected its appearance

7- And the loggias, more radiant than
   any architectural work

8- And his [Roger's] gardens of fresh herbage, where
   earthy existence reverts to splendor

9- And from the mouths of the lions in his fountain
   the waters of Paradise gush forth

10- And spring dresses the land
    with its beauty in radiant cloaks,

11- and transforms it, and crowns its countenance
    with bright and bejeweled garments

12- They perfume the eastern breeze
    at morning and evening.

(*Muʿjam*: 58–9; translated by Karla Mallette: *Kingdom*: 141–2) Ibn Bashrun's concluding verses in response to al-Buthayri's challenge (see translation in Mallette: *Kingdom*:142) may be read with a similar message:

1- In this land exalted Roger thrives, King of the Caesars;
   among the delights of a lengthy life and Sicily's pleasing beauties.

Abu Hafs ʿUmar ibn Hasan (*Muʿjam* #99:149–50) was a reputable Sicilian philologist and grammarian and who, according to his biographers, was widely respected for his well-crafted poetry. It was related that he had been arrested by the Normans and subjected to multiple punishments, the reasons for which we can only imagine. Why a scholar of such repute would fall out of favour with the Norman authorities remains a mystery not only from the scant biographical information but also from the 'edited' remains of a panegyric poem ibn Hasan wrote to King Roger in which he pleads for clemency.

The poem or at least the lines that remain of it are cast in the form of a love poem (*ghazal*) in which the lover (i.e. the poet) not only is rejected by the beloved but fails to encounter the beloved's phantom, even in sleep. What is immediately striking is Ibn Hasan's naming of 'Suʿad' as a beloved one whose rejection leaves him dejected, with the 'dark recesses of his heart' and soul. The evocation of Suʿad may very well be read as a reference to the opening line of the seventh-century Kaʿb ibn Zuhayr's panegyric to the Prophet Muhammad:

1- Suʿad is gone, my heart stunned (*matbul*)
   Lost in her traces, shackled (*makbul*), unransomed.⁹

The image of the heart as both 'unransomed' and 'shackled' would certainly resonate with Abu Hafs 'Umar's incarceration, and the intertextuality with a poem dedicated to the Prophet would undoubtedly win over Ibn Zuhayr's (Arabic-reading) audience's sympathy.

In his dejected condition, the poet evokes King Roger as an attentive and responsive lover, a common convention in neoclassical Arabic poetry that collapses the beloved (*mahbub*) with the panegyrized (*mamduh*) and as one who rewards all those he looks on with favour with sustenance (wine). The poet attempts to manipulate the conventional boast of bonding, an essential component to the relationship between the praiser and the praised in the Arabic panegyric, whereby he pleads his case (as a prisoner) for release. The following lines encompass attributes of generosity, courage and supernatural prowess that resonate as much with *Jahili* poetics as they do with post-Islam poetics and imply a contractual bond whereby the poet sells his praises to the patron for a reward. Once again, we have the commentary of the anthologist editing the poem concerning praising the infidel but offering excuses that Abu Hafs is writing his verses under duress and should not be held in shame for it.

1- He sought solace from someone other than his [beloved] Suʿad
   who might occupy the dark recesses of his heart and soul;

2- and he longed for a visit from his beloved's phantom when she spurned him,
   but his passion denied him the sweetness of sleep.

3- By God! Were it not for Roger who
bestows upon those dear to him the best of his love,

4- he would not refuse the cup of honor on the day of separation from her,
and he would behold the face of nobility in his [Roger] birth.

–

5- Eager in giving, with the eagerness of one who grasps a sword
he brandishes on the day of battle,

6- In the darkness [of war] his face shimmers [with the light of] dawn;
you would think the sunlight was among those who envy him.

7- Gemini arises where he stakes his tents
and the stars, the sun, and the moon are the pegs that secure his tents.

8- When matters are uncertain, his sword becomes a pen
that whitens the blackness [with the clarity] of its ink.

–

9- Oh King! who stands firm,
hardy and grounded, on the two feet of his obduracy.

10- the spirits of his enemies call out to him, and he disposed of them,
laughing, as they come face to face with the wide blade of his sheath.

Abu al-Daw' Siraj ibn Ahmad ibn Raja' (*Mu'jam* #44: 43–44) was a professional scribe whose literary merits as an accomplished poet were first recorded by the contemporaneous Sicilian anthologist, Ibn Bashrun. Ibn Bashrun cites him for being a 'keen observer, sharp witted, and creative and refined in the manner in which he composes his verses'. The entry in Abbas's collection suggests that the poet was the son of professional scribe and likely an employee of the Norman court as well. Jeremy Johns describes him as a member of a 'distinguished Palermitan family which provided the *qadi* (chief judge) of Palermo in three successive generations'.[10] We can also assume that he enjoyed stature and respect among the members of a dwindling Muslim community of legal and medical scholars.[11] The three poems whose extracts survive in this biography include a poem of response to a request for a loan of a book by a jurist, a poem in the form of a love song that treats trachoma and an elegy composed on the death of one of Roger II's sons. What is particularly noteworthy here is the brief but illuminating snapshot of the ties that bound members of this dwindling community of Arab intellectuals in what remained of Muslim Sicily.

1- A burst of sobs, and eyelids awash in tears
   a wave of grief, hearts wilting and bodies weak,

2- The radiant moon has vanished and gloom covers the earth,
   and everything steadfast, high and mighty, trembles.

3- Just as he stood up on two feet in all his beauty and radiance,
   and as every quest for glory takes pride in him,

4- does the horror of Death snatch him away, deceitfully,
   unexpectedly. How treacherous Death is.

5- It cast a dark shadow over the face of the moon,
   and just at it reached full illumination, its glow was dimmed.

6- It is only natural that tears be shed over him,
   tears like pearls and coral that trickle down the cheek,

7- Hearts ache with burning pain, and souls ail,
   grief intensifies and sorrows prevail.

8- Sadness is swapped and tear ducts well,
   a flood of watery tears mix with flames of grief.

9- His tents and his palaces mourn him,
   and swords and lances are sheathed in their loss.

10- The horses' neighing rise from their throats in their longing for him,
    and they can only be restrained, bridled and haltered.

11- The leaves of the thicket weep only for him,
    had the branches known, they would have preceded the doves in sorrowful cooing.

12- O how afflicted you are by such a gruesome loss, a cruel twist of fate,
    when patience is no where to be found and consolation lacking.

13- O how unimaginable it must be, this most horrific day,
   the mere sight of which has turned children's hair gray.

14- It was as if the town crier came forth to announce to the throngs,
   and they rose up in unison, just as they were.

15- And the wide open spaces contracted with the masses,
   and they all stood together, men and women side by side,

16- And their hearts were rent, not the sleeves of their robes,
   the nightingales chanted 'To God we return!' as minds and hearts trembled,

17- When once like doves they donned in gay white apparel,
   they now like crows cloak themselves in black.

What survives of the elegy amounts to seventeen lines that, despite the spectre of editorial deletions, display a remarkable thematic cohesion. Historical accounts report that Roger lost several sons, both young and matured, and it's not clear which one here is the eulogized. The third line's image of a child beginning to walk and the fifth line's metaphor of the 'moon-faced' attribute could suggest a youngster, while in lines nine and ten the evocation of tents, swords and horses in a state of mourning suggests a young man who had been in the service of his father's army.[12]

These verses, along with the remains of the two other poems cited in the biography, demonstrate Abu al-Daw's considerable talent and creativity in the use of the poetic conventions of antithesis (*tibaq*) and paronomasia (*jinas*) that were hallmarks of neoclassical Arabic poetry in those times. And keeping with literary tradition, the poem begins with the customary existential brooding and aphoristic statements common to *Jahili* poetry. The poet then proceeds by gradually casting the masses as the anguished lovers of the Arabic *ghazal* waning in the loss of the beloved. However, the poem is remarkable in several ways. First, there is scant mention of the deceased's personal qualities, a de rigueur component of Arabic elegy, and also little mention of Roger other than the couple of lines in which the poet addresses the bereaved father in the second person. Second, the poem expresses a public bereavement for a national or collective loss that is abstract and impersonal, accentuated by the repeated use of passive verbs. We find nothing in the way of the poet's personal relation to the bereaved father/king/patron or to the deceased, nor of any mental and emotional anguish (*tafajjuʿ*) that he personally feels over the loss, which would normally be essential ingredient in a successful Arabic elegy. Third and above all, when read in sequence, the poem's last five surviving lines conjure all the doom of the end of a world. From the reversal of the natural order (i.e. children's hair turning grey) to their appearance of a harbinger who summons the masses, with the people tearing out their own hearts instead of rending their clothing as would be typical in contemporaneous mourning practices, the poet ends his elegy with lines that go beyond expressions of grief over the death of a child or a young man. The sequence of images in these lines conforms to Islamic apocalyptic imagery, and they fit logically and aesthetically into the structure of the poem and the overall mood of the sad occasion, portending the signs of a bleak outcome. While an audience listening to them could understand and accept these lines, in all their hyperbole, as poetic speech appropriate to the occasion, the ominous warnings of a world coming to an end would resonate more forcefully with the Muslim community than with non-Muslim Arabophone audiences, given the political climate in which the poem was written.

ʿAbd al-Rahman al-Atrabanshi (*Muʿjam* #54: 54–55) was (assumedly) a professional poet whose name bears the origin of the city of Trapani, situated on the western coast of the island. Virtually nothing of his life survives in the archive other than the poem composed in praise of Roger II, commonly known as *al-Favara*. It remains until today the most familiar example of Muslim culture in Norman Sicily, having been cited numerously in classical Arabic biographical dictionaries as well as in nineteenth- and twentieth-century Italian scholarship. The fifteen-line poem, most recently analysed and translated into English by Karla Mallette, lavishes praise on Roger's palace and its gardens in a mixture of images that strongly suggest a love song (*ghazal*). The poem evokes brooks and palm trees, set against the sea, with fish-filled ponds in palatial gardens, replete with oranges and lemons. The analogy of two lovers seeking protection against an unnamed enemy is followed with the appeal, addressed in the second person (presumably to Roger) to provide the lovers with his protection. Missing in the extant verses are any direct personal attributes of King Roger (the subject of praise):

1- Oh, Favara of the two seas! in you, desires converge!
   In you life is pleasant, your view is majestic

2- Your waters are divided into nine streams;
   how lovely their divided flow!

3- At the convergence of your two seas, a battlefield of love
   and upon your two bays, desire encamps

4- How glorious is the sea of the two palm trees,
   and what the sea surrounding it contains is the greatest of all places

5- It is as if your waters, where they flow together, in their clarity
   were melted pearls, and the land were dusky skin

6- And as if the branches of the gardens stretched out
   to gaze on the billowing waters and smile

7- The fish swim in the clarity of her (???) water
   and the birds of her garden sing

8- The oranges of the island when they blossom
   are like fire blazing in branches of chrysolite

9- The lemons are like the yellow complexion of the lover
   who, having spent the night in torment of distance, laments

10- And the two palm trees like two lovers who choose
    as protection from the enemy, a castle well-fortified against them

11- Or as if misgiving clings to them, and they draw themselves up
    to frighten suspicion out of the one who suspects them

12- O two palms of the two seas of Palermo, may you always drink
    of the sustaining rain! May it not be cut off!

13- May you take pleasure in the passage of time, may it grant all your desires,
    and may history lull you to sleep

14- By God, protect with your shade the people of love,
for in the safety of your shade love finds protection!

15- This account of an eyewitness is not to be doubted: rather,
distrust the trivial descriptions based on hearsay.

(*Mu'jam*: 54–5; translated by Karla Mallette: Kingdom: 139–40)

On the surface of these lines, we see the poet intertwining various motifs of the *ghazal* – the jilted lover, sleepless nights and the appeal for protection against enemies. He also demonstrates his skill at *wasf* (description poetry), a de rigueur exercise at that time for poets in Sicily and al-Andalus. Here, he uses both literal and metaphorical language and figures and speech to draw graphic images of an ideal setting: the praise proper contains what Roger II has built of his palaces and gardens, having full advantage of what God (implicitly) has endowed to the paradisiac island of Sicily. The pervasive use of the dual, as Mallette points out, has multiple meanings, including a Qur'anic reference as well as a doubling for the two lovers of the *ghazal*.[13] I would add that it may also be a poetic tribute to the doctrine of dualism, a central theme in Fatimid theology and aesthetics, which, I have argued elsewhere, also found its way in earlier Muslim Sicilian panegyric poetry.[14]

The last four lines of the poem appear to be in a familiar position; that is, they read as closing lines in the convention of the traditional *du'a'*, a prayer or plea to God for safekeeping. What al-Atrabanshi does here is to address the two palm trees and pray that they 'always drink from the sustaining rain', which can only come from God. He also appeals to them, not to King Roger, the subject of the 'assumed' praise, to protect the people of love in the shade of their protection. The last line of the poem ends rather curiously, with the highly unusual conjuring of the image of the false reports that lovers of the *ghazal* are often subjected to at the hands of ill-wishers and jealous rivals. The contrast between an eyewitness, presumably the poet himself, and 'trivial descriptions of hearsay' leaves the audience with the disturbing image of hostile agents lurking about who cast a dark shadow over the entire poem, pointing once again in the direction towards our zone of contradiction.

Seduced by patronage: Ibn Qalaqis extols William II

Abu al-Futuh Nasrallah ibn ʿAbdallah ibn Makhluf ibn ʿAli ibn ʿAbd al-Qawi ibn Qalaqis, al-Lakhmi al-Azhari al-Iskandari, was born in the city of Alexandria (Egypt) in 532/1138 during the twilight years of the Fatimid dynasty in Egypt. The little we know of him from the bio-bibliography points to an elite traditional education (al-Azhar), access to court circles and a reputation as a highly skilled poet. He also happened to possess a smooth, beardless complexion, about which several lewd poems were composed. He was nicknamed 'the most honorable judge' (*al-qadi al-aʿazz*), but there is little evidence that he in fact practised law to any significant extent. It was also noted by his biographers that he was constantly on the move and travelled frequently.[15]

Ibn Qalaqis lived his relatively short life (of thirty-six years) in a time of political turmoil, witnessing the rapid succession of the last four Fatimid caliphates and the downfall of their dynasty in 1171. His first journey of significance was to Cairo, where he succeeded in connecting with court dignitaries and men of high position. Next, he travelled to Sicily in 563/1168, also during a period of the island's instability marked by political intrigues and conspiracies in and out of the Norman Court. There, he made the acquaintance of a Muslim chieftain, Abu al-Qasim ibn al-Hajar, with whom he established a friendly relationship and to whom, in gratitude for his patronage, he composed a collection of high-quality praise poems entitled *al-Zahr al-Basim fi Awsaf Abi al-Qasim*.[16] Subsequently, having barely spent two years in Sicily, Ibn Qalaqis set sail for Yemen. And eerily similar to his departure from Sicily, which was delayed for a period of time due to a shipwreck at sea from a storm, he encountered yet another storm and another shipwreck which ended in his drowning off the coast of the port city of ʿIydhab in the Red Sea in 567/1174.

The life of Ibn Qalaqis resembles that of Muslim Sicily's 'national' poet, Ibn Hamdis, in several ways. As a highly gifted and ambitious court poet himself, he was forced to seek patronage in a number of places beyond the boundaries of his native homeland; he participated in or, at least was privy to, the inner-court life of political machinations and jockeying for power and influence; and he had to contend with the challenges of conspiracies and shifting loyalties. He was witness, furthermore, to the clear and ominous signs of a rapidly changing world, especially around the wider Mediterranean Basin, where the

Islamic world was vulnerable to political and sectarian fragmentation and the increasing might of the Christian (read: European) Reconquest. Unlike Ibn Hamdis who lived a long life, Ibn Qalaqis died early in his career, and his time spent in Sicily, the subject of our interest here, was, as stated above, approximately two years.

In addition to the collection of poems he composed to his friend and benefactor, Ibn al-Hajar, Ibn Qalaqis bequeathed to posterity a panegyric he wrote and dedicated to King William II. The poet's arrival in Sicily, the reasons for which remain obscure, occurred during the transitional period between Kings William I and II, that is, during the regency of Queen Margaret of Navarra who controlled the reins of power until her young son could reach the legal age to rule. Unlike the fragments of poems composed to King Roger II discussed above, this poem, thirty-eight lines long, with a discernible beginning and end, appears to be uncut and intact. With that, one must keep in mind the context of composition and imagine what kind or level of the (assumed) relationship was there between the praiser and the praised. In drawing an analogy between Ibn Qalaqis's Norman panegyric and Ibn Hamdis's panegyric to the twelve-year-old Zirid Prince Hasan ibn 'Ali in 1123 on the occasion of the Muslim victory over the Norman navy at the Battle of Dimas off the coast of Tunisia, we cannot help but wonder where the poetics end and the politics begin. Or, in reading the poem, how much *convivencia* can we read between the crisscrossing of historical fact and poetic craft.

Under what circumstances or on what occasion might Ibn Qalaqis have composed this panegyric? Was it delivered orally or inscribed in text? These questions remain for historical speculation. In light of his anthology to Ibn al-Hajar, we can safely assume that there remained on the island a highly literate Arabic community who could read and appreciate the poem with, as we shall see, all its sophisticated use of language. In her study of the poet, Adalgisa De Simone reminds us that Ibn Qalaqis did indeed circulate among a segment of society given to feasting and celebrating the good life.[17] At this point, we can assume that by the later decades of the twelfth century, human traffic and cultural ties continued to flow between Sicily and the Muslim lands of the east, and that some degree of a shared 'high' culture – of which panegyric poetry was a savoured ingredient – had continued to flow since its heyday at the Kalbid Court nearly two centuries earlier.

Ibn Qalaqis's panegyric to the very young King William II consists of thirty-eight lines and is a monothematic 'occasional' *qasida* in the classical sense of the term.

1- To King William, son of William, did King Soloman bequeath his kingship, as did King David his rule.

2- The planets make use of him as a good-luck charm against the enemy, when he thrashes them with a sword of lightning and a spear of stars.

3- Not every crescent moon is like Sagittarius
gliding in the sky, piercing a luminous meteor with arrows.

4- For what is Victory but his army wherever it passes,
on the vast tracts of land or on the waves of the deep sea.

5- He possesses noble steeds which many mistake for ships
that loom large in the imagination.

6- His two armies are like rain clouds that never cease to hurl stones in war,
and like arrows, they strike their target [even] in peace.

7- He leads every charger [star] toward his enemies,
along with his sleek black (*duhm*) horses and well equipped (*duhm*) ships.

8- He sets out with his leonine battalions without the hunger for meat (*qaram*),
[merely] aiming toward a mighty (*qarm*) king.

9- The earth beneath the abodes quake from their roar,
as they strip the best of its habitation down to nothing.

10- They set their sights on seizing the port cities (*thughur*),
while their defenders devour the meal with toothless jaws (*thughur*).

11- All the estates bow down to him in submission,
like tiny stars that come face to face with the full moon.

12- For kingship is only for the one about whom the enemy says:
he is a deluge of generosity when he flows (*yahmi*), a lion when he protects (*yaHmi*).

13- How many sick of heart are there whose resolve he restored,
and how many frightened souls he resuscitated to good health.

14- He has been granted the light of the Lord by praying for guidance,
as he brings life to the dead and healing to the ill.

15- He has exceeded the Messiah's miracles
with what the edge of the sword (*husam*) taught him about striking (*hasm*).

16- It was a time that designated no intimate companion,
save one who brought him what the Lord apportioned of knowledge.

17- O, king (*malik*) of the world, who manages peoples' affairs
with the management of one who never assumed power (*mulk*) by force,

18- who gives advantage to the sword in war with resolve,
and who is keen in conveying his message to the utmost of understanding,

19- whose ancestors bear kingship that is well established,
and to whom the greatest of kings bear witness by acknowledgement.

20- Amongst them you are held in the highest esteem in the east and west,
enjoying security from darkness (*zalam*) and injustice (*zulm*).

21- You replace in equal measure fear with security,
corruption with justice, and loss with gain.

22- You don the crown of kingship with valor,
from which the crown of time falls down prostrating itself grudgingly.

23- You make both sides of the throne (*sarir*) sway in joy (*masarra*)
with the breeze of wind, by [your] righteous rule and forbearance.

24- From eminence (*fadl*) and patronage (*ifdal*), you gird the necks of palaces
with jewels well strung like pearls on a pendant.

25- And whoever into whose mouth the pearly teeth return with a kiss
because of your extensive generosity

26- bows down whenever your face appears in wakefulness,
just as the stars bowed down to Joseph in his dream.

27- You raise high the star of good fortune in magnanimity,
and you send the best of the shooting stars into battle.

28- Fates make use of what you always strove for,
and they act upon all on which you left your mark.

29- I reckon that the vicissitudes of time have given you sovereignty (*hukm*),
and they have taken an oath: Let there be no exit from your rule (*hukm*).

30- [You are one] who turned them toward justice with the turning of a skilled man,
who is as insightful to the outcome of events as he is understanding [of them],

31- Were he to be viewed in some misfortune
then he would snicker with good tidings in its scornful face.

32- Noble thoroughbreds disclose these good tidings
and they are like lean horses unrestrained [from being tied up].

33- As though they race, more knowledgeable of battle than the enemy,
not belted with harnesses (*huzum*) but only with resolve (*huzm*).

34- [They are] fully laden armadas with troops who imitate vipers
in what they spit out of their venom.

35- If they reach a port in the morning, then victory before noon swears an oath
that they will have the lion's share of the spoils of war.

36- Thus, may be the resolve of kings,
but how rarely do you see a king bringing what you brought of resolution.

37- I have composed this panegyric to you certain that you are the one
who clothes me with pride with what saved me from humiliation.

38- The twist of fate has turned into my obedient servant
when once I had only known the misfortune of adversity.

The opening line of the poem explicitly names King William II, son of King William I, as the subject of the panegyric and who, by historical calculations, was either still under his mother's regency or recently declared king (in 1171).

In either event, the teenager was not sufficiently experienced nor accomplished as king to be credited with many of the attributes listed herein by Ibn Qalaqis, as suggested above. Nonetheless, the poem is a virtuosic display of poetic skill, replete with sophisticated uses of the rhetorical figures of high classical Abbasid *badi'* (i.e. synonyms, antonyms, homonyms etc.), that, when read or heard, would be most pleasing to a literate and sophisticated audience. There is no attempt at a reworking of the classical thematic sectioning, nor are there hints of an amatory preface, nor a journey through hostile terrain. The poet draws on conventional panegyric images and motifs that he deftly weaves throughout the poem to give it an aesthetic unity and narrative cohesion. The 'praising' itself is refracted through several dominant binary oppositions: celestial versus terrestrial, human versus animal, land versus sea; and secondary binaries: strength versus weakness, justice versus injustice, and knowledge versus ignorance, all essential components of medieval panegyrics. These binaries, in the main, fall well within the 'horizons of expectations' of *Jahili* and Islamic Arabic poetics, but it is Ibn Qalaqis's evocation of 'land and sea' in this poem that resonates particularly powerfully with the historical significance of Muslim Sicily and Norman Sicily to the wider medieval Mediterranean world. What Fatimid naval power and skill accomplished, and what their Norman successors built on, defined the contours of war and peace that shaped and reshaped medieval Sicilian history, and the poet manipulates this quite effectively.

On the other hand, the poem lacks two standard features of Arabic panegyrics of the classical period: a personal relationship or bonding (real or imagined) between the poet and the praised, and I would extend this to the poet and the land; and explicit or implicit references to Islamic historical consciousness. The lack of these two features draws attention to some important distinctions between Ibn Qalaqis's poem and those penned by 'native' Sicilians. Apart from the obvious fact that a young king held by the tight grip of his protective regent/mother and her inner circle of court advisors would not be in a position of bonding (real or imagined) with a court poet, Ibn Qalaqis was very much the 'foreigner', and as a non-native Muslim Arab visitor to the island during undisputed Norman sovereignty and rule, he had no personal local experience to draw on. Although he may have enjoyed the good graces of his Muslim patron, Ibn Hajar, he would hardly be in a position to gain access to the palace against its bureaucrats and Norman barons hostile to Muslims. We can safely imagine him as one of those transient travellers passing through the island Ibn Jubayr would eventually warn about who were seduced by the Norman Kings into their patronage. Much of the praising verses are cast in the third person, with infrequent interjections of the second person, save for the last three lines of the poem. This renders the overall tone and sentiment of the poem as abstract and impersonal. Furthermore, and more significantly, there is no mention – in stark contrast to the poems to Roger II, not to mention the poems of Ibn Hamdis – of Sicily as 'sacred' space, as homeland or as idyllic paradise. The poem is suspended in both place and time, again, reinforcing the abstract and impersonal. The aim, as stated in the last two lines of the poem, is clear: *I am here at your service with hopes of escape from adversity and humiliation.*

Secondly, the poem is devoid of any Islamic references, images or theologically loaded language. There are, however, several references peppered throughout the poem that may be read as references to esoteric Fatimid Shi'ite doctrine, such as the centrality of reason and intellect in matters of faith, and the role of the leader to be divinely guided and, in turn, to guide the community to knowledge and understanding. But since these concepts were shared universal themes of Neoplatonism, they could very well have been understood as neutral enough not to offend Muslim sensibilities. However, the prevailing practice among anthologists of deleting lines of poems penned by Muslim poets in praise of the Normans using Islamic explicit language and imagery deemed inappropriate, sacrilegious or treasonous may very well have compelled Ibn Qalaqis to use caution and restraint in this regard. The poet opts instead for a historical continuum that bridges the Old and New Testament to suggest legitimation of King William as essential to the praise. Kings David and Solomon bequeath their kingship and rule to the Normans (line 1), and the (eleven) stars bow to King William as they did to the Biblical Joseph (line 26). Ibn Qalaqis uses the comparison of Jesus and his ability to work miracles (lines 14–15) as a way to praise his patron in the context of Christian history and theology. In this regard, Ibn Qalaqis echoes the Sicilian poets, 'Abd al-Rahman al-Buthayri and 'Abd al-Rahman al-Atrabanshi, as well as al-Idrisi in his *Introduction*, in their references to the Caesars, in order to make it clear that these praises were not of Islamic provenance. In a place and time when faith was of paramount importance to all aspects of political, social and literary life, and when political legitimacy was understood as having come from God, no credible poem of praise would be received without some reference to divine intervention. Additionally, after centuries of coexistence, the Muslims and Christians of twelfth-century Sicilian were sufficiently knowledgeable about each other's faiths, and apart from any residual debates among the religious scholars concerning the divinity of Christ, the Trinity, or the nature of prophethood that continued to divide them, they surely came to the realization that accusations of infidelity need no longer be taken literally. Thus, the impersonal, generic tone of the poem and the refrain from Islamic references keep the poem safe from would-be religious or political critics, while the references to God's hand and exquisite linguistic artistry give the poem both literary merit and historical value.

Nearly forty years had passed between the death of Ibn Hamdis and the composition of Ibn Qalaqis's panegyric to William II. Apart from the obvious differences between the two poets (i.e. their physical and political stances towards the Norman Court), they did share a passion and talent for Arabic poetry and poetics. Whatever their worldly aims and aspirations were – the liberation of a beloved homeland for Ibn Hamdis, and a sanctuary, albeit transient, from the pending dissolution of the Fatimid Empire in Egypt – both men sought and found comfort and stability in the centuries-old traditions of classical Arabic poetry and in all that it offered of mobility, dichotomy and advocacy. But whatever bound them together was unfastened by the forces of history. In those thirty years, Count Roger was coronated King Roger, and his empire building included not only incorporating the best of three cultures but also an aggressive expansion into the wider Mediterranean, where he succeeded in establishing Norman colonies throughout Ifriqiya. It was also in this brief but critical period when the might of the Christian Reconquest was exerting itself, especially through the influx of mainland Lombards into Sicily, the growth of Pisan and Genoese naval and mercantile power, and relentless pressure from the Vatican, much to the disadvantage of whatever remained of the Muslim community. The emigration from the island, particularly by the educated and professional elites, and the decreasing influence of Arabic culture and scholarship, however much they were still cherished by the Norman kings, took a toll on Sicilian *Dar al-Islam*.[18] Ibn Hamdis and Ibn Qalaqis stood at opposite ends of the spectrum of the zone of contradiction where invective and praise could be read as milestones of the Sicilian jihad.

***

When the historian Ibn al-Athir recorded his account of the downfall of Muslim Sicily, it should be recalled, he ended it with a description of Roger II's ascendency to rule on the island, stating that he

> followed the customs of Muslim rulers, kept in place [Muslim] court positions and other governing structures, and established a court of grievances that protected the rights of all citizens, winning, whereby, the loyalty and affection of the island's Muslim population.[19]

The passage above, when read literally, strongly suggests that the 'changing of the guard', or the establishment of a 'new world order', to use modern parlance, was not as traumatic or shocking to Muslim Sicilians as one might have imagined over the centuries. Also, given the fact that Ibn al-Athir's chapter on Muslim Sicily's downfall is replete, as indicated earlier, with descriptions of political divisiveness among Muslims, civil unrest and shifts in loyalties that paved the way for a successful Norman conquest, it would be natural that the Arab defeat came as little surprise to the Sicilians.

What I see as easing the transition, and central to Ibn al-Athir's praise of Roger II, as well as what the court poets extolled of Norman virtues and accomplishments, is the adoption of Muslim practices. The praise passages are constructed on the premise that Roger was seen (or imagined) as fitting into a continuum that began with the establishment and development of an Islamic 'state' two centuries earlier. Roger's reign was legible to Ibn Athir, as it must have been to contemporary Muslims, insofar as he adopted practices in line with Muslim political culture, and thus deemed rightfully deserving of praise for looking like and acting like a Muslim sovereign. In addition to the appropriation of Arabic royal titles and inscriptions, and in line with both earlier Kalbid Palermitan court custom as well as the wider Fatimid Empire centred in Egypt, Roger's legitimacy in the eyes of his Muslim subjects was derived from a shared set of values and attributes that applied to all those who ruled an *umma*. Long accustomed to the ethos and practices of *dhimma* (i.e. protection of peoples of other (scriptural) faiths) and to the complexities of cross-cultural conflict, the Sicilian Muslims were prepared for and resigned to the changes, as long as the rules applied.

In the *Chronicon* of Romuald of Salerno, we read that in the last years of his life, Roger II turned to religious matters and 'labored in every conceivable way to convert Jews and Muslims to the faith of Christ, and endowed converts with many gifts and resources'.[20] In the nearly half century of his rule (1105–54), Roger II presided over massive changes that clearly took Sicily into different directions, with extensive immigration of northern Italians and other Christians to the island and an increasingly acerbic Crusading rhetoric that applied pressure against any fostering of Muslim-Christian relations across the Mediterranean Basin. He also weathered the natural, existential changes in a man coming face-to-face with his own mortality. The rule of Roger II clearly falls into that zone of contradiction, wherein on the one hand, he established a kingdom and promoted a courtly culture that extracted the best of local traditions and practices by which he cultivated tolerance and learning, and on the other hand, he presided over an aggressive and assertive resurgence of Christian political, military and economic domination over Sicily and beyond its borders.

As long as King Roger remained accessible and responsive to his own defeated Muslim community and legible within the broader Muslim cultural and political idiom, and as long as the Norman Court continued to function as a contact zone for all of Norman, Byzantine and Muslim Sicily, we read the extant verses cited above as credible articulations of a coexistence that sang the praises of its chief architect. And given the loyalty to traditional poetic forms and adherence to Arabic as an imperial language, as Karla Mallette observed, we can make safe conjectures about the deleted portions of the poems at the hands of anthologists who either took it upon themselves or perforce were pressured by powerful (political, religious or cultural) patrons to police the Arabic language and its cultural production.

In my reading of the extant Arabic verses composed to Roger II, along with al-Idrisi's lavish praise of his patron in his introduction to *Kitab Rujar*, as testaments to a multicultural humanism that was a hallmark of the Norman Court of Sicily, I argue nonetheless for alternative readings of the Arabic panegyrics to the Normans, if only to bridge the gap between a highly abstract patronage poetics and between the political realities unfolding on the ground.

Firstly, I argue that these Arabic panegyrics of twelfth-century Sicily were penned against a tide of gradually increasing duress for the Muslim community. Whether composed by writers of prose or poetry, from (i) those who were well ensconced within the Court (*al-Idrisi*) or (ii) those who enjoyed limited access via trade, military service or profession (scribes, lawyers, physicians) or (iii) those who came to the island from outside (Ibn Qalaqis, Ibn Jubayr), it was clear that the Norman Court as a site for religious, linguistic and cultural synthesis and tolerance, however maintained and protected especially by Roger II, William II, and to project forward by Frederick II in the first half of the thirteenth century, was losing ground to the powerful forces of the Christian Reconquest.

Secondly, I argue that the extant verses to Roger II were as much a tribute to Muslim Sicily itself – something akin to what we might imagine in our own time to be 'national literature'. In the fashion of their compatriot Ibn Hamdis, in exile across the Mediterranean, these twelfth-century poets gave Sicily prominence, especially in their description (*wasf*) segments, imagining the island as sacred homeland and paradisiacal landscape, replete with a lush environment provided by God and luxurious palaces and gardens constructed by Roger II in the fashion of Muslim rulers. I read these poems as targeting a cultured, but dwindling, Arabic Muslim community anxious about its present and future, as much as they target Roger II and his palace functionaries who might – or might not – have understood them. In the vein of Ibn Hamdis's art, these verses extol Sicily as sacred space, but unlike Ibn Hamdis's vitriolic diatribes against the Norman conquest, they embrace what Roger was able to imitate and preserve of their customs and safeguard their existence on the island. Above all, I read these panegyrics as cultural-political capital with which the dwindling Arab community could negotiate their livelihood and survival in a world of rapid change and uncertainty. As long as Arabic poetry, in all its traditional language and form, thrived at court ceremonies, and as long as Arabic high culture and expertise penetrated the administrative and cultural sectors of government, the Normans could boast a kingdom like no other. These poems were reminders to both the victors and the vanquished of what Sicily was able to achieve by way of the nobler values of the greater jihad.

Finally, I read these poems as articulations of *fitna*: *fitna* as 'seduction' and *fitna* as 'chaos'. As Ibn Jubayr's diary shows, it was not just the power and wealth of the lucrative Norman royal patronage that seduced Muslims but also the presence of a non-hostile Christian population who, in choosing to live their lives with a degree of *convivencia*, challenged the Muslims of Sicily – reduced in numbers, political and economic power, and cultural significance – to maintain their Arab-Islamic identity. For all who lived on the island, whether they were employed as palace guards or soldiers, domestic servants, or even court poets, or whether they were young men or women seeking to marry Christian Sicilians, or – God forbid! – convert to Christianity, the reality of Muslim life of twelfth-century Sicily bestrode the dual meanings of *fitna* as seduction and chaos. Ibn Jubayr's anxieties about coexistence in a time of turmoil and his warnings against seduction emanated from his awareness of an historical dynamic in which Muslims were on the decline. Like Ibn Hawqal two centuries earlier, Ibn Jubayr could not help but marvel at the wonders of Sicily and at the same time sense the potential dangers of cross-cultural contact. The Sicily from Roger II to William II gradually produced a threatening environment, notwithstanding well-intended Norman Court patronage, in which the Lombard baron classes and a belligerent Crusader mentality were on the rise. For young Muslims living their lives in mid-twelfth-century Sicily, the worlds of *Dar al-Islam* and *Dar al-Harb* no longer existed on favourable Islamic terms. And at the same time, such a Manichaean world view lost its political and cultural significance in light of the centuries of sharing a common life. The Arab poets' evocation of the Caesars and Ibn Qalaqis's references to (old and new) Biblical figures are articulations of submission to these historical realities.

Postscript

In the third decade of the thirteenth century, the Muslim communities of western Sicily rose up in rebellion against their Christian governors. It had been some sixty years since the anti-Norman riots of 1160 and thirty-five years since the death of King William II. The 'Saracens', as they had come to be called since that time and henceforth, still made up a significant percentage of the population of the major urban centres of Palermo, Trapani and Agrigento, as well as areas of the adjacent countryside. The reasons for these public revolts can be clearly imagined given the steady decline of Arab and Muslim power and influence on the island. The 'the long-term malaise and brewing discontent in the Muslim community', as Alex Metcalfe aptly describes it,[1] were the understandable results of the vast changes taking place over the central Mediterranean, which came to the detriment of those Muslims who, by choice or per force, continued to inhabit the island.

Recently returning from an overseas adventure to consolidate his empire, King Frederick II made a radical decision to solve the *Saracen* problem. He rounded up as many of the island's Muslims and Jews he could and relocated them to the province of Apulia (Puglia) in the southwest of the Italian mainland. His aim was twofold: first, he wanted to rid Sicily, the crown jewel of his empire, of a major source of discontent in order to appease the island's powerful barons and to address the growing criticism, spearheaded by the Vatican, of his avoidance in fighting in the fifth Crusade; second, he intended to preserve the Muslim and Jewish Sicilian communities, protect them from their rapacious Christian enemies, and above all reap the benefits of their knowledge and skills. His goal to create an agricultural and mercantile hub centred around the city of Lucera, 11 miles northwest of the city of Foggia, was high-priority master plan to resolve the Saracen issue once and for all while expanding the economic bases of his realm.

It is Roger II, as we have seen, who features prominently in medieval Muslim Sicilian historiography as the founding father of a multicultural Norman Sicily. However, he has ultimately been eclipsed in world history by his grandson, Frederick II (1194–1250), who survives to this day as the most illustrious personality of medieval multicultural Sicily. Frederick was born to Constance (the daughter born posthumously to King Roger II) and Henry VI (1165–1197), a member of the Hohenstaufen dynasty and king of the Holy Roman Empire. In many ways, Frederick deserves the lion's share of credit for Sicily's reputation as the beacon of medieval Mediterranean multiculturalism and cosmopolitanism. He spoke numerous languages; he was a scholar and statesman who patronized the arts and scholarship from across the Mediterranean Basin; and he presided over a court that played a major role in the birth of Italian vernacular poetry (*la scuola siciliana*) that would guide Sicily into the future.

Like his grandfather, Frederick's rule and realm fall well within the 'zone of contradiction'. His epithet of *stupor mundi* (wonder of the world) captures the extraordinary image he held in both his own times and in perpetuity, and his titles – King of Sicily and King of Jerusalem – would sound contradictory even in his own time and place. His nicknames or labels span the positive and negative, depending upon how one viewed him: 'baptized sultan', 'antichrist' or 'messiah'; all connote ambivalence and contradiction.

The Kurdish historian, Abu al-Fida' Isma'il ibn 'Ali (1273–1331), has bequeathed to us an account of a visit to Apulia by Jalal al-Din ibn Wasil (1208–1298), historian, logician, judge and emissary who served in both the Ayyubid and Mamluke governments in Syria.[2] In 1260, the Mamluke Sultan Baybars dispatched Ibn Wasil on an embassy to King Manfred, son of Frederick. In his account, Abu al-Fida' reports an earlier deal or compromise (*munasafa*) that had been concluded between the Ayyubid sultan, al-Malik al-Kamil, and the Frankish emperor, Frederick II, whereby the Ayyubids would restore the Latin kingdom of Jerusalem in exchange for Crusader withdrawal from Egypt. Abu al-Fida' reports that Ibn Wasil described the emperor (Frederick II) as a man of distinction, a lover of philosophy, logic, and medicine, and partial towards the Muslims because he was raised in Sicily, where the majority of its inhabitants are Muslim.

In a later recording of Ibn Wasil's obituary in the year 1298, Abu l-Fida' again quoted Ibn Wasil as praising Emperor Frederick for possessing a (brotherly) affection (*musafiyan*) for the Ayyubid monarch, al-Malik al-Kamil, and added that both his sons and successors, King Conrad and King Manfred, (also) had a brotherly affection for Muslims and favoured their scholars. Quoting Ibn Wasil, Abu al-Fida' wrote: 'When I arrived [in Apulia], the Emperor Manfred welcomed me with honor and I resided with him in one of the towns in Apulia. I met with him frequently and found him to excel in the rational sciences.' He continued, 'In the city of Lucera, all the inhabitants are Muslims from Sicily, and there the Friday sermon is held, the banners of Islam wave, the call to prayer rings out, and many of the king's entourage are Muslims.'[3]

Abu al-Fida's account of Ibn Wasil's journey to Apulia echoes the many statements and sentiments of the previously mentioned historians, travellers and poets who lavished praises on the Norman kings and their successors. That is, as long as the Christian rulers of Sicily, from Roger II to Frederick II and his son Manfred, behaved in the manner of Muslim rulers and respected and protected their Muslim subjects and nurtured their culture, and as long as they remained faithful to the Arab Islamic codes of good government, they were deserving of praise. Ibn Wasil's snapshots of royal Norman Sicilian benevolence towards Islam and Muslims come, however, against the reality of Lucera as site of Muslim expulsion from the paradisiacal Sicily Ibn Hamdis ached for and the panegyrists of Roger II celebrated. On the one hand, the amicable relationship between Frederick and al-Malik al-Kamil was based on shared human values of intellectual curiosity and scholarly inquiry, reinforced repeatedly in Abu al-Fida's narrative, which were the hallmarks of both Islam's 'spiritual (greater) jihad' and the essence of the 'Norman synthesis'. On the other hand, the relationship was the product of continuous warfare, the 'physical jihad' and 'Crusades' of a long-standing Muslim-Christian contestation for power and dominance over the Mediterranean.

The world of Frederick II's Sicily and that of his son and successor, King Manfred, continued to exist as contested space in which, I have been arguing throughout, Sicily held a central position, and its Muslim 'citizens', to borrow a modern term, played a major role. Throughout the accounts, descriptions, praises and invectives of all those Arab poets, travellers and historians who told their stories about Islam in Sicily in the world of the medieval Mediterranean run the interlacing threads that quite often wove complex patterns of war and peace where the intersections of *Dar al-Islam* and *Dar al-Harb* were blurred, destabilized, trespassed and criss-crossed. Muslim Sicily, like Roman, Byzantine, Norman, and Bourbon Sicilies, had a 'rise and fall', as Ibn Khaldun would see it. But each of these Sicilian histories wrestled with tensions that lay between native and foreign, occupier and occupied, ruler and ruled, urban and rural, religious and secular, oppression and tolerance, war and peace.

In drawing towards my conclusion, I return to my earlier point about the fictional cosmos of modern Sicilian stories that draw from the Muslim era of the island's history. Here I cite a short story of Giuseppe Bonaviri (1924–2009), curiously but charmingly entitled, 'Jesus and Juha' (*Jesu e Giuffa*), which tells the story of an infant abandoned in a cave by his unmarried mother, Maria, and raised by a bereft mother sheep.[4] One day, when he was eight years old, he encounters a cobbler on his way to the village. The cobbler asks him if he is a Saracen, noticing his dark skin. The cobbler goes on to tell him that the village once belonged to them (i.e. the Saracens) and laments that 'these days we are like the spider dangling by a thread over the ravine'. When the boy asks for an explanation, the cobbler replies: 'I mean to say that our king and lord (may God Macone protect him!) Ased-ibn-Forat-Ibn-Sinan, a Great Doctor, was defeated by King Frederick, our most vicious enemy.' 'Watch out! Be careful,' the cobbler warns the boy.

The pairing of Jesus and Juha (known in Sicily and southern Italy as Giufa), the beloved character of Arabic folklore known for his simplicity of mind and his wisdom, might strike the reader as odd, given that the two characters lived in different historical and literary worlds. But to the Sicilian reader, or to those who know something about Sicilian history, the pairing bears a measure of logic and credence, given that the island, deeply ensconced in Christianity, was home to four centuries of Arab Islamic civilization. The choice of Juha/Giufa is also noticeably curious in that one would expect (the prophet) Muhammad to be the obvious counterpart to Jesus, but the story evokes a world of the everyday, of the simple men and women who shared a common life with their Muslim neighbours, a world that is celebrated, or at least reflected upon, in this and other stories in Bonaviri's collection.

The parallel pairing of the two characters in the cobbler's tale, Ased-ibn-Forat-Ibn-Sinan and King Frederick, is equally curious in that both men lived centuries apart. And, again, similarly the pairing bears historical logic in that these men are the bookends of the era of Muslim Sicily: Asad ibn al-Furat was the commander of the army that invaded Sicily in the early ninth century, which eventually brought Arabs and Islam to the island, and Frederick II expelled the Arabs from it four hundred years later. What links these two men together is that they were both scholars and warriors, combining what I have been arguing throughout, in Islamic terms, the spiritual (greater) and physical (lesser) jihad. As king of Sicily and emperor of the Holy Roman Empire, Frederick II commanded armies, embarked on imperial conquest and fought his enemies wherever they were found. He also was a student of many languages and a scholar interested in the sciences, philosophy, music and poetry. He authored a book on falconry, *De Arte Venandi cum Avibus*, promulgated a code of laws for his kingdom, *Liber Augustalis* (The Constitutions of Melfi, Syracuse, 1971), and hosted at his court and patronized scientists and translators who participated in the transmission of knowledge between languages and cultures.

No less impressive was Asad ibn al-Furat who, four centuries earlier, commanded the successful Muslim expedition that ushered Arabs and Islam into Sicily. Asad chose to pursue a scholarly career and studied the Islamic disciplines and law at the feet of the greatest scholars of his day, in his native Ifriqiya, as well as in the Hejaz, Iraq and Egypt. He authored an authoritative manual on Islamic jurisprudence and engaged in public disputations on the most critical issues in Muslim legal thinking. Recall the sermon he delivered on that early summer day in June 827 to his troops and the masses assembled at the port of Susa:

> Exert your minds and labor your bodies in the search and pursuit of knowledge; increase it and be patient with its intensity, for with it you will gain this world and the next.

The sermon helps us appreciate the rich significance of Bonaviri's coupling of Asad with Frederick to conjure an image of a Muslim Sicilian past.

The fictional cosmos of Bonaviri's *Novelle Saracene* collection is inhabited with a mixed population of kings and wizards, peasants and mystics, and a cast of colourful common folk with fixed and hybrid identities, collectively bearing witness to both a lived multiculturalism and rich story-telling traditions in which the island and its inhabitants have long taken pride. The Sicilian landscape of Bonaviri's stories is a mosaic dotted with mountains and valleys, caves and ravines, fields and forests that provide natural backgrounds to Sicily's kaleidoscopic history. Bonaviri's diptych image of Asad ibn al-Furat and Frederick II nonetheless captures all the complexities and contradictions that made the island's history. Above all, it vividly portrays the duality of war and peace that played a central role in it.

The Arab historians, poets, geographers and travellers who comprise the cast of characters in these five chapters recorded events, made their analyses and judgements, described, preached, warned, praised and vilified along the vertical and horizontal lines of war and peace in Muslim Sicily. They wrote between the literal and figurative meanings of jihad as they tried to make sense of what God wants and what men do. Theirs was a 'jihad of the tongue', as Sahnun would have it, using their words to engage the enemy, whoever he may be, and persuade and invite to God's cause. Few of them lived to see Muslim Sicily rising or falling, while many others wrote by unearthing the treasures of the historical and literary archives. But the stories they told through their observations, insights, emotions and experiences have left us a vast terrain of writing on which we can tread to comprehend a highly complex time and place of peace and war specific to the Mediterranean's largest island.

Notes

Preface

1 Bernard Lewis, *Islam from the Prophet Muhammad to the Capture of Constantinople* (New York, 1974), p. 99: Ibn Hawqal writes: 'I described their sect, which is unlike any other sect in Islam or any creed in any [Muslim] land and heresy, nor indeed does it resemble the beliefs of any other religion at all. They are tricksters [?]. The majority of the inhabitants of the cities, countryside, and the villages practice marriage with Christian women, the male children being tricksters [?] like their fathers, while the females are Christians like their mothers. They do not perform the prayer; they do not observe ritual purity; they do not give legal alms; they do not go on pilgrimages. Some of them observe the fast of Ramadan and then commit uncleanliness and wash themselves after it during the fast.'

2 'Abd al-Salam Sahnun ibn Sa'id, *al-Mudawwana al-Kubra li al-Imam Malik*, Part I (Beirut, 1986), pp. 367–9.

Chapter 1

1 'Abd al-Rahman ibn Khaldun, *al-Muqaddima*, 'Abd al-Salam al-Shadadi (ed.) (Casablanca, 2005), pp. 296–8.

2 Qur'an 47: 35. The translation is that of Ahmed Ali, *al-Quran: A Contemporary Translation* (Princeton, 1988).

3 See Abu Bakr 'Abdallah al-Maliki, *Riyad al-Nufus*, Husayn Mu'nis (ed.) (Cairo, 1951). The most complete accounts of these debates are provided in the entries of this volume: Abu 'Abdallah Asad ibn al-Furat ibn Sinan, pp. 172–89; and Abu Muhriz Muhammad ibn 'Abdallah, pp. 189–96. For a further study on Asad ibn al-Furat, see William Granara, 'Ibn al-Sabil: Crossing Boundaries in the Biography of Asad ibn al-Furat', *Scripta Mediterranea* XIX–XX (1998-9), pp. 259–67; and Umberto Rizzitano, 'Asad ibn al-Furat giuresconsulto dell'Ifriqiya', in *Storia e Cultura nella Sicilia Saracena* (Palermo, 1975), pp. 3–19.

4 *Siyar* is best translated as the 'literature of international relations'.

5   Al-Maliki, *Riyad al-Nufus*, p. 188.
6   Georges Marcais, 'Aghlabids', in *Encyclopedia of Islam (second edition)* (Leiden, 1960–2009), pp. 247–50. **Henceforth: *EI*.**
7   Mohamed Talbi, *L'Emirat Aghlabide 184–28* (Paris, 1966), pp. 213–4.
8   Michele Amari, *Biblioteca arabo-sicula* (Lipsia, 1857); Ibn al-Athir #35, pp. 240; Ibn Khaldun #50, pp. 474–5. **Henceforth: *BAS*.**
9   See Marius Canard, 'Fatimids', *EI* 2 (1965), pp. 850–62. Also Farhat Dachraoui, *Le Califat Fatimide au Maghreb 296–365 AH/909–975* (Tunis, 1981); and Antonino Pellitteri, *I Fatimiti e la Sicilia* (Palermo, 1996).
10 Kharijism began in early Islamic history as a movement of political opposition to the arbitration between the partisans of 'Ali and the forces of al-Mu'awiya ibn Abi Sufyan in 658. Its appeal in Ifriqiya, particularly among the Berbers, rests on its rejection of both the Sunni and Shi'ite notions of political legitimacy.
11 Raqqada, a medieval palatine town located *c.*5 miles southwest of Qayrawan, was the residence of the Aghlabid ruler Ibrahim II (r.875–902). It was briefly occupied by the first Fatimid rulers until they completed their city of al-Mahdiyya on the eastern coast of Tunisia. Raqqada survives in ruins and of late has become a major site for archaeological exploration.
12 The most complete genealogy of the author is given as al-Nu'man ibn Abi 'Abdallah Muhammad ibn Mansur ibn Ahmad ibn Hayyun al-Tamimi al-Isma'ili al-Maghribi Abu Hanifa. See A. A. Fyzee, 'Al-Qadi al-Nu'man', *EI* 6/51 (1935), pp. 953–4.
13 Abu Hanifa Muhammad al-Qadi al-Nu'man, *Da'a'im al-Islam wa Dhikr al-Halal wa al-Haram wa al-Qadaya wa al-Ihkam 'an Ahl Bayt Rasul Allah*, A. A. Fyzee (ed.) (Cairo, 1951).
14 Al-Qadi al-Nu'man, *Iftitah al-da'wa*, Farhat Dachraoui (ed.) (Tunis, 1975).
15 Ibid., pp. 256–7.
16 Edward W. Lane, *An Arabic-English Lexicon*, Part 6 (Beirut, 1976), p. 2398.
17 Al-Qadi al-Nu'man, *Iftitah*, p. 191.
18 Ibid., pp. 253–4.
19 Michele Amari, *Storia dei Musulmani di Sicilia*, Carlo A. Nallino (ed.) (Catania, 1933), II, pp. 168–9. **Henceforth: *SMS*.**
20 Ibn al-Athir reports widespread opposition in Ifriqiya: 'On Fridays a man known as al-Sharif conducted the post-sermon study sessions accompanied by the missionaries. They forced the residents of the town to attend and they invited them to join their sect. Those who accepted were treated well; those who did not were imprisoned. Only a small number actually complied. A large number of those who refused were put to death.' (*BAS* 35, p. 250).

Also, there was opposition from radical Kharijite elements. The persistent anti-Fatimid campaign, launched by Abu Yazid between 883 and 947 and culminating in the occupation of Qayrawan and the siege of Mahdiyya and Susa, was not put to an effective end until al-Mansur (r.946–53) staged a violent counter-campaign against him.

21 'Ali had been elected to rule Sicily by the people of Palermo while Abu Mudar Ziyadat Allah III was ruling as emir in North Africa. Amari suggests two reasons for his election: first, as a reaction against the parricide, and second, as a reaction against Ahmad ibn Abi al-Husayn's harsh rule. Citing a Greek manuscript found in the Vatican and describing it as being comparable to that of *Cronica di Cambridge (Cambridge Chronicle)*, (*BAS* 27), Amari writes: '*Sotto l'emirato di Ahmad ibn Abi al-Husayn ibn Rabah devi porsi una grave persecuzione contro i Cristiani di Sicilia*'. (Amari, *SMS* II, pp. 165–6, fn #3).

22 Amari, *SMS* II, p. 173.

23 The use of '*al-'Arab*' among the historians to describe those elements of the army that intervened to protect Ibn Qurhub's son is intriguing. It more than likely suggests elite and powerful Arab factions in the army, as opposed to Berber, Slav or other groupings.

24 Aleksandr A. Vasiliev, *Byzance et les Arabes*, Marius Canard (ed.) (Brussels, 1935–50), pp. 226–7. Vasiliev writes: 'There had been a reaction in Sicily against Ibn Qurhub on the part of the Berbers who refused to obey him and elected instead a man named Ja'far. The later succeeded in capturing Ibn Qurhub after concluding a treaty with the Byzantines, and he sent him to Fatimid court in Ifriqiya where he was put to death.'

25 Amari, *SMS* II, p. 173: '*Non ando guari ch'ei compiva maggior sagrifizio, gittandosi nella voragine della rivoluzione; non per leggerezza, non per vanita, non per ambizioni, ma ad occhi aperti; per religion d'animo generoso, quando conobbe che v'era da tentar con un dado contro centro, la liberazione della patria dall'Affrica insieme e dall'anarchia.*'

26 The anonymous author of the *Cambridge Chronicle* records several incidents like the following: 'Two officials came with Salim's son, al-Balazmi and al-Qalashani and they imposed fines on the people' (*BAS* 27, p. 170).

27 Again, the *Cambridge Chronicle* provides accounts that, although seemingly exaggerated, reveal a desperate situation: 'There was so much starvation at the time, in Palermo as well as in the countryside, that parents began to eat their children'; also, 'Agrigento was taken, starvation intensified and the fortress towns and countryside of Sicily were devastated'; and, 'In those days stealing and destruction increased, and the strong began to devour the poor' (*BAS* 27, p. 173).

28 See Umberto. Rizzitano, 'Kalbids', *EI* 4, pp. 496–7.
29 Ibid., Rizzitano describes the urgency of the appointment: 'Confronted by the chaotic situation caused by the rebellions in Palermo and Agrigento against the Fatimid representatives, the caliph al-Mansur deemed it logical and sensible to entrust Sicily's management to those whose fidelity was proven beyond doubt and who, moreover, could maintain a neutral stand between the rebels and the imams of Ifrikiya.'
30 Muhammad Abu al-Qasim Ibn Hawqal, *Surat al-Ard* (Beirut, 1979), p. 118. Also, see Adalgisa De Simone, 'Palermo nei geografi e viaggiatori Arabi del Medioevo', in *Studi Maghrebini II* (Naples, 1968), pp. 129–89.
31 Shihab al-Din al-Nuwayri, *BAS* 46, p. 441. The Egyptian historian Shihab al-Din al-Nuwayri (d.1333) succinctly describes it as follows: 'Rometta was captured after which many battles were fought between the Muslims and the Christians (infidels), including the Battle of the Straits. So many Christians died that the waters turned red. Then peace was made between al-Mu'izz and Domestico Nicephorus Phocas in 356, from whom he received gifts. Then al-Mu'izz notified the governor (of Sicily) al-Ahmad of the truce.'
32 Included in his list of military accomplishments was his defeat of the Hamdanid prince of Aleppo, Sayf al-Dawla, in 962, and the capture of Cyprus in 965. For a general discussion of his military and political accomplishments, see Romily Jenkins, *Byzantium: The Imperial Centuries AD 610–107* (New York, 1969), pp. 270–82.
33 Amari, *SMS* II, p. 377.
34 For a recent study on Sicilian Islam, see William Granara, 'Islamic education and the transmission of knowledge in Medieval Sicily', in J. Lowry, D. Stewart and S. Toorawa (eds), *Islamic Legal Education: Articles in Honor of George Makdisi* (London, 2004), pp. 150–73.
35 On the life and works of Ibn al-Khayyat, see William Granara, 'Rethinking Muslim Sicily's golden age: Poetry and patronage at the Fatimid Kalbid Court', *Alifba: Studi Arabo-Islamici e Mediterranei*, vol XXII (Palermo, 2008), pp. 95–108.
36 Ibn al-Athir, *BAS* 35, p. 274.
37 Ibid., p. 273.
38 The Arab historians differ on the exact date. See Idris, Hady Roger, *La Berberie Orientale Sous les Zirides, Xè-XIIè siècles* (Paris, 1962).
39 Ibn al-Athir, *BAS* 35, p. 275.
40 Ibid.

Chapter 2

1. Lane, *An Arabic-English Lexicon*, Book One, Part 2, p. 826.
2. Haydan White, 'The question of narrative in contemporary historical theory', *History and Theory* XXIII/1 (1984), p. 2.
3. Paul Ricoeur, 'Narrative time', *Critical Inquiry* 7 (1980), (Question 27: fn #53), p. 27.
4. H. White 'The value of narrativity in the representation of reality', *Critical Inquiry* 7/1 (Autumn 1980), p. 17.
5. Amari, *SMS*, pp. 367–81.
6. Ferdinando Gabotto, '*Eufemio e il movimento separatist nell'Italia Bizantina*', *La Letteratura*, v-vi (Torino, 1890).
7. John B. Bury, 'The naval policy of the Roman Empire in relation to the westen provinces from the 7th to 9th century', in *Centenario della Nascita di Michele Amari* (Palermo, 1910), pp. 21–34.
8. Vasiliev, *Byzance et les Arabes*, pp. 83–7.
9. The terminology employed in these late-nineteenth- to early-twentieth-century accounts of Euphemius resonate with nineteenth-century ideas of the nation-state, self rule and national independence. The reading of Euphemius as national hero and the claim that he sought to restore to Sicily a vestige of the Roman Empire echo the then current views within European imperialist discourse that included Mussolini's doctrine of '*Mare Nostrum*', as well as the civilization-decline theories in colonial French justification for its presence in Algeria.
10. Olivia R. Constable, *Housing the Stranger in the Medieval World* (Cambridge, 2003). On her comments on Sicily, see pp. 202–18.
11. Bronislaw Geremek, 'The marginal man', in Jacques Le Goff (ed.), *Medieval Callings* (Chicago, IL, 1990), pp. 34–72.
12. Ibid., p. 351.
13. Ibid., p. 358.
14. Roy Mottahedeh, *Loyalty and Leadership in an Early Islamic Society* (Princeton, NJ, 1980).
15. Ibid., p. 181.
16. Patricia Crone, 'Mawla', *EI* VI, pp. 874–82.
17. Ibid., p. 877.
18. Ibn al-Athir, *BAS* 37, p. 270.
19. Abu 'Uthman 'Amr al-Jahiz, *Rasa'il*, 'Abd al-Salam Muhammad Harun (ed.) (Cairo, 1964, 1979), pp. 139–82. Also Alfred F. L. Beeston (ed.), *The Epistle on Singing Girls of Jahiz* (Wiltshire, 1980).

20 It was suggested that Jawhara was a gift from the 'Abbadid prince al-Mu'tamid, although nothing in the *Diwan* supports this. See Zin al-'Abdin al-Sanusi, *'Abd al-Jabbar ibn Hamdis: Hayatuh wa Adabuh* (Tunis, 1983), p. 61.
21 Nachman Ben-Yehuda, *Betrayals and Treason: Violations of Trust and Loyalty* (Boulder, CO, 2001), p. 17.
22 'A fifth column is a group of people who clandestinely undermine a larger group, such as a nation, from within, to the aid of an external enemy. The term originated with a 1936 radio address by Emilio Mola, an insurgent general during the 1936–39 Spanish Civil War'. http://en.wikipedia.org/wiki/Fifth_column.
23 Hans Speier, *Treachery in War, Studies in War and Peace* No. 5, *Social Research* 7 (September 1940), pp. 258–79.
24 Abu 'Abdallah Muhammad al-Himyari, *Kitab al-Rawd al-Mi'tar fi Khabar al-Aqtar*, E. Lévi-Provençal (ed.) (Cairo, 1937), p. 88.
25 Speier, *Treachery*, p. 258.
26 Suzanne Pinckney Stetkevych, *The Poetics of Islamic Legitimacy* (Bloomington, IN, 2002), p. 119.
27 Robert D. King, 'Treason and traitors', *Society* 26/5 (1989), p. 39.
28 Enrico Pozzi, 'Le paradigme du traitre', in *De La Trahision* (Paris, 1999), p. 1.
29 Taqi al-din Ahmad ibn 'Ali al-Maqrizi, *Kitab al-Muqaffa al-Kabir: Tarajim Maghribiyyah wa-Mashriqiyya min al-Fatrah al-'Ubaydiyyah*, Muhammad al-Ya'lawi (ed.) (Beirut, 1987).
30 Jeremy Johns, *Arabic Administration in Norman Sicily* (Cambridge, 2002), pp. 80–8.

Chapter 3

1 Abu al-Fadl 'Iyad ibn Musa (al-Qadi), *Tartib al-Madarik wa Taqrib al-Masalik*, vol 4, Ahmad Bakir Mahmud (ed.) (Beirut, 1968), pp. 623–4.
2 al-Dawudi's *al-Nasiha fi sharh al-Bukhari* (now lost) is among the first commentaries from the medieval Muslim on al-Bukhari's (d. 256/870) magnum opus on *hadith*.
3 Abu Ja'far Ahmad ibn Nasr al-Dawudi, *Kitab al-Amwal*, Rida Shahada (ed.) (Rabat, n.d.), p. 7.
4 An anecdote relates that al-Dawudi's letter admonishing his Maliki colleagues for their cooperation with the Fatimid state was replied to with scorn: 'Be quiet, you who have no professor! (*Iskut lā shayka laka!*)'. Iyad ibn Musa, *Tartib*, p. 623.

5   See fn #1. Also, see Abdul-Wahhab al-Fili, Najib. *A Critical Edition of Kitab al-Amwal of Abu Ja'far Ahmad b. Nasr al-Dawudi (d. 401/H)*. PhD Thesis (University of Exeter, 1989). For a French translation, see 'Le regime foncier en Sicile au Moyen Age (IXè et Xè siècles)', in H. H. Abdulwahab and F. Dachraoui (ed. and trans.), *Etudes d'Orientalisme Dédiées à la Mémoire de Lévi-Provençal* (Paris, 1962). Also, see Cengiz Kallek, 'al-Dawudi: a North African Malikite observer of the economic disorder under the Fatimid Regime', *IIUM Journal of Economics and Management* 7/1 (1999), pp. 57–9.

6   Al-Dawudi, *Kitab al-Amwal*, Rida Shahada (ed.) (Rabat, n.d.), pp. 70–81. *Translation is mine*.

7   Meir. J. Kister, 'Land property and jihad', *Journal of the Economic and Social History the Orient* 24 (1991), p. 285.

8   Ibid., p. 311.

9   Abu al-Hasan 'Ali al-Mawardi, *al-Ahkam al-Sultaniyya* (Beirut, 1985).

10 It is not my intention to treat all works written within this genre during this period but rather those I believe to be most influential on al-Dawudi. Other prominent works include: Muhammad al-Shaybani (d.774), *Kitab al-Siyar*; Yahya ibn Adam (d.818), *Kitab al-Kharaj*; Abu 'Ubayd Sallam (d.841), *Kitab al-Amwal*; Abu Dawud al-Sijistani (d.890), *Sunan Abi Dawud*; Ibn Zanjawai, Hamid ibn Mukhlid (d.865), *Kitab al-Amwal*; Qudama ib. Ja'far (d.c.922), *Kitab al-Kharaj*. A. Ben Shemesh observes: 'A comparison between the theoretical precepts mentioned in the works of Abu Yusuf, Yahya ibn Adam, and Qudama ibn Ja'far reveal no differences worth mentioning.' See Ben Shemesh, *Abu Yusuf's Kitab al-Kharaj*, translated with introduction and notes by A. Ben Shemesh (Leiden, 1970), p. 32.

11 Malik ibn Anas, 'Kitab al-jihad', in Ahmad Ratib 'Armush (ed.), *al-Muwatta'* (Beirut, 1977), pp. 296–313.

12 John Wansbrough characterizes the *Muwatta'* as articulating a primarily 'apostolic theory of authority: first, in the sense of a paradigmatic behavior of the Prophet and his associates; second, in the sense of pronouncements on paradigmatic behavior by competent authorities'. Cited in Norman Calder, *Studies in Early Muslim Jurisprudence* (Oxford, 1993), p. 23.

13 Sahnun ibn Said, *al-Mudawwana al-Kubra*, pp. 367–402. I am aware of the question of authorship of this text, that is, Calder's assertion that it is not an authored text nor was its final form reached by way of a single authorial or redactional process. However, my intent is to show the current state of scholarship on these particular issues at the time. See Calder, *Studies*, p. 17. Also, Calder's

assertion that the composition of the *Mudawwana* was three decades prior to the *Muwatta'* has been persuasively contested. See Wael Hallaq, 'On dating Malik's *Muwatta'*, *UCLA Journal of Islamic and Near Eastern Law* 1 (2000–1), pp. 47–65.

14 Abu Yusuf Ya'qub, *Kitab al-Kharaj*, Ihsan 'Abbas (ed.) (Beirut, 1985).
15 Calder, *Studies in Early Muslim Jurisprudence*, pp. 106–7.
16 Ibid., p. 146.
17 Abu Yusuf, *Kitab al-Kharaj*, pp. 112–3. He writes: 'Leave the lands and the rivers to those who work on them so that they remain the bounty for [all] the Muslims; for if you apportion them to those who are here now, then nothing will remain for those who come after them.'
18 Calder emphasizes this point repeatedly in his article, 'The *Kitab al-kharaj* of Abu Yusuf'. He writes: 'Local and juristic materials advocating traditional payments and fixed sums were gathered, controlled, and redacted by government agents who submitted them to interpretative arguments designed to advocate taxation at capacity, according to government discretion, and usually in the form of a proportional tax.' Calder, *Studies in Early Islamic Jurisprudence*, p. 141.
19 Abu Yusuf, *Kitab al-Kharaj*, p. 174.
20 Dachraoui, *Le Califat Fatimide au Maghreb (909–975)*. My remarks here centre on the last chapter of his thesis, 'L'organisation judiciare', pp. 397–422.
21 For a comprehensive and more recent study on this subject, see Heinz Halm, *The Fatimids and Their Traditions of Learning* (London, 1997).
22 Abu al-'Arab Muhammad ibn Tamim and Muhammad ibn al-Harith al-Khushani, *Tabaqat 'Ulama' Ifriqiya*, Muhammad Ben Cheneb (ed.) (Beirut, n.d.), pp. 198–212. Also, for a discussion on these debates, see Sumaiya Hamdani, 'The dialectic of power: Sunni-Shi'ite debates in tenth century North Africa', *Studia Islamica* 90 (2000), pp. 5–21.
23 Al-Qadi al-Nu'man, *Iftitah al-Da'wa*, Farhat al-Dashrawi (ed.) (Tunis, 1975).
24 Al-Qadi al-Nu'man, *Da'a'im al-Islam wa Dhikr al-Halal wa al-Haram*, Asaf Fyzee (ed.) (Cairo, 1969).
25 Ya'qub Abu Yusuf, *Kitab al-Kharaj*, Ihsan 'Abbas (ed.) (Beirut, 1985), pp. 313–85.
26 Averil Cameron, *The Mediterranean World in Late Antiquity AD 395–600* (London, 1993), p. 84.
27 Emanuele Vaccaro, 'Sicily in the eighth and ninth centuries AD: A case of persisting economic complexity?' *Al-Masaq* 25/1 (2013), pp. 34–69. He argues for less hilltop-fortified sites and more rural settlements, 'characterized by the continuity of long-lasting large open sites, in many cases occupied until the Muslim and Norman period' (p. 61).

28 Ibn al-Athir, *BAS* 35, p. 228.
29 Al-Nuwayri, *BAS* 48, p. 435.
30 See Sayeed Sajjur Rahman, *The Legal and Political Thought of Ibn Abi Zayd al-Qayrawani (310–386) AH/922–996 CE*. Yale University Thesis (2009), pp. 58–60.
31 Khaled Abou El Fadl, *Rebellion and Violence in Islamic Law* (Cambridge, 2001), pp. 33.
32 Ibid., p. 8.
33 Granara, 'Islamic education', p. 156; see fn #18 for primary and secondary sources.
34 Mohamed Talbi, *Tarajim aghlabiyya* (Tunis, 1968), p. 105. 'As soon as [Sahnun] assumed the post of chief judge he dispersed from the Grand Mosque [of Qayrawan] those study groups who promoted heresy and he chased away the free thinkers. Among them were the Sufri and Ibadhi Kharijites, as well as the Muʿtazilites who would hold public disputes during which they demonstrated clearly their deviance [from the right path]. He forbade these people from leading the masses in prayer and from teachering the young. He forbade them from congregating and punished those who disobeyed his orders. He would make them march in circles and order them to confess publicly inside the mosque, confessing their guilt and declaring their contrition for their heresies.'
35 Al-Talbi, *Tarajim*, pp. 106–7.
36 See Alex Metcalfe, 'Orientation in three spheres: Medieval Mediterranean boundary clauses in Latin, Greek and Arabic', *Royal Historical Society: Transactions of the RHS* 22 (2012), pp. 37–55; and 'Language and the written record: Loss survival and revival in early Norman Sicily' (forthcoming). *N.B.: The author wishes to thank Prof. Metcalfe for an advanced copy of this article.*
37 Ibid., 'Language', p. 7.
38 Granara, 'Ibn al-Sabil: Crossing boundaries in the biography of Asad ibn al-Furat', pp. 19–20.

Chapter 4

1 Amin Maalouf, *Leo Africanus* (New York, 1989).
2 Al-Muʿtamid Ibn ʿAbbad was also a poet of considerable accomplishment. See Raymond Scheindlin, *Form and Structure in the Poetry of al-Muʿtamid ibn ʿAbbad* (Leiden, 1974).
3 ʿAli ibn ʿAbd al-Rahman al-Ballanubi, *Diwan*, Hilal Naji (ed.) (Baghdad, 1976).

4   Two major sources that preserve an abundance of information of Arabic Sicilian poetry are Ibn al-Qatta' al-Siqilli, *al-Durra al-Khatira fi Shu'ara' al-Jazira*, Bashir Bakkush (ed.) (Beirut, 1995); and 'Imad al-din al-Katib al-Isfahani, *Kharidat al-Qasr wa Jaridat al-'asr: Qism Shu'ara'al-Maghrib*, M. al-Marzuqi, M. al-Mitwi and G. Yahya (eds) (Tunis, 1966). The most recent and comprehensive edition is Ihsan 'Abbas (ed.), *Mu'jam al-'Ulama' wa al-Shu'ara' al-Siqilliyyin* (Beirut, 1994). See his introduction, pp. 5–12, for a survey of the classical Arabic sources for Sicilian Arabic poetry and poets.

5   There has been much written, in Italian, on the life and work of Michele Amari; see: G. Siragusta, 'Michele Amari', *CA* I (1910), pp. ix–xliv; G. Salvo Cozzo, 'Le Opere a Stampa di Michele Amari', *CA* I, pp. xlvii–cviii; Francesco Gabrieli, *La Stroiografica Arabo-Islamica in Italia* (Napoli: Guida Editore, 1975); and Illuminato Peri, *Michele Amari* (Naples: Guida, 1976). See also Karla Mallette, *European Modernity and the Arab Mediterranean* (Philadelphia: University of Pennsylvania Press, 2010).

6   Ibn Hamdis. *Il Canzoniere Nella Traduzione di Celestino Schiaparelli*, Stefania Elena Carnemolla (ed) (Palermo, 1998). See Carnemolla's *'Introduzione,'* p. 40; see also fn #49 for accounts of correspondence between Amari and Dozy and de Slane.

7   One such example is Amari's suggestion that Ibn Hamdis was forced into exile due to a scandalous love affair, basing his opinion on a literal reading a few lines in a poem. See Nallino's footnote #1 (*SMS* II, p. 593).

8   The first (Arabic) edition was titled and subtitled as follows: *Il Canzoniere di 'Abd al-Gabbar ibn Abi Bakr ibn Muhammad ibn Hamdis Poeta Rabo di Siracusa (1056–1133). Testo Arabo Pubblicato Nella Sua Integrita Quale Risultata dai Codici di Roma e di Pietroburgo, Coll'aggiunta di Poesie dello Stesso Autore Ricavate da Altri Scrittori da Celestino Schiaparelli,* a spese del R. Inst. Orien. in Napoli (Roma, 1897).

9   Stefania Carnemolla's new edition cited above of the Italian translation includes a superb introduction outlining the textual and scholarly history of Ibn Hamdis.

10 Zayn al-'Abdin al-Sanusi, *al-Wataniyya fi Shi'r Ibn Hamdis* (Tunis, 1950); and *'Abd al-Jabbar ibn Hamdis: Hayatuh wa Adabuh* (Tunis, 1983).

11 One of note: Sa'd Isma'il al-Shalabi, *Ibn Hamdis al-Siqilli: Haytuh min Shi'rih* (Cairo, n.d.).

12 Ihsan 'Abbas, *al-'Arab fi Siqilliya* (Cairo, 1959); 'Abd al-Jabbar Ibn Hamdis, *Diwan*, Ihsan 'Abbas, (ed.) (Beirut, 1959).

13 It may be of interest to the reader that Ihsan 'Abbas classifies Ibn Hamdis's poetry into four distinct categories: (i) the *'Siqilliyat'* or Sicilian odes, which include

all genres that express (Muslim) Sicily's wars with Christians and its loss to the Normans; recollections of his youth; poems lamenting his nostalgia; and elegies to close relatives, in which his exile from Sicily is a primary topos; (ii) long poems spontaneously composed to express his emotional states; (iii) description poetry that may be read as short pieces or clippings; and (iv) philosophical or didactic poems that may be either contemplative (aesthetic) or didactic (cautionary). *Diwan*, pp. 17–21.

14 Jaroslav Stetkevych, *The Zephyrs of Najd: The Poetics of Nostalgia in the Classical Arabic Nasib* (Chicago, IL, 1993), p. 60.

15 Amari, al-Sanusi, Gabrieli, and 'Abbas, whose works are cited above, amply treats Ibn Hamdis's nostalgia for Sicily. See also Andrea Borruso, 'La nostalgia della Sicilia nel diwan di Ibn Hamdis', *Bollettino del Centro di Studi Filologici e Linguistici Siciliani* 12 (1973), pp. 38–54; W. Granara, 'Remaking Muslim Sicily: Ibn Hamdis and the poetics of exile', *Edebiyat* 9/2 (1998), pp. 167–98.

16 Stetkevych, *The Poetics of Islamic Legitimacy*.

17 David Wasserstein, 'The library of al-Hakam II al-Mustansir and the culture of Islamic Spain', *Manuscripts of the Middle East* 5 (1990–1), pp. 101–2.

18 Stetkevych, *The Poetics of Islamic Legitimacy*, p. 74.

19 F. Gabrieli, 'Sicilia e Spagna', in *Dal Mondo dell'Islam* (Naples, 1954), p. 121.

20 Ahmad ibn Muhammad al-Maqarri, *Nafh al-Tib min Ghusn al-Andalus al-Ratib*, vol. III, Ihsan 'Abbas (ed.) (Beirut, 1968), pp. 616–17.

21 Suzanne Stetkevych, 'Ritual and sacrificial elements in the poetry of blood vengeance: two poems by Durayd ibn al-Simmah and Muhalhil ibn Rabah', *JNES* 45/1 (1986), pp. 31–43.

22 Carole Hillenbrand, 'Jihad poetry in the age of the Crusades', in Thomas F. Madden, J. Laus and V. Ryan (eds), *Crusades-Medieval World in Conflict* (Surrey, 2010), pp. 9–23:12.

23 I have discussed this poem from a different perspective and refer the reader to 'Sicilian poets in Seville: literary affinities across political boundaries', in Suzanne. C. Akbari and Karla Mallette (eds), *A Sea of Languages: Rethinking the Arabic Role in Medieval Literary History* (Toronto, 2013), pp. 199–216.

24 Muhammad ibn 'Abdallah Al-Himyari, *Al-Rawd al-Mi'tar fi Khabar al-Aqtar*, E. Lévi-Provencale (ed.) (Cairo, 1937), p. 87. Al-Himyari reports that when Yusuf and his army actually crossed the Straits and arrived in the city of Algeciras, the population greeted them warmly, and the 'mosques' and public squares filled with volunteers. He describes these as being among the poor people, suggesting that joining the army was, in addition to a religious calling, a means of employment in what must have been difficult economic times.

25 This is curious, given that he would compose twelve panegyrics to Tamim's son Yahya (r.1108–16); twenty-seven panegyrics to his grandson 'Ali (r.1116–21); and five to his great-grandson al-Hasan (r.1121–67). One likely explanation is that Ibn Hamdis was wandering from court to court in the first years of his exile from Seville, looking for the most appropriate patron.

26 W. Granara, 'Ibn Hamdis's *al-Dimas* qasida: memorial to a fallen homeland', in R. Baalbaki, S. Said Agha, and T. Khalidi (eds), *The Value of Poetry in Reconstructing Arab History* (Beirut, 2010), pp. 243–58.

Chapter 5

1 Muhammad ibn Muhammad al-Idrisi, *Nuzhat al-Mushtaq fi Ikhtiraq al-Afaq*, A. Bombaci et al. (eds) (Naples, 1970, 1978), pp. 4–5.

2 Johns, *Arabic Administration*, pp. 212–56. Also, for an insightful study on the palace eunuchs of twelfth-century Palermo, see Joshua C. Birk, 'From borderlands to borderlines: Narrating the past of twelfth-century Sicily', in James. P. Helpers (ed.), *Multicultural Europe and Cultural Exchange in the Middle Ages and the Renaissance* (Brepols, 2005), pp. 9–31.

3 Alex Metcalfe, 'The Muslims of Sicily under Christian Rule', in Graham A. Loud and Alex Metcalfe (eds), *The Society of Norman Italy* (Leiden, 2002), p. 297. Metcalfe writes: '… there can be no doubt that the creation of fiscal and legal divisions according to religion and the degree of autonomy that indirect rule thus afforded, contributed to the preservation of a Muslim consciousness, identity and a sense of community throughout the Norman period'.

4 Muhammad ibn Ahmad ibn Jubayr, *Rihlat Ibn Jubayr* (Beirut, 1964), pp. 293–352. For an English translation see *The Travels of Ibn Jubayr*, William Wright (trans. and ed.) (Leyden, 1907), pp. 336–52.

5 Lane, *An Arabic-English Lexicon*, Book One, Part 6, pp. 2335–6.

6 Karla Mallette, *The Kingdom of Sicily, 1100–1250* (Philadelphia, 2005), pp. 29–32.

7 James E. Montgomery, 'Dichotomy in Jahili poetry', *Journal of Arabic Literature* XVII (1986), pp. 17–18.

8 Ihsan 'Abbas (ed.), *Mu'jam al-'Ulama' wa al-Shu'ara' al-Siqilliyyin* (Beirut, 1994), pp. 42–4.

10 Johns, *Arabic Administration*, p. 88.

11 Adalgisa De Simone, 'Alla corte di Ruggero II tra poesia e politica', *Nella Sicilia 'Araba' tra Storia e Filologica* P. 6 (Palermo, 1999), pp. 3–15.

12 Johns, *Arabic Administration*, pp. 88–9. Johns speculates that it was neither the first son, Roger, nor the infant Henry, but more likely one of the middle sons, Tancred or Alfonso.
13 Mallette, *The Kingdom of Sicily*, p. 26.
14 Granara, 'Rethinking Muslim Sicily's golden age: poetry and patronage at the Fatimid Kalbid Court', pp. 95–108.
15 Abu al-'Abbas Shams al-Din ibn Khallikan, *Wafayat al-A'yan wa Anba' Abna' al-Zaman*, Ihsan 'Abbas (ed.) (Beirut, 1977), pp. 385–9.
16 Adalgisa De Simone, *Splendori di Sicilia in un'Opera di Ibn Qalaqis* (Soveria Mannelli (Calabria, 1996).
17 Ibid., p. 20. She writes: '*il poeta sembra vivere anche una vita di svaghi, partecipando a banchetti e gite in località siciliane che nomina e talvolta celebra in componimenti o in brevissimi frammenti, dal taglio a volte ironico, come accade nel caso del Ghirbal, e della Fawwara*'.
18 Alex Metcalfe, *The Muslims of Medieval Sicily* (Edinburgh, 2009), p. 289.
19 Ibn al-Athir, *BAS*, p. 278.
20 Graham A. Loud and Thomas Wiedemann (trans. and eds), *The History of the Tyrants of Sicily by 'Hugo Falcandus' 1154–69* (Manchester UK, 1998), p. 220.

Postscript

1 Metcalfe, *The Muslims of Medieval Sicily*, p. 276.
2 'Imad al-Din Isma'il Abu al-Fida', al-Mukhtasar fi Akhbar al-Bashar, *BAS* 47, pp. 404–23. See also, P. M. Holt (trans. and ed.), *The Memoirs of a Syrian Prince: Abu'l-Fida', Sultan of Hamah 1271–1331* (Wiesbaden, 1983), pp. 31–2.
3 Abu al-Fida', *BAS* 47, p. 419.
4 Giuseppe Buonaviri, *Novelle Saracene* (Palermo, 1981).

Bibliography

'Abbas, Ihsan, *al-'Arab fi Siqilliya* (Cairo, 1959).
'Abbas, Ihsan, *Mu'jam al-'Ulama' wa al-Shu'ara' al-Siqilliyin* (Beirut, 1994).
'Abdul-Wahhab al-Fili, Najib, *A Critical Edition of Kitab al-Amwal of Abu Ja'far Ahmad b. Nasr al-Dawudi (d. 401/H)*, PhD Thesis (University of Exeter, 1989).
Abou El Fadl, Khaled, *Rebellion and Violence in Islamic Law* (Cambridge UK, 2001).
Abu al-'Arab, Muhammad ibn Tamim, and Muhammad ibn al-Harith al-Khushani, *Tabaqat 'Ulama Ifriqiya*, Muhammad Ben Cheneb, ed. (Beirut, n.d.).
Abu Yusuf, Ya'qub, *Kitab al-Kharaj*, Ihsan 'Abbas, ed. (Beirut, 1985).
Al-Dawudi, Abu Ja'far Ahmad ibn Nasr, *Kitab al-Amwal*, Rida Shahada, ed. (Rabat, n.d.).
Al-Dawudi, Abu Ja'far Ahmad ibn Nasr, 'Le regime foncier en Sicile au Moyen Age (IXè et Xè siècles)', in Hasan H. Abdulwahab et Farhat Dachraoui (eds), *Etudes d'Orientalisme Dédiées à la Mémoire de Lévi-Provençal* (Paris, 1962), pp. 401–44.
Al-Himyari, Abu 'Abdallah Muhammad, *Kitab al-Rawd al-Mi'tar fi Khabar al-Aqtar*, E. Lévi-Provençal, ed. (Cairo, 1937).
Al-Idrisi, Abu 'Abdallah Muhammad, *Nuzhat al-Mushtaq fi Ikhtiraq al-Afaq* (Cairo, 1990).
Al-Isfahani, 'Imad al-din al-Katib, *Kharidat al-Qasr wa Jaridat al-'Asr: Qism Shu'ara' al Maghrib*, Muhammad Marzuqi, Muhammad al-Mitwi and al-Jilani. Yahya, eds. (Tunis, 1966).
Al-Jahiz, Abu 'Uthman, *Rasa'il*, 'Abd al-Salam Muhammad Harun, ed. (Beirut, 1991).
Al-Maliki, Abu Bakr 'Abdallah, *Riyad al-Nufus fi Tabaqat 'Ulama' al-Qayrawan wa Ifriqiya*, Husayn Mu'nis, ed. (Cairo, 1951).
Al-Maqarri, Ahmad b. Muhammad, *Nafh al-Tib min Gghusn al-Andalus al-Ratib*, Ihsan 'Abbas, ed. (Beirut, 1968).
Al-Maqrizi, Taqi al-Din Ahmad ibn 'Ali, *Kitab al-Muqaffa al-Kabir: Tarajim Maghribiyya wa Mashriqiyya min al-Fatrah al-'Ubaydiyyah*, Muhammad al-Ya'lawi, ed. (Beirut, 1987).
Al-Mawardi, 'Ali ibn Muhammad, 'Ali ibn Muhammad, *al-Ahkam al-Sultaniyya wa al-Wilayat al-Diniyya* (Cairo, 1966).
Al-Qadi al-Nu'man, Abu Hanifa, *Da'a'im al-Islam*, Asaf A. Fyzee, ed. (Cairo, 1951).

Al-Qadi al-Nu'man, Abu Hanifa, *Iftitah al-da'wa*, Farhat Dachraoui, ed. (Tunis, 1975).
Al-Qatta', Abu al-Qasim, 'Ali, *al-Durra al-Khatira fi Shu'ara' al-Jazira*, Bashir Bakkush, ed. (Beirut, 1995).
Al-Sanusi, Zayn al-'Abdin, *'Abd al-Jabbar Ibn Hamdis: Hayatuh wa Adabu* (Tunis, 1983).
Al-Sanusi, Zayn al-'Abdin, *al-Wataniyya fi Shi'r Ibn Hamdis* (Tunis, 1950).
Amari, Michele, *Biblioteca Arabo-Sicula* (Lipsia, 1857).
Amari, Michele, *Storia dei Musulmani di Sicili*, Carlo A. Nallino, ed. (Catania, 1933).
Al-Ballanubi, 'Ali ibn 'Abd al-Rahman, *Diwan*, Hilal Naji, ed. (Baghdad, 1976).
Ben-Yehuda, Nachman, *Betrayals and Treason* (Boulder, 2001).
Birk, Joshua, 'From borderlands to borderlines: Narrating the past of twelfth-century Sicily', in James P. Helfers (ed.), *Multicultural Europe and Cultural Exchange in the Middle Ages and Renaissance* (UK Brepolis, 2005), pp. 9–31.
Borruso, Andrea, 'La nostalgia della Sicilia nel diwan di Ibn Hamdis', *Bollettino del Centro di Studi Filologici e Linguistici Aiciliani* 12 (1973), pp. 38–54.
Bury, John B., 'The naval policy of the Roman Empire in relation to the Western Provinces from the 7th to 9th Century', in *Centenario della Nascita di Michele Amari* (Palermo, 1910), pp. 21–34.
Calder, Norman, *Studies in Early Muslim Jurisprudence* (Oxford UK, 1993).
Cameron, Averil, *The Mediterranean World in Late Antiquity AD 395–600* (London, 1993).
Cassarino, Mirella, 'Palermo experienced, Palermo imagined. Arabic and Islamic culture between the 9th and the 12th century', in Annliese Nef (ed.), *A Companion to Medieval Palermo: The History of a Mediterranean City from 600 to 1500* (Leiden, 2013), pp. 89–129.
Constable, Olivia R., *Housing the Stranger in the Medieval World* (Cambridge, 2003).
Crone, Patricia, 'Mawla', *Encyclopedia of Islam*, vol. VI, fasc. 111–2 (Leiden, 1989), pp. 874–82.
Dachraoui, Farhat, *Le Califat Fatimide au Maghreb 296–365 AH/909–975* (Tunis, 1981).
De Simone, Adalgisa, 'Alla corte di Ruggero II tra poesia e politica', in *Nella Sicilia 'Araba' Tra Storia e Filologica* (Palermo, 2000), pp. 3–15.
De Simone, Adalgisa, 'Ibn Qalaqis in Sicilia', in Biancamaria S. Amoretti e Lucia Rostagno (eds), *Yad-Nama: In Memoria di Alessandro Bausani*, vol. II (Rome, 1991), pp. 323–44.
De Simone, Adalgisa, 'Palermo nei geografi e viaggiatori Arabi del Medioevo', in *Studi Maghrebini II* (Naples, 1968), pp. 129–85.
De Simone, Adalgisa, *Splendori di Sicilia in un'Opera de Ibn Qalaqis* (Calabria, 1996).

Falcandus, Hugo, *The History of the Tyrants of Sicily by 'Hugo Falcandus' 1154–69*, Graham A. Loud and Thomas Wiedemann, eds. (Manchester UK, 1998).

Gabotto, Ferdinando, 'Eufemio e il movimento separatist nell'Italia Bizantina', in *La Letteratura* (Torino, 1890), pp. v–vi.

Gabrieli, Francesco, *Dal Mondo dell'Islam* (Naples, 1954).

Geremek, Bronislaw, 'The marginal man', in Jacques Le Goff (ed.), *Medieval Callings* (Chicago, 1990), pp. 346–72.

Granara, William, 'Fragments of the past: Reconstructing Palermo's Jewish neighborhood: 973–149', in Susan G. Miller and M. Bertagnin (eds), *Architecture and Memory of the Minority Quarter of Muslim Mediterranean City* (Cambridge MA, 2010), pp. 35–55.

Granara, William, '*Ibn al-Sabil*: Crossing boundaries in the biography of Asad Ibn al-Furat', *Scripta Mediterranea* XIX–XX (1998–9), pp. 259–67.

Granara, William, 'Ibn Hamdis', in Terri DeYoung and Mary St. Germain (eds), *Essays in Arabic Literary Biography 92–135* (Weisbaden, 2011), pp. 145–50.

Granara, William, 'Ibn Hamdis's *al-Dimas* qasida: Memorial to a fallen homeland', in Ramzi Baalbaki, Saleh Said Agha, and Tarif Khalidi (eds), *The Value of Poetry in Reconstructing Arab History* (Beirut, 2010), pp. 243–58.

Granara, William, 'Islamic education and the transmission of knowledge in Medieval Sicily', in Joseph E. Lowry, Devin J. Stewart, and Shawkat M. Toorawa (eds), *Law and Education in Medieval Islam: Studies in Honor of George Makdisi* (London, 2004), pp. 150–73.

Granara, William, 'Remaking Muslim Sicily: Ibn Hamdis and the poetics of exile', *Edebiyat* 9 (1998), pp. 167–97.

Granara, William, 'Rethinking Muslim Sicily's golden age: Poetry and patronage at the Fatimid Kalbid Court', in *I Fatimidi e il Mediterraneo* (Palermo, 2008), pp. 95–108.

Granara, William, 'Sicilian poets in Seville: Literary affinities across political boundaries', in Karla Mallette and Suzanne C. Akbari (eds), *A Sea of Languages: Rethinking the Arabic Role in Medieval Literary History* (Toronto, 2013), pp. 199–216.

Hallaq, Wael, 'On dating Malik's *Muwatta*', *UCLA Journal of Islamic and Near Eastern Law* 1 (2000), pp. 47–65.

Heinz, Halm, *The Fatimids and Their Traditions of Learning* (London, 1997).

Hamdani, Sumaiya, 'The dialectic of power: Sunni-Shi'i debates in tenth century North Africa', *Studia Islamica* 90 (2000), pp. 5–21.

Hillenbrand, Carole, 'Jihad poetry in the age of the Crusades', in Thomas Madden et. al. (eds), *Crusades: Medieval Worlds in Conflict* (Surrey, 2010), pp. 9–23.

Ibn Hamdis, 'Abd al-Jabbar, *Diwan*, Ihsan 'Abbas, ed. (Cairo, 1960).

Ibn Hamdis, *Ibn Hamdis: Il Canzoniere*, Introduction by Stephania E. Carnemolla (Palermo, 1998).

Ibn Hawqal, Muhammad, *Kitab Surat alArd* (Leiden, 1967).

Ibn Jubayr, Muhammad Ibn Ahmad, *Rihla* (Beirut, 1964).

Ibn Jubayr, *The Travels of Ibn Jubayr*, William Wright, trans. & ed. (Leiden, 1907).

Ibn Khaldun, 'Abd al-Rahman, *al-Muqaddima*, 'Abd al-Salam al-Shadadi, ed. (Casablanca, 2005).

Ibn Khallikan, Abu al-'Abbas Shams al-Din, *Wafayat al-A'yan wa Anba' Abna' al-Zaman*, Ihsan 'Abbas, ed. (Beirut, 1977).

Ibn Qalaqis, Nasr Ibn 'Abdallah, *Diwan Ibn Qalaqis*, Siham al-Furayh, ed. (Cairo, 2001).

Idris, Hady Roger, *La Berberie Orientale sous les Zirides, Xè-XIIè Siècles* (Paris, 1962).

'Iyad Ibn Musa, Abu al-Fadl, *Tartib al-Madarik wa Taqrib al-Masalik*, Ahmad Bakir Mahhmud ed. (Beirut, 1968).

Jenkins, Romilly J., *Byzantium: The Imperial Centuries AD 610–1071* (New York, 1967).

Johns, Jeremy, *Arabic Administration in Norman Sicily* (Cambridge, 2002).

Kallek, Cengiz, 'Al-Dawudi: a North African Malikite observer of the economic disorder under the Fatimid regime', *IIUM Journal of Economics and Management* (1999), pp. 57–92.

King, Robert, 'Treason and traitors', *Society* 26/5 (1989), pp. 329–38.

Kister, Meir J, 'Land property and jihad', *Journal of the Economic and Social History the Orient* 34 (1991), pp. 270–311.

Lane, Edward William, *An Arabic-English Lexicon* (Beirut, 1976).

Malik ibn Anas, *al-Muwatta'*, Ahmad Ratib 'Armush, ed. (Beirut, 1977).

Mallette, Karla, *The Kingdom of Sicily, 1100–1250: A Literary History* (Philadelphia, 2005).

Marcais, Georges, 'Aghlabids', in *Encyclopedia of Islam* (Leiden, 1960), pp. 247–50.

Metcalfe, Alex, 'Language and the written record: Loss survival and revival in early Norman Sicily' (forthcoming). N.B. The author wishes to thank Prof. Metcalfe for an advanced copy of this article.

Metcalfe, Alex, *Muslims and Christians in Norman Sicily: Arabic Speakers and the End of Islam* (London, 2003).

Metcalfe, Alex, *The Muslims of Medieval Italy* (Edinburgh UK, 2009).

Metcalfe, Alex, 'Orientation in three spheres: Medieval Mediterranean boundary clauses in Latin, Greek and Arabic', *Royal Historical Society: Transactions of the RHS* 22 (2012), pp. 37–55.

Montgomery, James E., 'Dichotomy in jahili poetry', *Journal of Arabic Literature* XVII (1986), pp. 1–20.

Mottahedeh, Roy, *Loyalty and Leadership in an Early Islamic Society* (Princeton, 1980).

Mottahedeh, Roy and Ridwan al-Sayyid, 'The idea of the jihad before the Crusades', in A. Laiou and R. Mottahedeh (eds), *The Crusades from the Perspective of Byzantium and the Muslim World* (Washington DC, 2001), pp. 23–9.

Pellitteri, Antonino, *I Fatimiti e la Sicilia* (Palermo, 1996).

Pozzi, Enrico, 'Le paradigme du traitre', in *De La Trahison* (Paris, 1999), pp. 1–33.

Rahman, Sayeed Sajjur, *The Legal and Political Thought of Ibn Abi Zayd al-Qayrawani (310–386 AH/922-996 CE)* (Yale University Thesis, 2009).

Rizzitano, Umberto, *Storia e Cultura nella Sicilia Saracena* (Palermo, 1975).

Rizzitano, Umberto, 'Kalbids', *Encyclopedia of Islam* 4 (1974), pp. 496–7.

Sahnun, 'Abd al-Salam Ibn Sa'id, *al-Mudawwana al-Kubra li al-Imam Malik* (Beirut, 1990).

Speier, Hans, 'Treachery in war', *Studies in War and Peace 5. Social Research* 7/3 (1940).

Stetkevych, Jaroslav, *The Zephyrs of Najd: The Poetics of Nostalgia in the Classical Nasib* (Chicago, 1993).

Stetkevych, Suzanne Pinckney, *The Poetics of Islamic Legitimacy: Myth, Gender and Ceremony in the Classical Arabic Ode* (Bloomington, 2002).

Talbi, Mohamed, *L'Emirat Aghlabide 184–28* (Paris, 1966).

Talbi, Mohamed, *Tarajim aghlabiyya* [Biographies Aghlabides: Extraites des Madarik du Cadi 'Iyad] (Tunis, 1968).

Vaccaro, Emanuele, 'Sicily in the eighth and ninth centuries AD: A case of persisting economic complexity?' *Al-Masaq* 25/1 (2013), pp. 34–69.

Vasiliev, Aleksandr A., *Byzance et les Arabes*, Marius Canard, ed. (Brussels, 1935–50).

Wasserstein, David, 'The library of al-Hakam II al-Mustansir and the culture of Islamic Spain', *Manuscripts of the Middle East* 5 (1990–1), pp. 101–2.

White, Hayden, 'The question of narrative in contemporary historical theory', *History and Theory* 1 (1984), pp. 1–33.

White, Hayden, 'The Value of narrativity in the representation of reality', *Critical Inquiry* 7/1 (1980), pp. 5–27.

Index

Abbasid caliphate 2, 5, 21, 71, 131
'Abbas, Ihsan 104, 158, 198 n.8
'Abd al-Jabbar ibn Hamdis: His Life and Work (al-Sanusi) 103
'Abd al-Masih 149–50
'Abd al-Rahman al-Atrabanshi 165–7, 174
'Abd al-Rahman ibn al-Qasim 8
Abou El Fadl, Khaled 90
Abu al-'Abbas ibn Ibrahim ibn Ahmad ibn al-Aghlab 13–15, 19–20
Abu al-Daw' Siraj ibn Ahmad ibn Raja' 162–5
Abu al-Fida' Isma'il ibn 'Ali 182–3
Abu al-Futuh Yusuf ibn 'Abdallah 28, 30–4
Abu al-Hasan 'Ali al-Rub'i. *See* Ibn al-Khayyat
Abu al-Qasim ibn al-Hasan 28
Abu Fihr. *See* Muhammad ibn 'Abdallah ibn al-Aghlab
Abu Ishaq Ibrahim II. *See* Ibrahim II (Aghlabid ruler)
Abu Muhriz Muhammad ibn 'Abdallah 6–8, 56, 94
Abu Tammam 104–5
Abu 'Uthman Sa'id ibn Muhammad 80
Abu 'Uthman Sa'id ibn Muhammad 90
Abu Yazid Makhlad b. Kayrad
    anti-Fatimid campaign 25
    Kharijite rebellion of 25–6, 71, 79, 189 n.20
Abu Yusuf, Ya'qub 75, 78
    advice to Harun al-Rashid 79
    Kitab al-Amwal 82
    Kitab al-Kharaj 75–7, 194 nn.17–18
    powers of *imam* 77
    study of *Sawad* 78–9
advocacy, classical Arabic *qasida* 157, 175
Aghlabid dynasty of Ifriqiya 37
Aghlabid dynasty in Sicily 3, 9–14
    against Christians 17
    deterioration of 17

Muslim Sicilian history 87
    problems encountered by 84
    in search of enemy at Qayrawan 4–9
Agrigento 18, 34, 88
    Berbers of 23
    evolution of 84
    Khalil ibn Ishaq to 24
    local militias 89
    Muslims (anti-Fatimid) of 23
    Palermo's battle with 13–14
Ahmad, Aziz 22
al-'Abbas ibn al-Fadl 11–12, 50
    attack of Castrogiovanni 58–9
al-Ahkam al-Sultaniyya (al-Mawardi) 75, 193 n.9
al-Akhal (Ahmad) 31, 33–4, 62
al-Andalus 124
    Castro on 67
    inhabitants 55
    Muslim Spain 1, 5, 109, 145, 148, 156
    petty kingdoms of 118, 122
'al-'Arab', use of 189
al-Asadiyya, works on Islamic law (Asad) 8, 94–5
al-Buthayri, 'Abd al-Rahman 158–60, 174
al-Da'a' im al-Islam (al-Qadi al-Nu'man) 75, 80–1
al-Dawudi, Abu Ja'far Ahmad ibn Nasr 69, 83, 85
    al-Nasiha fi sharh al-Bukhari 192 n.2
    early life and death 69–71
    Kitab al-Amwal 71–2, 74, 80, 82, 192 n.3, 193 n.6
    on land/property issues 72–3
    law and order 91
    letter to colleagues 192 n.4
    masalih mursala, principles of 83
    political resistance 97–8
    powers of *imam* 77
    on Sahnun 93
    scholarship 70

Sicilian jihad 91, 97
takfir wa al-hijra 89
al-Favara 165
Alfonse VI, King 54
    against al-Mu'tamid 57, 100, 124, 144
    and Yusuf 129
al-Hasan ibn 'Ali 25–6, 28
al-Hasan ibn al-Samsam 33–4, 41
al-Himyari, Abu 'Abdallah Muhammad 57, 192 n.24, 197 n.24
al-Idrisi, Abu 'Abdallah Muhammad 144–5, 155
    birth and family 145
    Book of Roger 145
    Introduction 146, 174
    Norman 146
    vs. Roger II 146–7
'Ali ibn Muhammad ibn Abi al-Fawaris 20
'Ali ibn 'Umar al-Balawi 19–20
al-Jahiz, Abu 'Uthman 51
al-Jawad, Ibn Abi 93
al-Khalisa 33, 88–9
al-Malik al-Kamil 182–3
al-Maliki, Abu Bakr 'Abdallah 75, 187 n.3
al-Mansur 16, 25–6
al-Mawardi, 'Ali ibn Muhammad 75, 193 n.9
Almoravids 52, 54, 57, 60–1, 130
al-Mudawwana (Sahnun) 75–7, 95
al-Mu'izz ibn Badis 16, 26, 28, 32–3, 71, 130
al-Mu'jam 158
al-Mu'tamid ibn 'Abbad 52. *See also* Ibn Hamdis, 'Abd al-Jabbar
    and King Alfonse VI 57, 100, 124, 144
al-Mutanabbi 104
al-Muwatta' (Malik) 75–6
al-Mu'zz li-din Allah 70, 80
al-nafal (reward) 76, 78
al-Nasiha fi sharh al-Bukhari (al-Dawudi) 192 n.2
al-Nuwayri, Shihab al-Din 4, 39, 190 n.31
    tax collectors 86
al-Qadi al-Nu'man, Abu Hanifa 8, 16, 75–6, 80, 85, 94, 97–8, 188 n.13
    al-Da'a'im al-Islam 80–1
    jihad 97
    powers of *imam* 81–2

al-Qa'im 14, 21, 23–4, 62
al-Samantari, Abu Bakr 'Atiq 59
al-Sanusi, Zin al-'Abidin
    political poetics 103–4
    works on Ibn Hamdis 103
al-shari'a (Islamic law) 7
al-takfir wa al-hijra (principle) 69
al-Tunbudhi, Mansur ibn Nasr 5–7, 95
al-Zahr al-Basim fi Awsaf Abi al-Qasim (Ibn Qalaqis) 168
ama (women servant) 51–2
Amari, Michele 4, 18, 20, 22, 189 n.25, 196 n.5, 196 n.7
    account of Euphemius 39, 63
    Biblioteca arabo-sicula 67, 188 n.8
    early life 102
    observation on jihad 91, 149
    political poetics 103–4
    reasons for election 189 n.21
    shift in agrarian policies and structures 84
    Storia dei Musulmani di Sicilia 35–6, 38–9, 188 n.19
anti-Aghlabid campaign 7, 14, 17
anti-Fatimid campaign, Abu Yazid's 25
anti-Fatimid revolts 72, 89, 91
Apulia 23, 181–3
Arabian Peninsula 2, 4–5, 47
Arabic Administration (Johns) 198 n.2, 199 n.12
An Arabic-English Lexicon (Lane) 188 n.16, 191 n.1, 198 n.5
Arabic panegyrics 61, 146
    from *Jahiliyya* to Islam 121
    to Norman 146
    philological aspects of 147
    of twelfth-century Sicily 155–7, 178
Arabo-Islamic political legitimacy 61
Arabo-Sicilian history 29
Arabs 4, 23, 32–4
    caliphates 2
    Euphemius and 40
    fitna 152
    historical consciousness 2
    and Islam 185
    lands conquered by armies of 4
    Nafh al-Tib 118
    into Sicily 45
    warriors 8

Asad ibn al-Furat 3, 6–9, 91–3, 184–6
    academic journey 94
    al-Asadiyya 8, 94–5
    attack of P/Balata 38
    chief judgeship 94–5
    command of Sicilian expedition 45
    education 92
    jihad 92
    Muslim prisoners issue 94
    peace treaty 56
    Sahnun's rivalry with 95

Bani Ziri (Zirids) 130, 139
The Battle of al-Dimas 65, 139, 169
The Battle of al-Zallaqa 57, 100, 124, 129, 144
The Battle of the Straits 27, 42–3
The Battle of Uhud 122, 129
Bedouin (Arabian tribes) 131, 156
    armies 73–4
    and pagan 157
    recounting on pre-Islamic poetry 2
Ben-Yehuda, N. 55, 192 n.21
Berbers
    of Agrigento 23, 85
    Almoravid warlord 54, 57, 100
    Arab elite and 5–6, 15
    Ibn Qurhub 22
    against Ja'far 50–1
    Kutama 5, 15, 18, 21, 24, 28, 30
    petty kingdoms 130
    rise of Fatimids 79
betrayal. *See* treason/treasonous acts
Biblioteca arabo-sicula (Amari) 67, 188 n.8
Bonaviri, Giuseppe 184–6, 199 n.4
Book of Roger (al-Idrisi) 145
Bury, John B. 39–40, 191 n.7
Byzance et les Arabes (Vasiliev) 40, 189 n.24
Byzantium 6
    'Abbas attack of 58–9
    defeats of 27, 37
    and Fatimid 24, 27
    Kalbid dynasty against 3
    latifunda system 44
    military aggressions against 22
    Muslim prisoners issues 94
    mutiny against 39

    recapture of Calabria 32–3
    rule in Sicily 37
    violation of treaty 6, 94

Calabria 14, 18, 20–1, 23, 26–8, 32–3
Calder, Norman 193 nn.12–13, 194 n.18
caliphs/caliphate
    of Abbasid 2, 5, 21, 71, 131
    in Baghdad 5, 7, 14, 32
    of Fatimid 16, 18, 23, 26, 62, 70, 72, 80, 130
    Iberian Peninsula 5
    Umayyad 2, 92
Cambridge Chronicle (anonymous) 189 nn.26–7
Cameron, Averil 84
Carnemolla, Stefania Elena 196 n.6, 196 n.9
Castro, Americo 67, 110
Castrogiovanni (modern Enna) 10–11, 34, 38
    conquest of 58–9
Christians
    al-Mu'tamid against 57
    Christian Reconquest 109, 122, 124, 130, 144, 175, 178
    Ibn Qurhub 20
    from Italian mainland 148
    jihad against 12, 88
    Muslim-Christian contestation 62
    Muslims convert to Christianity 153
    relationship with Muslim 26, 45, 150, 152, 177
    Saracens 148
    surrendered to Islamic rule 10
    treaty (nontaxable) 26
Christ Pantocrator, mosaic of 98
The *Chronicon* of Romuald of Salerno 177
chronological narration 36
The Church of Saint John of the Hermits 67
configurational dimension of narration 36, 39
Constable, Olivia R. 191 n.10
Constantinople 9, 14, 24, 26–7, 37–8, 40, 88–9
Crone, Patricia 48
cross-cultural conflict 44, 54, 65, 67, 98, 153–4

cross-religious relationships 26, 49, 150, 152, 177
crossroads of civilization, Sicily 45, 100

Daʿaʾim al-islam (al-Nuʾman) 16, 75, 80, 188 n.13, 194 n.24
Dachraoui, Farhat 80, 188 n.9, 194 n.20
Dar al-Harb (non-Muslim world) 43–5, 54, 96, 109–10, 116, 154, 179, 183
Dar al-Islam (Muslim world) 7, 42–5, 54, 62, 179
    with Dar al-Harb 45, 110, 183–4
    groups/categories of citizens 47–9
daʿwa, proselytizing mission 15, 81
De Arte Venandi cum Avibus (Frederick II) 185
'defender of the faith' 9, 16, 61, 121, 137, 139
De Simone, Adalgisa 169, 190 n.30, 198 n.11, 199 n.16
dhimma (protection to people) 48, 62, 110, 116, 176–7
dhimmi 49, 148
dichotomy, classical Arabic *qasida* 156–7, 175
diwan (Ibn Hamdis) 101–2, 105, 109, 146
    ʿAbbas's edition of 104
    on bravery and *poetics of jihad* 112–15
    jihad motif 111
    leaving Sicily and travelling to Ifriqiya 106–7
    panegyric to al-Muʿtamid 119–23, 125–9
    Schiaparelli's edition of 102–3
    sermon to his compatriots on fighting jihad 140
    sub-genres 104
    'Tamim panegyric' 131–8

Egypt
    Abu al-Futuh Yusuf to 31
    al-Muʿizz to 28
    Fatimid dynasty of 26, 32, 101, 131, 168, 175
episodic dimension of narration 36, 39
Epistle on Singing Girls (Jahiz) 51
espionage in Muslim frontier societies 55–6

'Eufemio e il movimento separatista nell'Italia bizantina' (Gabotto) 39
Euphemius 36–7, 94, 191 n.9
    Amari's account of 39, 102
    assassination of 38, 40
    Bury on 39–40
    defeat of Byzantines 37
    Gabotto on 39
    and Ibn al-Thumna 34, 41, 49, 63, 66
    love affair 38, 40
    national hero 40–1
    P/Balata and 37
    Speier on 56
    spy of consequence 56
    Vasiliev on 40
    and Ziyadat-allah 6, 37
Europe xx
European Byzantinist version (narration) 38
The Excursion of One Longing to Cross the Horizons. See *Kitab Nuzhat al-Mushtaq fi ikhtiraq al-Afaq* (al-Idrisi)

Fatimid dynasty in Sicily 15–19
    appeal to Muslims of Sicily 80
    and Byzantium 27
    capital 70
    dismantling Old Palermo 89
    Muslim Sicilian history 87
    problems encountered by 84
    against Sunnis of Ifriqiya 79–80
Fatimid dynasty of Egypt 26, 32, 100, 131, 168, 175–6
Fatimid Mahdi mission 14–16, 28
fifth column/columnist
    account 192 n.22
    George of Antioch 66
    vs. spy 55–6
fiqh (legal writings and jurisprudence) 29, 74, 78
fitna (Ibn Jubayr) 148–54, 178–9
    cross-cultural/cross-religious contact 153–4
    internal divisions/breaking of ranks 152
    Lane on 151
    temptation/seduction 148, 152
foreign invaders (target for Sicily) 4, 44, 46–7, 102, 104–5

Frederick II, King 178, 185–6
   and al-Malik al-Kamil 183
   birth and family 182
   De Arte Venandi cum Avibus 185
   Ibn Wasil on 182
   Liber Augustalis 185
   on Saracen problem 181
   zone of contradiction 182
fuqaha' (religious scholars) 6

Gabotto, Ferdinando 39, 191 n.6
Gabrieli, Francesco 103–4, 116–17
George of Antioch 64, 66, 152–3
   cathedral built by 152–3
   and Ibn Hamdis 65
   to Ifriqiya 64–5
   modern fifth columnist 66
Geremek, Bronislaw 45–6, 191 n.11
ghazal (love poem) 101, 106–7, 114, 161, 164–5, 167
ghazi (warrior) society 45

hadith (prophetic saying and deeds) 2, 74, 77
Hanafi (Sunni) 47
   Kitab al-Kharaj (Abu Yusuf) 75
   madhhab 95
   Qayrawani 80
Hanafi school of Sunni Islam 75, 79
Harun al-Rashid 5, 75–6
   advice from Abu Yusuf 79
Hillenbrand, Carole 124, 197 n.22
historical consciousness process 2–3, 157, 173
The History of the Arabs in Sicily ('Abbas) 104

Iberian Peninsula 4–5, 8–9, 57
Ibn Abi Khinzir, al-Hasan ibn Ahmad 18–21
Ibn al-Athir 4, 31, 35, 39, 176
   on 'Abbas attack of Byzantium 59
   on Abu'Affan 85
   anecdote 49, 54
   on Ibrahim II 13
   Muslim Sicily's downfall 176
   praise of Roger II 176
   reports of 19, 49, 188 n.20
Ibn al-Hajar, Abu al-Qasim 168–9, 173

Ibn al-Khatib, Lisan al-Din 2
Ibn al-Khayyat 30, 190 n.35
Ibn al-Thumna 30, 34, 41, 49, 61, 63, 66
Ibn Bashrun 158–60, 162
Ibn Hamdis, 'Abd al-Jabbar 195 n.2
   and al-Mu'tamid 100, 118, 129
   al-Sanusi's work on 103
   Christian Reconquest 109, 124, 130, 144
   diwan (anthology) (*see diwan* (Ibn Hamdis))
   early life 99–100
   exile 52, 60–1, 101, 105, 116, 144, 157, 178, 196 n.7
   Gabrieli's work on 103
   and George of Antioch 65
   Hamdisian-favoured themes 136
   to Ifriqiya 100, 131, 144
   invectives on Roger II 145
   Jawhara (*see* Jawhara (slave girl))
   khiyana 66
   literary genres 101, 104–6
   literary–political implications 108–9
   and modern critics 102–4, 109, 117
   neoclassicism 104–7
   Norman armies 144
   to North Africa 144
   panegyrics 60–1, 100–1, 104–23, 169
   poetics of jihad 110–11, 115–18, 123, 138–40
   poets of Arabian wastelands 111
   qasida 104–9, 111, 114, 124–6
   Sicilian interlude 60–1
   siqilliyat 53
   'Tamim panegyric' 131–8, 157
   warrior-poet 118–29
   at Zirid court 130–41, 144
Ibn Hasan, Abu Hafs 'Umar 160–2
Ibn Hawqal, Muhammad Abu al-Qasim 23, 154, 179, 187 n.1, 190 n.30
   comments on Sicilian Muslims' 43
   criticisms 42, 96
   on jihad 43
   neighbourhood 27
   Surat al-Ard 42–3, 190 n.30
   on treacherous acts 44
   visit to Sicily 41–2
Ibn Jubayr, Muhammad ibn Ahmad 155, 179
   on Cefalu 150

Christian Sicilian 152
fitna (*see fitna* (Ibn Jubayr))
   to God 152
   on King William II 149, 151–2
   on Messina 149
   on Norman civilization 152–3, 174
   Palermo 150
   Rihlat Ibn Jubayr 198 n.4
   to Sicily 149
   temptation/seduction 153
Ibn Khaldun, 'Abd al-Rahman 35–6, 39, 131, 184
   diplomatic mission 2
   early years and family 1
   to Granada 2
   Kitab al-'Ibar 3
   Muqaddima 3
   revolts 1
   thesis of cycles (life span of nation) 3
Ibn Qalaqis, Nasr Ibn 'Abdallah 179
   al-Zahr al-Basim fi Awsaf Abi al-Qasim 168
   anthology to Ibn al-Hajar 168–9
   journey 168
   panegyric to King William II 170–4
   poems to King Roger II 169
   resemblance of Ibn Hamdis 168–9
Ibn Qurhub, Ahmad 62, 189 n.24
   case of 19–23
   on Sicilian politics 86
Ibrahim II (Aghlabid ruler) 12, 15, 188 n.11
   Ibn al-Athir on 13
   orders from Ifriqiya 14
   revolt 13–14
Ibrahim I ibn al-Aghlab 5
Ifriqiya 3, 5, 11–12
   Aghlabid dynasty of 10, 12, 37
   Fatimid's power in 79, 83
   Ibn Hamdis to 100, 131, 144
   relationship with Sicily 15
   Zirid princes 32
Iftitah al-Da'wa (al-Nu'man) 16, 80, 188 n.14, 194 n.23
Il Canzoniere Nella Traduzione di Celestino Schiaparelli (Carnemolla) 196 n.6
imam (leader) 17
   conduct of 81
   powers of 77, 82

   of *umma* 71–2, 77
Islam from the Prophet Muhammad to the Capture of Constantinople (Lewis) 187
Islamic conquest of Sicily 3, 5, 8–9, 42, 44
   Aghlabid-Byzantine relations 56
   freed slaves 48–9
   mawali 48
   military slaves 49
   wala' 48–9
Islamic jihad. *See also* jihad campaign in Siciliy
   Da'a'im al-islam (al-Nu'man) 80
   Amari's observation 149
   against Christian 88
   conditions for fighting in jihad 76
   holy war/holy peace 110
   Ibn Hamdis 109
   literature of 74–83
   manpower and financial support 85–6
   modes of 76
   Sahnun's 91–8
Islamic law
   al-Asadiyya 8
   al-shari'a 7
   benign treatment of slaves 52
   flexibility to reach non-Muslims 88
Islamic Maghreb 7
Islamic Spain 110
Isma'ili theology 80

Ja'far 28–32, 50, 189 n.24
Jahiliyya (pre-Islamic) poetry 105, 109–11, 114, 117, 121–2, 124, 137, 161, 164
Jalal al-Din ibn Wasil
   Abu l-Fida' on 182–3
   on Frederick II 182
jariya (women servant) 52
Jawhara (slave girl)
   al-Mu'tamid 192 n.20
   Ibn Hamdis's elegies to 52–3
   loyalty 53–4
   non-Arab 54
Jesu e Giuffa (Bonaviri) 184
'Jesus and Juha.' *See Jesu e Giuffa* (Bonaviri)
jihad campaign in Siciliy 9–15, 50. *See also* Islamic jihad
   foreign troops to assist 23

Ibn Hawqal on 44
Kalbid 25
rift in commanding 50
jizya (protection tax) 10, 38, 48, 74
Johns, Jeremy 64, 162, 192 n.30
　Arabic Administration 198 n.2, 199
　　n.12

Ka'b ibn Zuhayr 161
Kalbid dynasty in Sicily 25–30
　against Byzantium 3
　collapse of 96
Khafaja ibn Sufyan 11
　assassination 12, 50
　as governor of Sicily 12
　to Palermo 11–12
Khalil ibn Ishaq 23–4, 28, 88–9
Kharijism/Kharijites 5, 37, 47, 188 n.10
　Abu Yazid 24–6, 71, 79
　political movement of 5, 15
khiyana (betrayal) 35, 59, 66
The Kingdom of Sicily (Mallette) 198 n.6
King, Robert 61–2, 192 n.27
Kister, M. J. 73–4, 193 n.7
Kitab al-Amwal (Treatise on Finance) 192
　n.3, 193 n.6
　Abu Yusuf's 82
　al-Dawudi's 71–2, 74, 80, 82
Kitab al-'Ibar (Ibn Khaldun) 3
Kitab al-Kharaj (Abu Yusuf) 75–7, 194
　nn.17–18
*Kitab Nuzhat al-Mushtaq fi ikhtiraq al-
　Afaq* (al-Idrisi) 145
Kutama Berbers tribe 5, 15, 18, 21, 24, 28,
　30, 79

Lane, Edward William 35, 151, 188 n.16,
　191 n.1, 198 n.5
latifunda system 44, 84
Le Califat Fatimide au Maghreb
　(Dachraoui) 188 n.9, 194 n.20
Leo Africanus (Maalouf) 99
Lewis, Bernard 187 n.1
Liber Augustalis (Frederick II) 185
literary history of Normans 154–67
　classical Arabic *qasida* 155–7
　hasab and nasab 155
　languages 155
　Mallette's study 154–5

Maalouf, Amin 99
madhhab
　Hanafi 95
　Maliki 92, 94–5
　Sunni 79
maghazi (accounts of campaigns) 2, 74
Mahdiyya (Tunisia)
　Fatimid court in 23–4
　Zirid court in 32, 60, 100–1, 130
Malik ibn Anas 7–8, 70, 193 n.11
　al-Muwatta' 75–7
　Asad and 94
　martyr 76
　modes of jihad 76
Maliki Sunnism 16, 29, 75
Mallette, Karla 154–5, 165, 177
　The Kingdom of Sicily 198 n.6
Manfred, King 182–3
Marcais, Georges 9
marginalization, social. *See* social
　marginalization
martyr, Malik's definition of 76
mawali of Muslim Sicily 48, 55
mawla 48
Medieval Sicily 45, 49, 51
Mediterranean island of Sicily 4, 45, 84,
　157, 186
Metcalfe, Alex 93, 148, 181, 195 n.36
　The Muslims of Medieval Sicily 199
　　n.18
　The Society of Norman Italy 198 n.3
Michael of Antioch 64
migration
　and colonization 45
　of North Africans into Sicily 90
military slaves of Muslim Sicily 49
mobility, classical Arabic *qasida* 155–6,
　175
modes of discourse (history and literature)
　36
monolithic Sicilian jihad 96
Montgomery, James 156, 198 n.7
Mosaic of Christ Pantocrator 98
Mottahedeh, Roy 46, 191 n.14
Muhammad b. Mansur Al-Qadi al-
　Nu'man 80
Muhammad Hasan al-Shalabi 71
Muhammad ibn 'Abdallah ibn al-Aghlab
　10–11, 50

Muhammad ibn al-Hasan al-Shaybani 8, 94–5, 193 n.10
mujahid/mujahidin (holy warrior) 14, 43, 90, 116
muqasama (proportional taxation) 78
'*musha'midhin*' 47
Muslims
    of Agrigento 23
    against Christian governors 181
    conversion to Christianity 153
    frontier societies 55
    ideal jihad 97
    non-Arab 48, 110
    relationship with Christians 26, 45, 56, 62, 150, 152, 177
    of third century 5
Muslim Sicily
    fall to Norman invasion 148
    in first century 84
    history 5, 10, 12, 35, 41, 66–7, 86–7, 89
    mawali of 48
    rifts within 90
The Muslims of Medieval Sicily (Metcalfe) 199 n.1, 199 n.18
Mu'tazilite/Mu'tazilizm 75, 95

narration (history and literature)
    chronological 36
    configurational dimension of 36, 39
    episodic dimension of 36, 39
    European Byzantinist version 38
    nativist Italian version 38
    nonchronological 36
neoclassicism, Ibn Hamdis's 104–7
Neoplatonism 174
Nicephorus (Phocas) II 27
non-Arab Muslims 48, 110
non-Muslim military assistance 88
Normans 31, 33–4, 49
    al-Idrisi 146
    capture of Syracuse and Noto 131
    defeat of Islam 147
    George and 65
    invasion of Muslim Sicily 148
    literary history (*see* literary history of Normans)
    poets and court patronage 154–67
    Sicilian Arabic poetry 147–8
Norman Synthesis 148, 183

North Africa xx, 31, 131
    anti-Fatimid campaign in 25
    Ibn Hamdis to 144
    Kutama Berbers from 24
    manpower and financial support to jihad 86
    patrons and Sicilian Muslims 86–7
    support for Sicily 89
    third Islamic century 92
    Zirids of 34, 54
Noto, Sicily 12, 34, 60, 100, 124, 131, 138, 144, 147
Novelle Saracene (Bonaviri) 185, 199 n.4

Otto I, Emperor 27
Otto II, Emperor 27–8

Palermo 3, 87, 181
    al-Hasan 26
    Arabs of 23
    battle with Agrigento 13–14
    capital city 12, 63, 90
    Cefalu to 150, 152
    conquered by Muslim armies 10
    evolution of 84
    Ibn Jubayr 150
    Ibn Qurhub in 21
    Jug of Mazzara del Vallo (Regionale Galleria) 34
    Khafaja ibn Sufyan 11–12
    local militias 89
    Muslim invasion in 44
    slav(e) quarter in 23
panegyrics
    Arabic (*see* Arabic panegyrics)
    Ibn Hamdis 54, 60–1, 101, 104–23, 169
    to King Roger II 158–67
    to King William II (Ibn Qalaqis) 170–5
    between poetic and political legitimacy 108–18
    to Prophet Muhammad (Ka'b ibn Zuhayr) 161
    'Tamim panegyric' 132–8, 140
    at Zirid court 130–41
Patriotism in the Poetry of Ibn Hamdis (al-Sanusi) 103
P/Balata (Byzantine governor of Sicily) 8
    refused orders from Euphemius 37

Poetics of Islamic Legitimacy (Stetkevych) 108, 197 n.18
polytheists (*mushrikin*) 82, 88
Prophet Muhammad 4, 15, 83, 184
    Ka'b ibn Zuhayr's panegyric to 161
    views on poet 110

qasida 101, 108–9
    aspects of 155–7
    classical Arabic 99, 105, 110, 122
    eleventh-century 114
    Ibn Hamdis's 104–6, 108, 111, 124, 129
    Jahiliyya 117
    monothematic 140, 170
    tripartite 107, 155
qayna (women servant) 51
Qayrawan (Tunisia) 12, 19
    Abu Muhriz 56
    Aghlabid court in search of enemy 4–9
    Asad to 94
    chief judge for 7–8, 92, 94–5
    court of Ziyadat-allah in 47
    Hanafis 80
qiyas (reasoning by analogy) 77, 83

Rabbah, Ahmad ibn Abi al-Husayn ibn 11, 20, 58–9
raqiq (women servant) 51
Raqqada (Tunisia) 15–16, 18–19, 21
    new Fatimid government from 87
    occupied by Fatimid rulers 188 n.11
ribat, Sicilian 42, 47
Rihlat Ibn Jubayr (Ibn Jubayr) 198 n.4
Riyad al-Nufus (al-Maliki) 187 n.3, 188 n.5
Rizzitano, Umberto 190 n.29
Roger II, King 64, 151, 154, 161, 164, 175, 178–9, 183
    Abu al-Daw's panegyrics to 162–5
    Abu Hafs's panegyrics to 160–2
    al-Atrabanshi's panegyrics to 165–7
    al-Buthayri's panegyrics to 158–60
    vs. al-Idrisi 146
    Arabic panegyrics 147, 158, 177
    characteristics 143–4
    in *Chronicon* of Romuald of Salerno 177
    Ibn al-Athir's praise of 176
    Ibn Hamdis's invectives on 145
    mosque restored as church by 67
    multicultural Norman Sicily 182
    zone of contradiction 177

Sadat, Anwar 69
Sahnun, 'Abd al-Salam Ibn Sa'id 72–3, 83, 186
    al-Dawudi on 93
    al-Mudawwana 75–7, 95, 193 n.13
    as chief judge 92, 94
    conditions for fighting in jihad 76
    education 92
    jihads 91–8
    land for soldiers 93–4
    legitimacy of jihad 97
    'no documentary proof' 93
    rivalry with Asad 95
Salim ibn Rashid 62, 66, 89
    army 88
    Muslims of Agrigento against 23
    regional agent/tax collector against 88
    Sicilians against Khalil 24
Saracens 148, 181, 184
Schiaparelli, Celestino 102
Seljuk Turks 130
Shemesh, Ben 193 n.10
Shi'ites Islam/Shi'ism 5, 47
    caliphal legitimacy 17
    Fatimids 16, 20, 22, 29, 79, 85, 130–1, 174
    Kutama Berbers 5
    Mahdis 70
Sicilian jihad movement 9–15
Sicilian-Maghribi-Egyptian axis 26
Sicilian-North African relationship 89
Sicily xx
    Aghlabid (*see* Aghlabid dynasty in Sicily)
    Andalusian privateers in 91
    Arab invasion and settlement of 45, 84
    cities xvii, xviii
    crossroads of civilization 45, 100
    Fatimid (*see* Fatimid dynasty in Sicily)
    foreign invaders/invasion 4, 44, 46
    inhabitants 55
    Islamic conquest of (*see* Islamic conquest of Sicily)
    Islamic period in 93
    Kalbid (*see* Kalbid dynasty in Sicily)

Mediterranean island of 4, 45, 84, 157, 186
North Africans into 90
provinces xvi
relationship with Ifriqiya 15
separated civilizations 96–7
testing ground of jihad 91, 98
united Sicilian front 23–5
urban development of 84
Siciulo-Arabic historical documentation
Persians/Africans of Muslim armies 47
terms of women servants 51–2
sira (biographies of Prophet) 2, 74
Siyar 7, 43, 187 n.4
slaves, Muslim Sicily 48–50
benign treatment 52
dependence on 84
freed 49
Jawhara (*see* Jawhara (slave girl))
master-slave relationship 52
slave corps 30, 50
soldier-slaves 49–51
social marginalization 44–6
foreign domination/shifts in government 46
and loyalties 44, 46–50
migrations of people 45
religious/legal perspective 46
The Society of Norman Italy (Metcalfe) 198 n.3
Southern Italy xix, 18, 22, 27, 33
Speier, Hans 55, 192 n.23, 192 n.25
on Euphemius 56
fifth columnist *vs.* spy 55–6
modern warfare 58
spy, categories of 55–6
Stetkevych, Jaroslav 105, 107
Stetkevych, Suzanne 108, 111, 192 n.26, 197 n.21
Storia dei Musulmani di Sicilia (Amari) 35–6, 38–9, 188 n.19
Sufism 3, 150
Sunni Islam 5, 20, 32
Aghlabid 85, 91, 97
against Fatimid Shi'ism 22, 79
Hanafis 47
Maliki 16, 29, 70, 75, 85
and Shi'ites 2, 5, 88
Sicilians' 88–9

Surat al-Ard (Ibn Hawqal) 42–3, 190 n.30
Syracuse 10–12, 111, 149
to Byzantine control 37, 40
evolution of 84

Talbi, Mohamed 9, 195 n.34
Tamim ibn al-Mu'izz 60–1, 64–5, 157
Ibn Hamdis's panegyrics to 131–8
Taormina, sicily 12, 20, 27, 42
Tarajim aghalbiyya (Talbi) 195 n.34
taxation, forms of
agricultural products 31
jizya (protection tax) 10, 38, 48, 74
kharaj (land tax) 78, 93
muqasama (proportional taxation) 78
tax collector 85–9
treaty 26, 81
tribute 37, 57
Thiqat al-Dawla 29
traitors, types of 63–4
treason/treasonous acts 40, 49–50, 54–5, 136, 144
anecdote 44, 66–7
associated concepts 55
betrayal 35, 50, 55, 59
citizen's allegiance 62–3
Euphemius's 37, 41
examination of 66
khiyana 35, 59, 66
King's study on 61–2
military confrontation 55
as moral depravity 58–61
Muslim-Christian contestation 62
natural disasters 55
traitors 63–4
tyrants (*ahl al-baghiy*) 82, 91

'Ubayd Allah 15–16, 18, 80
ulema 6, 8, 37, 56
against Isma'ili usurpers 85
Maliki 71
'Umar ibn 'Abd al-'Aziz 92
'Umar ibn al-Khattab 73, 83, 93
on division of land 77–8
policies in al-Sawad (land and tax) 74, 78, 90–1, 94
Umayad caliphate of Levant 2, 92
umma, Islamic nation 4–5, 7, 74, 77, 88, 91, 98, 176

urbanization 45
    Palermo 12, 181
    urban development of Muslim Sicily 84
'Uthman ibn 'Affan 73

Vaccaro, Emanuele 194 n.27
Val Demone island 4, 19, 28, 87–8
Val di Mazara island 8, 10, 18
Vasiliev, A. A. 22
    Byzance et les Arabes 40, 189 n.24

wait-and-*see* strategy 6, 56
Wansbrough, John 193 n.12
waq'at al-majaz (The Battle of Straits) 27
wasifa (women servant) 51
Wasserstein, David 110
White, Hayden 36, 191 n.2, 191 n.4
William II, King 151, 154, 178–9
    Arabic panegyrics 147
    Ibn Jubayr on 149, 151–2
    Ibn Qalaqis extols 168–79
    projection of 150–1
    statue of 141

Yahya ibn Fityan al-Tarraz 65, 154
Ya'ish 28

Ya'qub b. Ibrahim Abu Yusuf. *See* Abu Yusuf, Ya'qub
Yusuf Tashufin 57, 100, 129, 144

Zirid dynasty 32–4, 130
Ziri ibn Manad 71
Ziyadat-allah, Abu Muhammad 5, 45
    call for jihad 96
    chief judges of 6–8, 56
    commanders 10
    economic and political control 10
    fleet force 8
    military intelligence 6
    peace treaty with Byzantium 6, 56
    response to Euphemius 37
    Val di Mazara island 8, 10
Ziyadat-Allah II
    Asad's appointment 92
    death of 85
Ziyadat-allah III, Abu Mudar 14, 18, 189 n.21
    murder of father 19–20
    overthrown 15
zone of contradiction 146, 149, 151, 154, 167, 176–7, 182

Plate 1 Jug of Mazzara del Vallo, Museo, Regionale Galleria, Palermo.

Plate 2 The Church of Saint John of the Hermits (San Giovanni degli Eremiti): A sixth-century church converted into a mosque during Muslim rule and restored as a church by Roger II *c.*1136, Palermo.

Plate 3 Mosaic of Christ Pantocrator in the royal Palatine Chapel (Cappella Palatina) commissioned by Roger II *c.*1132, Palermo.

Plate 4 Statue of William II at the front of the Cathedral of Monreale (begun by William II *c.*1174), Monreale (Sicily).